SanDiego

CALIFORNIA'S CORNERSTONE

By Iris H. W. Engstrand

San Diego: California's Cornerstone

a pictorial and entertaining commentary on the growth and development of San Diego, California

By Iris H. W. Engstrand

Dedicated to my daughter
Kristin and her friends so they
may understand and appreciate
the city in which they live.

Publishers:
  Larry P. Silvey
  Douglas S. Drown
Editor:
  Ellen Sue Blakey
Associate Editor:
  Peggi Ridgway
Art Director:
  Rusty Johnson
Historical Photo Editor:
  Thomas L. Scharf
Assistant Art Director:
  James Michael Martin
Project Director:
  Tim Colwell
Contributing Editor:
  Roger Conlee

San Diego: California's Cornerstone is sponsored by The San Diego Chamber of Commerce.

San Diego: California's Cornerstone is one of The American Portrait Series published by Continental Heritage Press. Others include:

Charlotte: Spirit of the New South
Cleveland: Prodigy of the Western Reserve
Columbus: America's Crossroads
Des Moines: Capital City
Detroit: American Urban Renaissance
Fort Worth: The Civilized West
Houston: A History of a Giant

Los Angeles Two Hundred
The San Antonio Story
San Jose: California's First City
The Saint Louis Portrait
The Tulsa Spirit

Prologue

San Diego is more than a city. It is an entire geographic region — the most southwesterly corner of the United States. It is unique because it is surrounded by large areas of open space — the Pacific Ocean to the west, Camp Pendleton to the north, the Laguna Mountains to the east and (except for the city of Tijuana) the barren mesas and mountainous areas of northern Baja California to the south. That formation makes it distinct, and San Diegans take great pride in being separate. They savor the achievements they have made despite — and because of — the region's relative isolation.

The city is the cornerstone of the area's development. It was the first settlement in upper California, the place where European contact with the native inhabitants was first made. Whether the small outpost prospered and grew, or merely stood still, depended a great deal upon its natural geographic advantages.

With its nearly ideal climate, the city has been handsomely blessed by nature. But San Diego also depended upon the aggressiveness and foresight of its people. San Diego was fortunate; it always had

men and women of vision.

It has survived the difficult times through the hard work of individuals. In later years when fate seemed to deal the city a hand second to Los Angeles or San Francisco, San Diego's leaders sought workable solutions to its problems. And often what seemed to be a disadvantage was turned to an advantage. When plans for a railroad link failed, the lack of easy access gave the city a chance to pace itself and plan future growth more carefully than many cities.

And that is what *San Diego: California's Cornerstone* is about. It provides, for the reader, identification with San Diego's past, an awareness of its present, and concern for its future. It fits the pattern of individual life into the broad spectrum of human development. Hopefully the result is pride in understanding and being a part of San Diego.

Sponsors & Benefactors

The following San Diego firms, organizations, institutions and individuals have invested toward the quality of this historic book and thereby expressed their commitment to the future of this great city and to the support of the book's principal sponsor, the San Diego Chamber of Commerce.

AAA Credit Service
Arthur Andersen & Co.
Architectural Engineering Products Co.
Donald C. Armbruster
Associated Engineers
*Atlas Hotels, Inc.
August Building Company
*Avco Community Developers
BankCal - The Bank of California, N. A.
Benton Engineering, Inc.
Mr. & Mrs. Philip Henking Benton
Mr. & Mrs. Robert Harrison Benton, Jr.
Mr. & Mrs. Robert Harrison Benton, Sr.
Bumble Bee Seafoods
C. & M. Meat Packing Corporation
CEP Associated
Cabrillo Crane & Rigging Corporation

Calbiochem-Behring Corp.
*California First Bank
California Meter Service
California World Title Company
Catholic Community Services
Charles W. Christensen & Associates
E. F. Cook & Associates, Ltd.
*The Copley Press, Inc.
Deems/Lewis & Partners, Planning and Architecture
*Del Mar Thoroughbred Club
Dibble Electronics, Inc.
Draheim Steel, Inc.
Dylon Corporation
Charles A. Ekstrom Company
El Camino Mortuary and Memorial Park
Empire Realty
Employee Benefits Insurance Co.
*The FedMart Corporation
First Affiliated Securities, Inc.
First Federal Savings & Loan Association of San Diego
*Foodmaker, Inc.
Frazee Paint and Wallcoverings
Mrs. S. Robert Frazee, Jr.

*General Atomic Company
*General Dynamics
James C. Gilchriest
Stanley F. Gizienski
*M. H. Golden Company
Gray, Cary, Ames & Frye
Steven C. Haley
The Hartley Company
Mr. & Mrs. Donald J. Hartley
The Hartley Family
Hasstech, Inc.
Fred A. Heilbron
Helix Imperial Harbour Development Corporation
Mr. & Mrs. Charles Frederick Henking
James T. and Margery Hill
*Home Federal Savings & Loan Association of San Diego
*Hotel del Coronado
*E. F. Hutton Life Insurance Company
ITT Continental Baking Co., Inc.
IVAC Corporation
*Imperial Corporation of America
Jennings, Engstrand & Henrikson
Johnson Forms Management

3. San Diego looking from N. E. Coronado

*KGTV10
*Kelco, Division of Merck & Co., Inc.
Kettenburg Marine/Division of Whittaker Corp.
King Container Company
Krommenhoek/McKeown & Associates, AIA
Kyocera International
Reuben E. Lee
James R. Libby and Associates
Lloyd Pest Control
McGladrey Hendrickson & Co.
Lynn McLean, Inc., Realtor
Maches and Baughman Accountancy
    Corporation
Maxwell Laboratories, Inc.
Mepco/Electra, Inc.
NCR Corporation
*National Steel and Shipbuilding Company
*National University
Nielsen Construction Company
Nelson & Sloan Materials and Concrete
Northwestern Mutual Life
Office Center Company
Olson Construction Company
*Pacific Southwest Airlines
Parliament Builders

Peat, Marwick, Mitchell & Co.
Mildred Penick
T. B. Penick & Sons, Inc.
Mr. & Mrs. Vennero Pernicano
Porter International Incorporated
*Rohr Industries, Inc.
*Roman Catholic Diocese of San Diego
San Diego Convention & Visitors Bureau
*San Diego Federal Savings and Loan Association
*San Diego Gas & Electric
San Diego National League Baseball Club, Inc.
*San Diego Trust & Savings Bank
San Diego Unified Port District
San Diego Unified School District
Sandaire
*Science Applications, Inc.
*Scripps Clinic and Research Foundation
Scripps Memorial Hospital
Sea World
Sears, Roebuck and Co.
Security Pacific Bank
Service Auto Parks Corp.
Sevier Engineering, Inc.
Walter & Mary Smyk
*Solar Turbines International

*Spectral Dynamics Corporation
Spectrum Printing
Spin Physics, Inc.
Sullivan, Jones & Archer
*The Sumitomo Bank of California
Harry L. Summers, Inc.
*Teledyne Ryan Aeronautical
*Trusthouse Forte, Inc. - TraveLodge
    International, Inc.
University Mechanical Engineers &
    Contractors
*University of San Diego
*Van Camp Sea Food Company
Vernitron Control Components
Weldmac Manufacturing Company
Wells Fargo Bank, N. A.
Wendy's of San Diego, Inc.
Western Airlines
Rolland E. Wick
Willis and Lang An Accountancy Corporation
Woodward-Clyde Consultants
Robert C. and Christie A. Wright

* Denotes Corporate Sponsors. The histories of these
organizations and individuals appear in a special section
beginning on page 177.

Contents

Chapter I

The untamed land

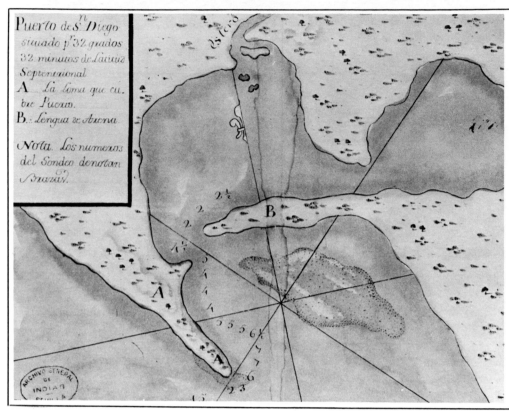

EXPLORER'S CHART: *Early Spanish map of San Diego Bay*

During its early years, San Diego's cultural progress and economic development were conditioned primarily by its position at an almost inaccessible edge of the North American continent. Fronting on a great expanse of ocean, it was backed—almost isolated—by mountains and desert. These natural barriers gave the region a distinct identity. Geographic remoteness shaped the life of its aboriginal inhabitants and established the settlement pattern of later colonizers. At first, communication by sea, moderate temperatures and available fertile land made living close to the ocean desirable. The early settlers stayed along the coast even though rainfall was erratic. Prevailing westerly winds, low clouds and frequent fog provided important sources of moisture for the land.

San Diego's recorded history is but a moment in geologic time. About 80,000 years ago, during the latter part of the Ice Age, a slightly curving coastline protected an area considerably different from today. Point Loma stood as a separate island, and Crown Point to the north formed a bay mouth bar across the ancestral Mission Bay. The mainland consisted of a broad mesa continually cut deeper and deeper by the rushing San Diego River. Finally a canyon 500 feet deep and 2,000 feet wide separated Linda Vista from Mission Hills. Throughout many centuries, the river carried mud and debris into the open sea, building up a delta to tie Point Loma to the mainland, closing off Mission Bay from San Diego Bay and creating a flat area at the base of Presidio Hill. Farther south, storm winds, nearshore north-moving currents and an eddy on the lee side of Point Loma caused sediment from the Tia Juana River to build up long sandy spits forming North Island and South Island to create Coronado and enclose San Diego Bay. Thus the area took on essentially its present

> *Geographic remoteness shaped the life of its aboriginal inhabitants and established the settlement pattern of later colonizers.*

shape and the river wandered between San Diego and Mission Bay.

Modern commercial and military demands have seen San Diego's port grow to harbor the world's largest ships. By extensive dredging, two new "islands"—Shelter and Harbor—have been created for man's use. Much of the area in Mission Bay, once silted up and clogged by sediments, has been made into a recreational park. Still, natural forces never cease to alter the landscape. Savage storm waves and constant winds work away at the jagged shoreline, eventually to carve new rocky inlets, form irregular sandbars and erode the long, white beaches. Secluded coves become imperceptibly larger; and sometimes the soft, overhanging cliffs, no longer finding support, tumble and fall into the sea—carrying man's creations with them. Both nature and man give and take.

Northerly from the Mexican border, the sandy shoreline rims a long coastal plain from which the natural harbor is cut. The coastal strand of Coronado with its characteristic dunes offers a number of woody perennials—shore sandbur, white-leafed saltbush, iceplants and lupine. Gulls, snowy plovers and many tiny invertebrates such as sand crabs and sand fleas call this home. To the north, Sunset Cliffs and La Jolla feature surf-beaten beaches where reefs and rocky formations extend from the shore and form tidepools. There are surf grasses, seagulls and an infinite variety of marine life. Farther north, the white beaches are broken by a shelf of sandstone that forms sculptured promontories and shallow caves near the water's edge. Where seasonal and small rivers empty into the sea, a number of tidal lagoons and salt marshes are formed. These include mudflats with low herbs or shrubs such as sea blite, salt grass and cord grass. The clapper rail, common egret, snowy egret, black brant, marsh hawk, Savannah sparrow, western sandpiper, least tern and other shorebirds find a home along with saltmarsh mosquitoes and the saltmarsh fly. Butterflies hover and sail; mice and rats scurry about.

But not all of San Diego is coastline. Much of the county consists of chaparral and oak-covered hills and mountains. The word "chaparral" comes from the Spanish *el chaparro* meaning the evergreen scrub oak. Spanish riders wore leather pants or *chaparajos* (chaps) to protect their legs from the dense prickly cover which was an effective barrier to ground travel by man and large animals. These brush-covered hills and mountains—dissected by branching arroyos that contain running water only during the rainy season—rise higher and higher toward the east and culminate in elevated areas where scattered forests of live and deciduous oaks, incense cedar, yellow pine, sugar pine, California juniper and other coniferous trees grow. To the northeast, Mount Palomar is 6,138 feet high, and in the southeast, Cuyamaca Mountain reaches an elevation of 6,515 feet. This part of the Peninsular Province mountain mass is still being uplifted. The Palomar, Volcan and Laguna mountains are thought to be upraised fault blocks.

Beyond the mountains, the Colorado Desert contains the present below-sea-level Salton Sea, a great brackish inland lake. Its ancestral waters were at times connected with the Gulf of California. The Colorado River in ages past brought down and deposited vast amounts of silt that formed the rich soils of the Imperial Valley, a part of San Diego County until 1907. The Anza-Borrego Desert State Park produces a spectacular wildflower show each spring.

The characteristic bushy growth of the hillsides and mesas is relieved by riparian woodlands of alder, cottonwood, oak, sycamore and maple along rivers such as the San Luis Rey and Santa Margarita. In addition to what people consider natural vegetation, San Diego features two man-created biotic communities with a coastal orientation—cismontane urban and cismontane rural. The first includes a great variety of introduced trees, most of which are today considered a part of the natural landscape. Olive, eucalyptus, many palms, jacaranda, bougainvillea, acacia and others from Africa, Australia, South America, Asia and various

Cathedral Rock at La Jolla.

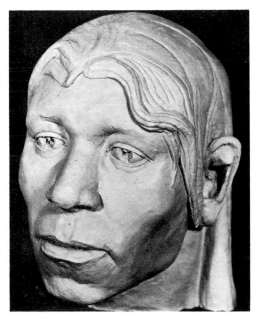

EARLY DWELLER: San Diego's sculptor Donal Hord's idea of a Kumeyaay or southern Diegueño Indian, an early inhabitant of the southwest coast.

parts of the United States abound. Private and public landscaping, dependent upon the use of water imported from long distances outside the county, have made luxuriant gardens out of areas where formerly only scrub oak could survive. In rural areas, cultivated croplands, pastures, fruit orchards of lemons, oranges and avocadoes, truck gardens, vineyards and fields of flowers have provided important revenues and new beauty throughout San Diego County. These areas are inhabited not only by man but by oppossums, gophers, rats, skunks, coyotes, rabbits, mice and several kinds of snakes. Planted areas host a seemingly insurmountable number of garden snails. Doves, quail,

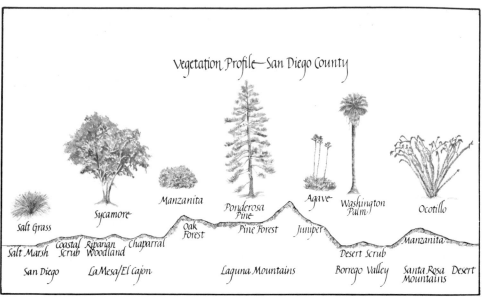

Vegetation Profile—San Diego County

Salt Grass · Sycamore · Manzanita · Ponderosa Pine · Agave · Washington Palm · Ocotillo

Salt Marsh · Coastal Scrub · Riparian Woodland · Chaparral · Oak Forest · Pine Forest · Juniper · Desert Scrub · Manzanita

San Diego · La Mesa/El Cajon · Laguna Mountains · Borrego Valley · Santa Rosa Mountains · Desert

hawks, pigeons, sparrows, finches, mockingbirds, blackbirds, starlings, and hummingbirds grace the skies, while ladybugs, butterflies and sowbugs are also well-known residents.

PLANTS AND PEOPLE: Biotic communities of southern California (above) go from salt marsh to pine forest to desert scrub. From birds in the area, a feathered ritual garment was made for Cinon Mataweer (Duro), the last great shaman of the northern Diegueño (below), who wears sacred owl, hawk and eagle feathers.

Prior to European contact, San Diego's natural food supply provided for a relatively larger Indian population than in other areas of the United States. Although natives in the region never reached the dense numbers that existed in central Mexico and Peru, estimates generally run about 10,000. These were divided between two major linguistic groups. In the extreme south and east, including adjacent areas of Baja California and Arizona, the majority of Indians belonged to the Hokan-Siouian family. Yuman was a subfamily of this group and was divided into the Ǩamia toward the east and northern and southern Diegueño (or Kumeyaay) toward the coast. These Indians displaced two prehistoric cultures—the San Dieguito dating from 7,000 B.C. and the La Jolla from about 5,000 B.C. A migration of Yuman-speaking peoples around 1,000 B.C. brought new artifacts and created the cultural complex that eventually interacted with the Spaniards. In north county the Indians belonged to the Uto-Aztecan family, linguistically (but distantly) related to the Aztecs of Mexico. Its Shoshonean subfamily included the Luiseño, Cupeño and Cahuilla whose descendants still live on the same lands.

By the mid-eighteenth century, despite their linguistic differences most of the region's Indians shared common cultural characteristics. They were generally an attractive, healthy and good-humored people who had a highly specialized hunting and food-gathering economy based upon vast ecological knowledge. The staple food supply, the acorn, was rather elaborately ground, leached, rinsed and prepared into a kind of gruel to which seeds, berries or other fruits were added for variety. They also consumed currants, wild plums, bulbous roots, the stalks of sage and yucca and different kinds of rushes. Deer, rabbits, ground squirrels, quail and ducks provided game. Coastal Indians ate shellfish and caught other kinds of fish in nets fashioned from milkweed, nettles or a kind of fiber called *ixtle.* Nets were also used to snare rabbits and other small game. Roasted grasshoppers were a delicacy for the Cupeños in the grassy valley of San Jose near today's Warner's Ranch.

Because of the moderate climate and limited building materials, Indian lodgings consisted of pole frames covered with bark, brush, cattails or other woven grasses in the shape of a dome. Usually their villages, or *rancherías* as they were called by the Spanish, consisted of 40 to 75

dwellings for sleeping purposes. These were semi-permanent during the winter and scattered at intervals of a few miles — some near today's downtown, others flanking Mission Valley and several more along the coast. Inhabitants of different villages quarrelled over food sources when supplies were scarce, but they were not warlike as a rule. Clothing was minimal; the men usually wore nothing and the women favored a kind of double woven skirt tied at the waist. In winter all wore cloaks around their shoulders made from sea otter, rabbit or deer skins. Fiber sandals were preferred for long journeys. Men tied up their long hair while women let it hang freely. Both sexes practiced tattooing with vertical lines or simple patterns although the women exhibited more elaborate markings.

The women were skilled basket makers and wove a variety of designs. Baskets served for carrying goods, storage, plates and many other uses. Pottery making was not widespread although some had apparently learned it from Indians living in the Colorado River region. Men made fishing and hunting nets from local fibers, shaped knives and arrowheads from stone and carved bows from willow, alder or ash. Coastal dwellers built simple rafts from cattail reeds and other floatable material.

All groups enjoyed recreation. Their games often involved batting a wooden ball about with a curved stick, guessing where a particular nut or stone was hidden or tossing carved rings in the air and catching them on a stick. Village ceremonies concerned significant transitional periods in the life of the individual — puberty, marriage and death. Coming-of-age rites were often the most elaborate. For girls, the celebration centered upon

INDIAN LINES: Portraits by H.B. Mollhausen show the Indians who were directly or indirectly involved with the Dieguenos – the Yuma (top left) and the Mojave (top right), directly, and the Chemehuevi (center left) and the Cocopah (center right), indirectly. Mollhausen was an illustrator who accompanied the Colorado Exploring Expedition of 1857-58. During this time, tribal boundaries of southwest Indian tribes were delienated (above), although these tribes were not warlike by nature.

preparation for marriage and child-bearing. Boys often drank a jimsonweed potion to envision future achievements. Special songs were sung by the elders and taught to the young people. Religious beliefs varied in complexity throughout the region but usually included ideas about life after death, a God-creator and supernatural forces.

The marriage ceremony was important and brought families together for a feast of several days. Nevertheless, if the marriage failed, new partners could be found for the couple. If a partner died, a new spouse was generally sought within the family group. The Diegueño had a general idea of a soul and when questioned about the death of a relative would answer, "He went to the stars." Because the spirits of the dead were believed able to return to make requests or occasionally do evil things, it was important that proper funeral rituals be conducted. The body was cremated the day after death and later the deceased's possessions were burned. Some evidence for prone burial has come to light through excavation of very early Western Diegueño sites, but cremation was the general practice. The concept of amassing material possessions or leaving an estate did not exist.

Although needs were limited primarily to food, clothing, weapons and ceremonial items, an economic network based upon the barter system functioned in the area. The Cahuilla supplied the Diegueño with roots, bulbs, cattail sprouts, yucca leaves, mescal, pine nuts, manzanita berries and mesquite beans. The Cahuilla received gourd rattles from the Quechan and basketry caps from the Chemehuevi. The Diegueño supplied acorns, tobacco, baked mescal roots, yucca fibers, sandals, baskets, carrying nets and eagle feathers to the Kamia and Cocopa and acorns to the Mojave. In turn, the Diegueño received salt from the Cocopa, gourd seeds from the Mojave, vegetables and salt from the Kamia. The Cupeño and Los Coyotes Cahuillas often exchanged goods through the use of shell money.

Despite their political disunity, the Indians of southern California had a wide range of contacts and lived in an active, orderly and self-sufficient manner. The natural evolution of their lifestyle was interrupted by European contact and left them with three options — to resist, to withdraw or to cooperate. Each was tried with varying degrees of success. But their goal was always the same — the preservation of their own political sovereignty and cultural integrity. Despite occupation of the San Diego area by

HOUSES, KEEPERS: Luiseño Indian women, circa 1893, stand beside a dwelling (top); the short woman was reported as being 128 years old at the time of the photo. The Luiseño's mountain-style wood and bark-slab house (above) was built on Palomar Mountain.

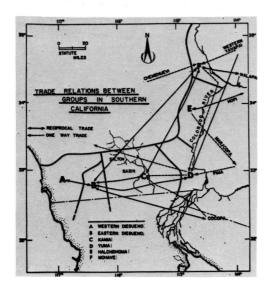

Indian trade routes before Spanish colonization

The natural evolution of the Indian lifestyle was interrupted by European contact and left them with three options - to resist, to withdraw or to cooperate.

non-Indians for more than 200 years, these first arrivals never lost their foothold. Their descendants presently number some 7,500 in the county and control 118,000 acres of federal land. They not only survived secularization of the missions under Mexico, the American conquest and ensuing problems of the 1850s and 1860s, they attracted congressional support as early as 1873 when John G. Ames investigated the state of former mission Indians and others residing in the area. Described as "homeless wanderers who have been dispossessed of their lands by white settlers," they retained their separate identity. In 1874 when there remained probably fewer than 1,000 Indians in the area, special commissioner Charles A. Wetmore toured the county and recommended the foundation of several small reservations and the reestablishment of Roman Catholic missionary work. As a result, in 1875, President Ulysses S. Grant by executive order set aside land for nine Indian reservations — Portrero, Cahuila, Capitan Grande, Santa Ysabel, Pala, Agua Caliente, Sycuan, Inaja and Cosmit. In the 1880s, additional lands were set aside for Indian use by the executive orders of Presidents Hayes, Arthur, Cleveland and Harrison. On various occasions, however, these same presidents issued other executive orders that restored portions of these lands to the public domain.

After the appearance of Helen Hunt Jackson's *Century of Dishonor* and her immensely popular novel *Ramona* during the 1880s, efforts were made to create permanent reservations for these Indians. In 1891, the Mission Indian Relief Act was passed empowering the Secretary of the Interior to appoint three commissioners to select a reservation for each group of Indians residing in California. In 1893, trust patents were issued for the Campo, Cuyapaipe, La Jolla, La Poste, Laguna, Manzanita, Pauma, Rincon and Yuima reservations. Subsequently, patents were also issued for the Santa Ysabel, Inaja, Cosmit, Barona Ranch, Viejas and Los Coyotes reservations. The federal government purchased some 3,438 acres to add to the Pala reservation in 1903 to accommodate Indians who had been displaced from Warner's Ranch. In 1910, the San Pasqual reservation was also patented.

In the final quarter of the nineteenth century, the federal government began to pass special laws to aid Indians throughout the country. Homestead law provisions were extended to Indians in 1875, and the Dawes Severalty Act of 1887 provided for the allotment of land to individual Indians with citizenship after 25 years. During the early twentieth century, additional special acts were passed. A statute of 1919 gave citizenship to all Indians who had received an honorable discharge from service in World War I. In June 1924, all remaining non-citizen Indians living within the territorial limits of the United States were given citizenship.

Additional special legislation authorized the bringing of suits against the United States for its Indian wrongs. Pursuant to an act passed in May 1928, a federal Court of Claims awarded the California Indians $5 million in 1944. Two years later, Congress then passed the Indian Claims Commission Act, a comprehensive act aimed at settling the Indian claims once and for all. The California Indians received an award of $29 million in 1965 for the taking of their lands and other damages. The hopes of resolving old conflicts by this legislation were too great. Additional claims against the United States relating to Indian land and water rights were still pending in early 1980.

San Diego's first inhabitants changed the natural environment very little. Subsequent generations altered the landscape to provide for themselves and their families. Today the region maintains a balance between old-timers and newcomers, urban dwellers and rural farmers, and those who prefer the natural setting in contrast to landscaped gardens. Increased population pressures will make future planning decisions more difficult.

Chapter II

The founding of San Diego

1542-1821

The Pacific voyage of Juan Rodríguez Cabrillo sailing under the flag of Spain in 1542 marked the first time that Europeans recorded their impressions of San Diego. Entry into the bay climaxed a series of maritime expeditions that had carried the cross and sword from the Iberian peninsula through the West Indies and Central America to the shores of Nuñez de Balboa's South Sea. Hernán Cortés, conqueror of the Aztec empire in 1521, established Spanish control in Mexico and promoted the discovery and exploration of Baja California in the mid-1530s. A constant search for wealth by some and a fervent desire to Christianize by others set into motion the events that led Rodríguez Cabrillo, a companion of Cortés and colonizer of Guatemala, to make his epic journey to Alta California.

Rodríguez Cabrillo's two ships, the *San Salvador* and *La Victoria,* built on the coast of Guatemala, set sail from the Port of Navidad, Mexico, on June 27, 1542, to explore remote and uncharted areas of the North Pacific — hopefully to find the Northwest Passage, a short-cut to Oriental riches. Their immediate goal was California — perhaps named for the mythical island of Amazon women described by Spanish novelist Ordoñez de Montalvo in a sixteenth-century adventure story called *Las Sergas (Deeds) of Esplandían.* Queen Calafia and her female subjects had "no other metal than gold" on their island whose craggy shores could have resembled California. Less romantically the name might have resulted from a combination of *cálida* meaning hot or *cal* meaning limestone joined with *forno,* an old Castilian form of *horno* or oven. To some, the arid desert lands of the lower peninsula may have suggested a hot oven or limekiln.

On September 28, 1542, Cabrillo and his companions headed their ships into San Diego Bay, anchored on the lee side of Point Loma near Ballast Point and stepped ashore. They were greeted by friendly Indians, "handsome and well built," wearing animal skins. The natives called their land Guacamal. Cabrillo christened the "closed and very good port" San Miguel Archangel (the name lasted only until the next explorer arrived). The men exchanged gifts with the natives and departed after a few days. The expedition stopped at several of the Channel Islands and during a short stay at *La Posesión* (later known as San Miguel Island), Cabrillo broke his shoulder. When the wound worsened they returned to *La Posesión,* where Cabrillo died. He was buried on shore in January 1543. The others, following Cabrillo's dying command, explored as far north as Cape Mendocino but returned to Mexico when a heavy storm prevented their continued search for gold or other riches.

It was nearly 60 years before the Indians of Guacamal again received European visitors. Sebastián Vizcaíno, merchant and veteran of the Manila Galleon trade with the Philippine Islands, sailed from Acapulco on May 5, 1602. He commanded the *San Diego, Santo Tomás, Tres Reyes* and a small auxiliary ship. His company of 200 men included a cosmographer and three Carmelite friars. Vizcaíno entered San Diego bay on November 10, noting its good anchorage and abundant natural resources. "On the 12th of said month, which was the day of the glorious San Diego {de

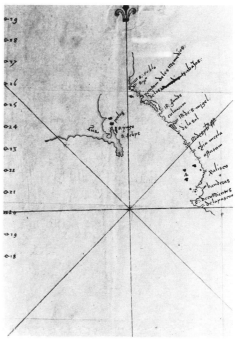

THE SPANISH IMPRINT: The search for wealth and the desire to Christianize set into motion the events that led Juan Rodriguez Cabrillo (above) to make his epic journey to California. He was a companion of Cortes who early charted the area (top). The Christian influence grew into "Mission Life" (left) as pictured in Jon Helland's mural.

Sebastián Vizcaíno

Alcala], almost everyone went ashore; they built a hut, said mass [and] celebrated the feast of San Diego." Since they did not recognize it as Cabrillo's San Miguel, they named the port after Diego, a Spanish saint who had performed his labors at the University de Alcalá de Henares near Madrid during the mid-1400s. He was canonized as Saint Didacus in 1588.

At the crest of Point Loma, Father Antonio de la Ascensión discovered "another good port" [Mission Bay]. Here the land was fertile, the variety of fish numerous and gold pyrites were abundant along the water's edge.

The Indians conducted Vizcaíno and others to their *rancherías* where women, dressed in animal skins, were cooking food in pots. After a friendly visit, the expedition sailed on November 20. Vizcaíno bestowed many other place names that remain today, including that of his first choice for California's capital port — Monterey.

Although Alta California continued to attract attention for a possible Manila Galleon port, no further attempts to explore or colonize the area were made during the next 167 years. Instead, Spain maintained her interest in the region of northern Mexico and established presidios and missions throughout the Southwest. The Jesuit mission chain in Baja California (begun in 1697 at Loreto) extended from the southern tip to northern portions of the peninsula. Alta California, however, remained solely occupied by Indians until the late eighteenth century when expulsion of the Jesuits, threatened Russian expansion into Alaska and availability of funds combined to provide the impetus for northward penetration.

Actual colonization and settlement of San Diego resulted from the efforts of several individuals. The driving force was José de Gálvez, a powerful and energetic representative of Spain's King Carlos III who had, since 1765, carried out a number of reforms in Mexico. Gálvez developed the plan for occupation of Alta California while surveying the west coast port of San Blas in 1768. He selected the personnel and wrote out lengthy instructions to leaders of four separate expeditions — two by sea and two by land — designed to reach San Diego in 1769. He gained viceregal approval of his plan and then sailed to La Paz to supervise operations. With unusual insight, Gálvez appointed Baja California's Governor Gaspar de Portolá — a well-qualified army officer from Lerida, Spain — to head the military force. He placed Father Junípero Serra, president of Franciscan missions in California, in charge of religious conversion.

Father Serra, born Miguel José in Petra on the Spanish island of Mallorca in 1713, first reached America with a party of missionaries in 1749. He gave up a prestigious career as professor of theology in Palma de Mallorca to labor among the Indians of the New World. He served with great success for nine years among the Pamé Indians in the Sierra Gorda mountains of eastern Mexico. Gálvez chose him to lead the Franciscans who would replace the expelled Jesuit priests in fourteen missions of Baja California and to help carry the cross to San Diego and Monterey. Gálvez chose wisely. Serra's zeal — despite poor health and a lame leg — never wavered until his goal of missionization to the north was realized.

The maritime branch of the Alta California expedition prepared the way for overland occupation. Two ships, the *San Carlos* (under Vicente Vila) and the *San Antonio* (commanded by Juan Pérez) left from La Paz on January 9 and February 15, 1769, carrying supplies and about 100 persons. Contrary winds, strong currents and faulty navigational information caused considerable delay, especially for the *San Carlos*. Both

THE FORCE: Colonization and settlement of San Diego resulted from the efforts of many. One driving force was José de Gálvez (above), the energetic representative of Spain's King Carlos III (top). Seen in a rare portrait shortly before his death, circa 1787, Gálvez was responsible for planning the expedition to occupy and settle the ports of San Diego and Monterey.

Serra's zeal - despite poor health and a lame leg - never wavered.

ships reached the port of San Diego in late April with a majority of crew members suffering from scurvy or some communicable disease. More than 60 men died on the beach in a makeshift hospital tent during the first few months. A third ship, the *San José* — scheduled to deliver needed supplies — disappeared at sea.

Two overland parties left the northern peninsula in March with equipment, food, animals and Indian personnel from the former Jesuit missions. The first (led by Captain Fernando de Rivera y Moncada of the Loreto presidio with Mallorcan Father Juan Crespí as diarist) successfully blazed the trail for the second party (headed by Portolá) with the spiritual guidance of Father Serra. All reached San Diego by July 1, 1769 and set up an encampment on a hill where the presidio would be built. Even though sickness had taken its toll, there were still enough men to continue the march northward. On July 14, Portolá led an overland expedition in search of Monterey, the port Vizcaíno thought appropriate for the capital of California. Failing to recognize Monterey, they came upon the expansive San Francisco Bay on November 1, 1769. Father Crespí recorded their discovery and the party returned to San Diego in early spring without having achieved its original goal.

Two days after Portolá's departure, the four Franciscan fathers — Junípero Serra, Juan González Vizcaíno, Fernando Parrón, and Francisco Gómez — blessed a site on Presidio Hill as Mission San Diego de Alcalá, the first in Alta California. They built a brush chapel and within a short time began construction of a small adobe church. Their early days were spent caring for the sick and dying Spaniards and making friends with the local Indians after some minor skirmishes. Finally, in March 1770, the *San Antonio* arrived with needed supplies from Baja California. Plans were made for further settlement. This time the search for Monterey proved successful, and Father Serra officiated at the founding of the presidio of Monterey and Mission San Carlos Borromeo on June 3. When the news reached Mexico City, cathedral bells rang out in honor of Spain's success.

FATHERS' BLESSING: In 1769, four Franciscan fathers blessed a site on Presidio Hill as Mission San Diego de Alcala; among them, Father Junípero Serra (top). The mission, which was the first European settlement on the west Pacific coast, was moved inland in 1774. The Serra Museum and Presidio Park (above) were later rebuilt on the original site.

ife in San Diego proceeded at a slow pace while soldiers and missionaries struggled to cultivate the land. Some of the married families lived in brush huts within the presidio complex, and the children learned their catechism from the priests. In 1772, members of the Dominican order took over the missions of Baja California and freed a number of Franciscans for service in the newer missions of Alta California. Among those who served San Diego were Father Luis Jayme (1771-1775), a native of Mallorca and Father Vicente Fuster (1773-1777) from Aragon. Both were in residence in August 1774, when poor soil and lack of water forced reestablishment of the mission six miles inland. The new site (where the mission stands today) was close to the San Diego River and included the Diegueño village of Nipaguay. Despite their slow beginning, the Franciscans baptized more than 100 Indians during the first five years, and about 97 made their home at the mission.

Spain continued to strengthen her claims over the north Pacific regions with the 1774 voyage of Juan Pérez to parallel 54° 40′ just north of the Queen Charlotte Islands and by recruiting colonists for the California settlements. During that year, Juan Bautista de Anza opened a 2,000-mile overland trail from the presidio of Tubac, Arizona, to Mission San Gabriel. This linked California with the Spanish Southwest. Dominican fathers laid the foundations for Mission Nuestra Señora del Rosario south of Ensenada in March 1774. The presidio at San Diego reached its largest number by January 1, 1775. At the fort — commanded by Lieutenant José Francisco de Ortega — were a sergeant, one corporal and 23 soldiers. A corporal and four soldiers formed the mission guard.

Rations at the presidio were scarce. Married women obtained extra food for their families by making tortillas for bachelor soldiers and preparing meals for them in exchange for additional corn and beans. New crops were planted at the mission in hopes of more abundant provisions.

After a record baptism of 60 Indians in October 1775, events suddenly took an abrupt turn at Mission San Diego. The Diegueños were unhappy about the mission's location at Nipaguay and resentful of Spanish intrusion. Encouraged by native leaders, they planned a simultaneous assault on both mission and presidio. On November 5, 1775, approximately 600 natives burned the mission buildings and cruelly killed Father Luis Jayme. Two others died and many suffered wounds, but the presidio escaped attack. The Indians were contrite after their unsuccessful attempt to destroy the mission. They feared the soldiers' reprisal, and abandoned further plans for destruction. Slowly they returned to the mission as converts. Fathers Fermín Francisco de Lasuén, a Spanish Basque, and Gregorio Amurrió from Calahorra joined Father Fuster, the surviving missionary at San Diego, in December 1775. The Franciscans moved to Presidio Hill with their converts and resumed construction of the chapel at the entrance to Mission Valley.

During early 1776, Governor Rivera and Lt. Colonel Anza both made tours of Diegueño villages. They reported no apparent unrest. Father Serra arrived in San Diego aboard the *San Antonio* in July and supervised the mission's reconstruction at the Nipaguay site. The mission was slowly rebuilt with the help of Indians and sailors from the *San Antonio* who made adobe bricks, dug trenches and gathered stone. The Franciscans baptized their first convert at the new Mission San Diego de Alcalá on December 8, far removed from events taking place in Philadelphia.

Peace and progress typified the final days of Spain's control over California from 1776 to 1821. Father Lasuén who succeeded Serra as father president of the missions served at San Diego from 1777 through 1784. During this period the mission took the form of a large quadrangle surrounding a spacious courtyard. Lasuén's annual report to Serra in 1783 described the church as 30 *varas* (yards) in length by 5 ½ in width

SOUTHWEST STRUGGLE: Susaan Kliech (above), one of the last Diegueño Indians. The early Indians were not happy about the mission's location, shown on map (top right) and in 1775, burned the mission buildings. The Mission San Diego de Alcalá lay in ruins (below, right) by the mid-1880s.

On November 5, 1775, approximately 600 natives burned the mission buildings and killed Father Luis Jayme.

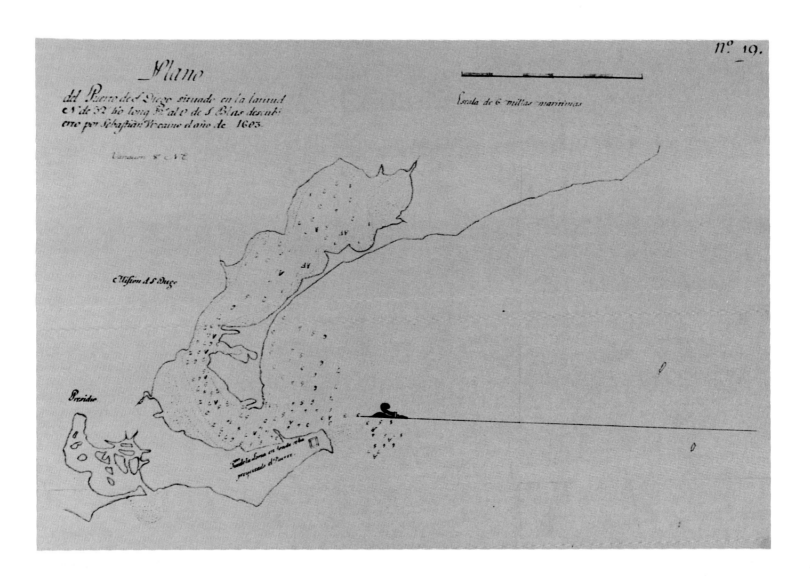

Nº 613.   San Diego Mission from the South West.   Nov 28th 1888.

(84-by-15 feet) "with walls two adobes thick, its large beams of pine, with corbels of oak and over that eleven unpolished beams of alder and poplar" supported by the same to form the roof, which was covered by tule and dried mud as a precaution against fire. The passageway extending along the south side was nearly ten feet wide with pillars and brackets of oak. "The entire aspect, especially the interior of the church and sacristy, is attractive, clean, and pleasing, because of the excellent ensemble achieved by the skill of the workers in using the resources of the mission. Thanks be to God."

Indians worked in the gardens, orchards and fields to produce the necessary beans, chick-peas, lentils, corn, wheat and barley for themselves and their livestock. Because of a shortage of water and lack of prime soil, the harvest at San Diego was generally less abundant than at other missions. Nevertheless, by 1783, the Franciscans had performed 966 baptisms and supported a live-in population of about 800. A number of Indians in the back country preferred to remain aloof.

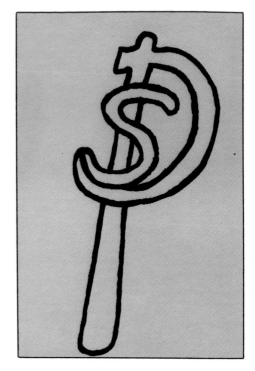

The role played by members of the San Diego presidial company in developing the Pueblo of Los Angeles in 1781 was significant. The first three *rancheros* in the Los Angeles area (and also in California) were Juan José Domínguez, Manuel Nieto and José María Verdugo of San Diego who were granted three large ranchos for cattle raising in 1784. A few retired soldiers chose to stay near the presidio and grow vegetables, raise some chickens and herd two or three milk cows. Since large scale cattle ranching was restricted to outlying areas, several others eventually moved to Los Angeles. The population at the San Diego presidio in 1791 included 112 men and 85 women. Fifteen local Indians worked there as servants.

San Diego remained relatively isolated until 1793 when British Captain George Vancouver visited the harbor on his return from the Pacific Northwest. He reported to London that the fine port was poorly defended and could be better protected from Point Loma. Any country able to take over the area would have an excellent potential for trade with the Orient. The Spanish forces, taking heed of the guarded threat, built Fort Guijarros at today's Ballast Point near the entrance to the harbor.

The little brig *Betsy* became the first American ship to enter San Diego Bay when it took on wood and water in 1800. Word of abundant sea otter and the high price of their fur in China had spread throughout the East Coast after several Americans visited the Pacific. In 1803 Spanish authorities prevented the ship *Alexander* from smuggling 500 otter skins out of the port. Later that year, the brig *Lelia Byrd* was stopped for the same reason. Fired upon from Fort Guijarros, the *Lelia Byrd* answered with a few shots. The "Battle of San Diego" was the only instance in which harbor defense guns were put into action. Before long, other ships manned by "Boston-men" entered into trading activities on the California coast.

Indian converts at Mission San Diego spent their days cultivating fields and tending livestock. The padres directed the building of a dam upstream in Mission Gorge to provide a more adequate water supply for irrigating crops. Nevertheless, Mission San Luis Rey de Francia founded in 1798 became the agricultural center for the region. The opening day ceremony, presided over by then Father President Lasuén, brought together a multitude of nearby Indians, and 54 children received baptism. Father Antonio Peyrí, a native of Tarragona, witnessed the mission's establishment and remained there as senior priest for 34 years. His wisdom, energy and architectural talent created buildings well known for their beauty and utility, and the mission fields stretched far inland. Father Peyrí founded Mission San Antonio de Pala as a branch or *asistencia* of San Luis Rey in 1816. Standing in a pleasant river valley in the foothills

MISSION ECONOMY: *Indian converts spent their days at Mission San Diego cultivating fields and tending livestock marked with the mission's brand (top). It was, however, Mission San Luis Rey de Francia (above) that became the agricultural center for the region; it later fell to ruin (right), photographed circa 1901. Mural (above) by Richard Gabriel Chase.*

east of today's Pala Mesa, the building is still in active use as a parish church for the local Indians. During the Spanish period, it served the large and cooperative Indian population working the grain fields of the area. The *asistencia* grew rapidly to rival the mission in importance and at its peak embraced more than 1,000 converts. Both Mission San Luis Rey and its sub-mission furnished agricultural produce to other areas and carried on brisk trading activities.

During construction of Mission San Diego's fourth church, a great earthquake on December 8, 1812, shook the buildings and caused structural damage. Fathers Fernando Martín and José Sánchez concluded that flared wings should be added to the façade as buttresses against future tremors that rolled on a north-south axis. They worked on the church during the next year and held dedication ceremonies for the building completed in its present form on November 12, 1813. Five years later, in 1818, the *asistencia* of Santa Ysabel was founded 60 miles east of San Diego to serve a group of 250 Indians who lived in the picturesque valley. Although it remained small, the permanent adobe buildings included a chapel, a granary and some houses; the number of Indians reached 450.

Until 1821, when revolutionary troops in Mexico succeeded in overthrowing Spain's government, San Diego remained essentially a religious and military outpost. When word of independence reached the distant port settlement, San Diegans raised the Mexican flag on April 20, 1822, amid appropriate festivities and swore allegiance to their new leaders. The only sadness was experienced by soldiers who had to cut off their long braids—symbols of the old regime. Spanish control over San Diego ended as it had begun—quietly and without violence. The cross and the sword, however, had left a permanent impression. The name itself—San Diego de Alcalá, conversion of Indians to the Catholic faith and interaction of Spaniards and Indians in agriculture, architecture and arts and crafts, all marked the beginning of a new way of life.

San Diegans raised the Mexican flag on April 20, 1822, amid appropriate festivities and swore allegiance to their new leaders.

Chapter III

San Diego under Mexico

1821-1846

After Mexico won its independence from Spain, California passed into a new era. The presidial soldiers and their families who lived on the hill, released from royal restrictions, began to think in terms of a permanent civilian town as founded in Los Angeles. The first person who probably moved down to the flat area below the hill was Captain Francisco María Ruiz, a native of Loreto in Baja California. Ruiz served as the last Spanish-appointed commandant of the presidio. He started an early garden and helped lay the foundations for several houses on the present site of Old Town. In 1823 he received the first private land grant in San Diego County — *Rancho Los Peñasquitos* (little cliffs). Captain Ruiz represented the new trend — less emphasis upon military matters and more interest in town building and ranching. The presidio literally began to crumble away.

One of the most famous residents of early San Diego was Pío Pico, the last Mexican governor of California. His family typified those living in the southern region during the years that spanned three epochs — Spanish, Mexican and American control. The Picos were involved in all aspects of political, military, social and religious life. Pío's father José María was of mixed Spanish, Indian and African ancestry. He came to San Diego from Sinaloa, Mexico, accompanied by his Sonoran-born wife María Eustaquia to join other presidio families in 1782. Their eldest son José Antonio was born on the hill in 1794 while Pío was born at Mission San Gabriel in 1801. Seven daughters and son Andrés, born in San Diego in 1810, completed the family. Because the elder Pico died in 1819 and José Antonio was in the service, Pío took charge of the household in San Diego. When they moved into the pueblo during the early 1820s, several other families had built houses in the area west of the plaza to the north and south. Pío opened up a small store where he sold liquors, provisions, chairs and shoes. He frequently traveled to Los Angeles, to the missions and to the frontier of Baja California to sell goods and bring back cattle and other products. He also gambled. Brother Andrés preferred the military and achieved a reputation as "brave, reckless, jovial, kind-hearted and popular." He never married although his sisters all found husbands locally. Pío's brothers-in-law included members of the Carrillo, Alvarado and Arguello families. His wife María was an Alvarado.

Closely associated with the Pico family were the Carrillos. Joaquín Carrillo, founder of the most numerous branch, came up from Baja California sometime after 1800. His cousin Guillermo had arrived earlier with Father Serra's entourage in 1769. The Carrillo house (on what is

FOUNDING FAMILIES: One of the most famous residents of early San Diego was Pío Pico (above, second from right), the last Mexican governor of California. He is shown (left to right) with niece Marianita, wife Leonora Pico and niece Trinidad Ortega. Cave Couts (left, standing) married a daughter of early-day settler Juan Bandini and later became owner of the 2,219-acre Rancho Guajome, where this photo was taken in the late 1860s, with seven of his eight children.

now Calhoun Street) may have been San Diego's first. Joaquín's daughter Josefa eloped in 1829 with American sea Captain Henry Delano Fitch, causing quite a stir in the conservative Catholic pueblo. Since Fitch's rival for Josefa's hand was Governor José María Echeandía (the man responsible for moving California's capital to San Diego), the couple's hasty departure for Valparaiso, Chile, without a proper church wedding was the talk of the town. Nevertheless, Josefa's family finally forgave her, and in time, Henry became a prosperous merchant and trader in San Diego, dealing with the many Boston ships that frequented the port. Their large family occupied the Carrillo home, and Fitch later served as a justice of the peace.

Governor Echeandía's problems during his six-year term from 1825 to 1831 involved a number of issues more serious than a lost sweetheart. These included the proposed secularization of the missions (for which he offered a plan of voluntary freedom with education), unrest among soldiers and non-mission Indians, and the arrival of foreigners by sea and land. Relaxed regulations had allowed French, British, American, Dutch and Russian ships to put in at San Diego for trade and supplies, but they often avoided paying custom's duties through various smuggling activities. A more serious threat, however, was the arrival of the first overland party from the growing United States—a group of mountain men led by Jedediah Smith of Missouri's Rocky Mountain Fur Company. Governor Echeandía rightly feared that once given an opening wedge, Americans would soon be coming to California in large numbers. He refused Smith and his men permission to stay. When James Ohio Pattie arrived in San Diego in 1829 with his father and a party of trappers from New Mexico, they were housed in the local jail. Although Pattie gained his freedom by helping cure a smallpox epidemic, further warnings were issued to parties seeking entrance.

After 1831—following Echeandía's ouster during a period of political unrest—Mexican policy was relaxed to allow Americans or others to enter the province and become naturalized Mexican citizens. This required conversion to Catholicism if they wanted to remain. Many men did so during the 1830s and married into local families.

EARLY SETTLERS: Migrating from Mexico to help settle San Diego were José Antonio Carrillo (top) and Juan Lorenzo Bruno Bandini (above, left) and daughter (above, right).

San Diego fought to keep the capital in the south. But as political fortunes vacillated between centralists and federalists in Mexico, repercussions were felt in California. Pío Pico and others supported Carlos Carrillo for governor, and Pico himself actually served twenty days in the post in 1832. Nevertheless, the southern group lost. When Brigadier General José Figueroa arrived as governor of California in January 1833, the capital was officially returned to Monterey. Residents of San Diego — then numbering 432 — appealed to the legislature assembled there that San Diego be granted official *pueblo* or town status, complete with municipal officers. Approval of a new civilian government was granted on June 4, 1834 and put into effect on January 1, 1835. Elected officials were Juan María Osuna, first alcalde (mayor); Juan Bautista Alvarado and Juan María Marrón, councilmen, and Henry Fitch, city attorney. They were installed by presidio commandant Santiago Argüello who agreed to supply Osuna with an inventory of documents in the "archives of San Diego."

By the mid-1830s, an historic town was beginning to take shape in San Diego. The Juan Bandini home southeast of the plaza was a center for political discussions and social activity. Juan's father José, a native of Spain, had migrated to Lima, Peru, where his children were born. Juan, a merchant, arrived in California in 1818 and in 1822 married María Dolores Estudillo. They became the parents of five children. After Maria's death, Juan married Refugio Argüello, and they also had five children. The large Bandini house, originally one story, had fourteen rooms and elegant furnishings. A kitchen and two storerooms were separated from the main house by an

TO SAN DIEGO BY SEA: Richard Henry Dana (above) came to California from Boston aboard the brig Pilgrim (right) and later, in his book Two Years Before the Mast, named San Diego as "the best place in California to land."

arcade. The Estudillo house across the path had twelve rooms surrounding a spacious courtyard. Its builder, José Antonio Estudillo was a native of Monterey, well educated and congenial. He and his wife María Victoria Domínguez had eleven children who, with all the others, made the plaza a lively area. Because the mission church was so far from town, the Estudillos had a little chapel built inside their home with guest quarters for the priest.

Richard Henry Dana, visiting California from Boston aboard a hide and tallow trader, saw San Diego in the summer of 1835 with shipmate Jack Stewart. Dana later recalled in his best-selling book *Two Years Before The Mast* that San Diego was decidedly the best place in California for landing and taking on board hides. Because the harbor was small and land-locked, vessels could lie within a cable's length of the smooth, sandy beach. Dana and Stewart paid a visit to the "old ruinous presidio" overlooking the small settlement of "about forty, dark-brown looking huts, or houses, and two larger ones, plastered" belonging to the Bandini and Estudillo families. They noticed that wood was scarce, and few trees grew in the area. For recreation they visited the local grog-shop, then rented some horses to ride out to the mission. There they ate "baked meats, frijoles stewed with peppers and onions, boiled eggs, and California flour baked into a kind of macaroni" which, "together with the wine, made the most sumptuous meal" they had eaten since Boston.

Dana enjoyed his stay in California but his strict puritanical background showed up frequently. He liked the violin and guitar playing but thought the men "thriftless, proud, and extravagant, and very much given to gaming ... The women had but little education and a good deal of beauty." What Dana may not have appreciated (among other aspects of California living) were the difficulties in building an adobe house. The three-foot deep walls of the typical one-room shelter of the Spanish-Mexicans required about 1,000 mud blocks. These were shaped in a rude mold to an average size of sixteen inches in width and twenty in length. Blocks were generally three to six inches thick and weighed from twenty to forty pounds. Straw was preferred as binding for the adobe substance, but inferior strengtheners such as shells, sticks, birds' nests and reeds were often necessary. The more prosperous homes were L-shaped or

Dana enjoyed his stay in California but his strict puritanical background showed up frequently.

U-shaped around an interior courtyard. The use of wood for flooring was practically unknown before 1835; the earth on the site was stamped to a degree of smoothness and occasionally hardened by watering. Glass was rare, and the lack of building timber prevented the addition of a second story. Two-story dwellings came later when lumbering operations began.

Dana's companion Jack Stewart married Rosa Machado, daughter of prominent San Diego resident José Manuel Machado. Machado and his wife María Serafina Váldez, parents of twelve children, provided at least three adobe houses near the plaza for their various offspring. (The Machado-Stewart and Machado-Silvas adobes have currently been restored.) Daughter Juanita, whose first husband Damásio Alipaz died in Sonora in 1835, later married first American settler Thomas Wrightington of Fall River, Massachusetts. Wrightington had left the brig *Ayacucho* in 1833 to remain in San Diego. He kept a general store featuring liquors, dry goods, shoes, bread and fruits. (The Machado families have many descendants in San Diego today.)

MEXICAN LIFE: The home of José Antonio Estudillo (above) had twelve rooms surrounding a spacious courtyard. Prepared in the typical Mexican oven (right) were "baked meats, frijoles stewed with peppers and onions, boiled eggs and California flour baked into a kind of macaroni," according to a visitor from the East.

A major change occurred in California with the secularization of the 21 Franciscan missions during Governor Figueroa's administration. The missions had been designed as temporary institutions, and local officials pointed out that they had long since fulfilled their obligations of conversion and training. The priests thought that the Indians were not yet ready for assimilation and objected to any change. But those with an eye on the extensive and prosperous mission lands thought otherwise. Authorities in Mexico City agreed that the time had come for a change and approved a general decree of secularization in August 1833. Effective in California the following year, the governor's decree placed Mission San Diego under civilian control on September 30, 1834, with a portion of the land going to the Indians. Joaquín Ortega became administrator of mission properties in April 1835, at a salary of $50 per month, to be paid from proceeds of mission products. Pío Pico took over the secular administration of Mission San Luis Rey that same month, but, according to his memoirs, "considered that all this property belonged by right and justice to the Indians." He received some 15,000 sheep, but all the cattle were wild and scattered since Father Peyri had departed the year before to retire in Spain. (The Indians had literally cried when the good priest left, but Father Peyri had not wanted to remain through the secularization period.) Although some mission administrators were well intentioned, the task of supervising Indians removed from the rigid mission discipline was enormous. Little by little, individual Indians—because of a lack of protection, training and/or motivation—lost or gave up lands assigned to them. Soon private ranchos took the place of mission farm and grazing lands.

Some of the Indians organized a little pueblo called San Dieguito in November, with 34 ex-mission families, while others searched for work as artisans in the pueblo or as workers on nearby ranchos.

Of the local residents who received grants of land for ranchos during the early Mexican period, some had been military men while others were prosperous merchants. All were well connected politically and had sufficient means at their disposal to qualify for a minimum grant of four square leagues (4,436 acres per square league). Santiago Argüello, whose father and brothers had been governors, received in 1829 Rancho Tia Juana, a sizable rancho extending from south of San Diego Bay to the site of present Tijuana in Mexico. Argüello and his wife Pilar Ortega also needed room to raise their 22 children. Other ranches granted by Governor Echeandia that year included Jamul (8,926 acres to Pío Pico); Janal (4,436 acres, to José Antonio Estudillo) and Otay (6,637 acres to Magdalena Estudillo.)

Because of frequent changes in the governorship and the problems of secularization, few grants were made during the 1830s. Many of the

Cave Johnson Couts

former mission holdings and other lands of San Diego County were granted to private owners by Governor Manuel Micheltorena during the period from 1841 to 1844. One of the largest was Rancho Santa Margarita y Las Flores — 133,440 acres stretching along 35 miles of coastline from Oceanside to Orange County and inland to Fallbrook. It was granted to Pío and Andrés Pico in 1841 and 1844. Some 300 Indians lived within the grant at Las Flores, a village founded in 1822 around an *asistencia* of Mission San Luis Rey. The smallest was Cañada de los Coches, a 28.33-acre hog farm within present-day El Cajon, granted to Doña Apolinaria Lorenzana, a devout woman who had been brought to California as an orphan in 1800. Because of her charitable deeds, she was called *La Beata* (The Devoted One). She had previously been given Rancho Jamacha (8,881 acres) as a reward for her services.

Other ranchos granted by Micheltorena included 8,824 acres called San Dieguito (later known as Rancho Santa Fe) to Juan María Osuna; Agua Hedionda (13,311 acres including much of today's Carlsbad) to Juan María Marrón; Las Encinitas (4,431 acres) to Andres Ybarra; Rincon del Diablo (today's Escondido — 12,653 acres) to Juan Bautista Alvarado, Los Vallecitos de San Marcos (8,877 acres) to José María Alvarado; Rancho San Bernardo (17,763 acres) to British sea captain Joseph F. Snook, husband of María Antonia Alvarado and Santa María (now the site of Ramona) — (17,708 acres) to British sea captain Edward Stokes, husband of Refugio Orega. Stokes and his father-in-law José Joaquin Ortega also received Rancho Santa Ysabel (17,719 acres) a year later. The 13,309-acre Pauma Rancho deep in Cupeño Indian territory was granted to José Antonio Serrano.

The area that became known as Warner's Ranch resulted from the combination of two prior grants. Silvestre de la Portilla received Rancho Valle de San Jose (17,634 acres) in 1836. A grant of 26,688 acres to José Antonio Pico in 1840 was called Rancho San José del Valle and included the Indian *ranchería* of Agua Caliente. Both Pico and Portilla abandoned their *ranchos* because of Indian attacks. Jonathan Trumbull Warner — a native of Connecticut who had come to California in 1831 from Santa Fe, New Mexico — had passed through the valley and noticed its fertility. He became a Mexican citizen and in 1837 married Anita Gale, a ward of Pío Pico's widowed mother Doña Eustaquia. Warner applied for both *ranchos* in 1844, citing their abandonment and received a grant of the entire San Jose Valley. He built an adobe house and trading post four miles south of Aqua Caliente and encouraged the Indians of the hot springs settlement to work for him.

Placenames

Agua Caliente: hot water.
Agua Hedionda: stinking water.
Ballena: whale.
Bonita: pretty.
Borrego: big horn sheep.
Buena Vista: good view.
Campo: field.
Chula Vista: pretty view.
Coronado: crowned (from Mexico's Coronado Islands).
Cuca: a root used as a substitute for coffee.
Cuyamaca: (Indian) rain above.
Dehesa: pasture.
Del Cerro: of the hill.
De Luz: of the light.
Del Mar: of the sea.
Descanso: rest.
Dulzura: sweetness.
El Cajon: the box.
El Camino Real: the main road.
Encanto: charm, enchantment.
Encinitas: little live oaks.
Escondido: hidden.
Guajome: (Indian) home of the frog.
Guatay: (Indian) large.
Jamacha: (Indian) wild squash.
Jamul: (Indian) slimy water.
Janal: (Indian) spongy ground.
La Jolla: the jewel.
La Mesa: the plateau, tableland.
La Presa: the dam.
La Punta: the point.
Las Flores: the flowers.
Las Pulgas: the fleas.
Linda Vista: pretty view.
Loma: hill.
Loma Portal: gateway to the hill.
Los Peñasquitos: the little cliffs.
Mesa Grande: large plateau.
Miramar: view of the sea.
Miramesa: view of the plateau.
Morena: brown.
Otay: (Indian) brushy.
Pala: trowel.
Palomar: pigeon coop.
Pauma: (Indian) I bring water.
Potrero: pasture.
Rincón del Diablo: Devil's corner.
Solana: sunny place.
Tia Juana: Aunt Jane.
Tierrasanta: holy land.
Tijuana: shortened form of Aunt Jane.
Valle: valley.
Vallecito: little valley.
Viejas: old ones.
Vista: view.

Shortly before the end of the Mexican period, Pío Pico finally realized his dream of becoming governor and established his headquarters in Los Angeles. During his term of office from February 22, 1845, to August 10, 1846, he did not forget his friends in San Diego and granted a number of sizable ranchos. One of the largest was Rancho El Cajon — 48,799 acres given to María Antonia Estudillo de Pedrorena, wife of Spanish-born Miguel de Pedrorena, a merchant and trader who held several local offices. The grant included present-day El Cajon, Lakeside, Santee, Bostonia and land east to El Monte Park. The Pedrorena family built a large adobe home near the center of Lakeside and a smaller one near the eastern end of Mission Gorge. Among the smaller grants was Cuca Rancho of 2,174 acres near Pauma Valley granted to María Juana de los Angeles Soberanes. It remained for some years in the hands of her daughter, wife of Gregorio Trujillo.

Other grants made by Governor Pico during 1845 included much of the county's agricultural and grazing lands, but these did not remain for long in the hands of their original owners. Many of the activities associated with these lands are of a later period. Rancho Cañada de San Vicente y Mesa del Padre Barona (13,316 acres) was granted to Juan Bautista López but deeded to Domingo Yorba in 1850. The southern part of the tract became the Barona Indian Reservation, named for Mission Father Josef Barona. The 2,219-acre Rancho Guajome (near Vista), given to Indian brothers Andrés and José Manuel, was in turn sold to Abel Stearns of Los Angeles. It later passed into the hands of Stearns' sister-in-law Isadora Bandini and her husband Cave J. Couts. Pico also granted nearby Rancho Buena Vista to an Indian, Felipe Subria, who gave it to his married daughter, Marie La Gradia Dunn. Its 1,184 acres were also acquired by Couts. The expansive Cuyamaca Rancho of 35,501 acres was granted to Agustín Olvera, an early resident of Los Angeles whose family gave Olvera Street its name. Olvera only visited the ranch occasionally and allowed several squatters to make their homes there. Rancho Guejito y Cañada de Palomía, (13,298 acres near Lake Wohlford) was granted to José María Orozco, a justice of the peace in San Diego who hosted countless fiestas at his large adobe ranchhouse.

Governor Pico granted San Diego's *alcalde* Pedro C. Carrillo and his wife Josefa Bandini a 4,185-acre tract called Península de San Diego. It lacked water and turned out to be unsuitable for grazing cattle. Even though Pedro won his battle with the pueblo over the rancho's boundaries, he decided to unload his barren land to Captain Bezer Simmons of the American ship *Magnolia* for $1,000 in 1848. Simmons did much better. On the mainland side of the bay, Rancho de la Nación (26,631 acres of presidio grazing lands) was granted to Pico's brother-in-law John (Juan) Forster of Liverpool, England. Forster's holdings also included Rancho Santa Margarita y las Flores (which he purchased from Andrés and Pío Pico) and Rancho San Felipe near the Banner Grade crossing toward Julian. Forster resided near San Juan Capistrano and in 1865 sold La Nación, the ranch which would later embrace National City and Chula Vista. The 9,972-acre Rancho San Felipe was originally granted to an Indian, Felipe Castillo, who transferred it to Forster. The 13,322-acre Monserrate Rancho was granted to Ysidro María Alvarado who built a small adobe home on the north side of the San Luis Rey River and carried on some ranching activities. A smallpox epidemic took the lives of many in the area during the 1860s, although son Tomás lived there with his family until the late 1870s.

The final area disposed of during the Mexican period was Rancho de la Misión San Diego de Alcalá — 58,875 acres stretching from the pueblo boundaries to El Cajon and from National City to today's Clairemont. It included present Linda Vista, Miramar, Mission Gorge, Allied Gardens, Del Cerro, San Carlos, Kensington, San Diego State University, La Mesa,

Santa Maria Rancho, where fine Merino sheep were a specialty.

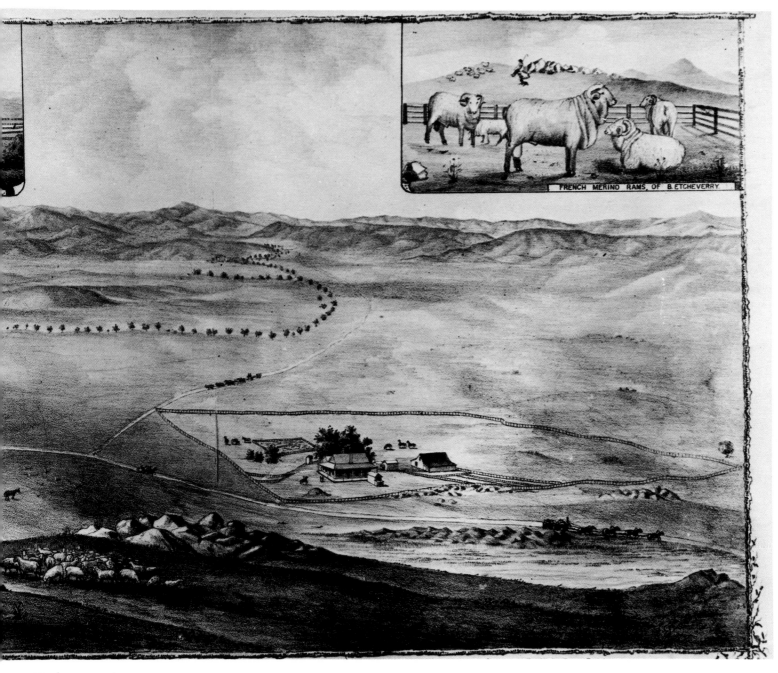

FRENCH MERINO RAMS, OF B. ETCHEVERRY.

Encanto and Lemon Grove. Pío Pico turned over the choice land to Santiago Argüello "in consideration of past services," and the deed was drafted June 8, 1846, in Los Angeles. Argüello was to pay the mission's debts, support the priests and maintain religious services. A death knell for the mission was sounded, however, when American troops occupied mission buildings during the American conquest of San Diego.

The Mexican War brought changes to San Diego, and the arrival of so many newcomers gradually transformed the way of life. In many ways, the changeover was peaceful and the adoption of new customs merely a continuation of the influence exerted by a number of non-Mexicans such as Philip Crosthwaite, a young Irishman who reached California in 1845. Crosthwaite—having lost the toss of a coin for the only berth on an eastbound ship—decided to stay in San Diego permanently. He married María Josefa López, settled in the pueblo and leased the ex-mission ranch lands from Argüello in 1848. He joined Henry Fitch, Abel Stearns, Edward Stokes, Juan Warner, Joseph Snook and others who tried to help San Diego manage a smooth transition from Mexican to American rule. Inevitably, tortillas gave way to white bread. Life in Southern California would never be the same.

Pío Pico, while governor of California did not forget his friends in San Diego and granted a number of sizable ranchos.

Legacy of the ranchos

Rancho Guajome (far right)

Rancho Las Encinitas (below)

Rancho land grants, San Diego County
(center right)

Original chapel of Rancho Guajome
(center below)

Rancho Guajome residence interior (far
right below)

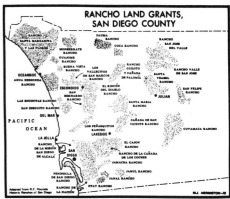

RANCHO LAND GRANTS,
SAN DIEGO COUNTY

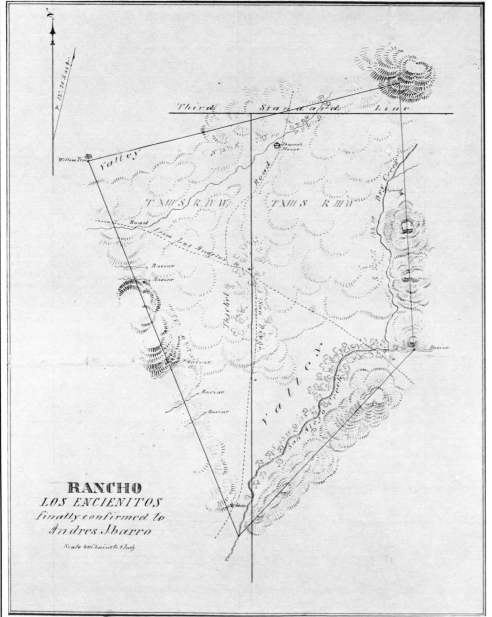

RANCHO
LOS ENCIENITOS
finally confirmed to
Andres Ibarro

Scale 40 chains to 1 inch

OLD AND NEW: Among the first buildings in New Town of 1850 was the San Diego Hotel (center), later called Dunnell's Hotel or the New San Diego Hotel. Old Town (below) continued as the center of activity around the short-lived time when the Bear Flag Republic flew its distinctive flag (left).

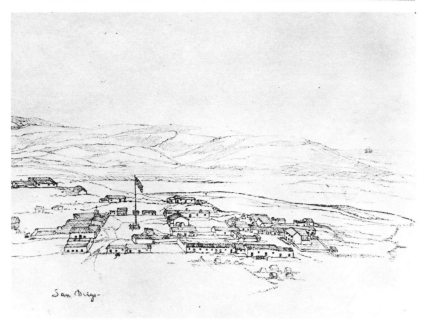

Chapter IV

A time of change

1846-1870

The Mexican War in 1846 abruptly altered the course of California history and significantly changed the structure of society in San Diego. Although never directly involved in the mainstream of the war, San Diegans felt the repercussions of events taking place on distant fronts. In the spring of 1846, American troops under Captain John C. Frémont camped near Monterey to survey "topographical features" of the nearby landscape. Mexican suspicions had been aroused ever since Americans had captured Monterey in 1842 under the mistaken belief that the United States was at war with its nearest neighbor. Asked by Mexican officials to leave the area, Fremont's troops headed toward Oregon — only to return to Sutter's Fort in Sacramento in June 1846, to support a group of American immigrants who had risen independently against Mexican control to establish the Bear Flag Republic. Since war against Mexico had been officially declared over problems in Texas the previous month, the three-week-old republic ended when the United States Navy raised the American flag over Monterey on July 9. Northern California fell to the invaders in short order.

On July 29, 1846, the *USS Cyane* under Commander Samuel F. Dupont sailed into San Diego Bay bringing John Fremont, the scout Kit Carson and a battalion of California volunteers to secure the southland. Lieutenants Stephen C. Rowan (United States Navy) and William A. Maddox (United States Marine Corps) went ashore with a Marine guard and raised the American flag in the plaza near the Estudillo house. For a time, there was little opposition. Dupont stayed in the home of Juan Bandini and commented that his host had long been a friend to the Americans and was ready for the change. There was music and dancing every night and, according to Dupont "Don Juan, although over sixty, is the most indefatigable and active of the dancers, saying it is *muy inocente*. His son-in-law, Don Pedro Carrillo, was educated in Boston and speaks English well. Don Miguel Pedrorena also speaks it fluently. These people are all intelligent and make it a much more agreeable place than Monterey...."

John Fremont was especially impressed by San Diego's surrounding countryside and wrote in his memoirs: "Among the arid, brush-covered hills south of San Diego we found little valleys converted by a single spring into crowded gardens, where pears, peaches, quinces, pomegranates, grapes, olives, and other fruits grew luxuriantly together, the little stream acting upon them like a principle of life. This southern frontier of Upper California seems eminently adapted to the cultivation of the vine and the olive. A single vine has been known to yield a barrel of wine, and the olive trees are burdened with the weight of fruit."

TROOP LEADERS: John C. Fremont (top), "The Pathfinder" who came to San Diego with Commander Samuel F. Dupont (above).

Ten days after the American flag was raised in the plaza, Fremont rode north with his battalion on a beautiful sorrel horse given to him by Juan Bandini. Other Mexican residents of San Diego—including members of the Osuna, Carrillo, Marrón and Machado families—failed to follow the appeal of Bandini and Santiago Argüello not to resist the Americans.

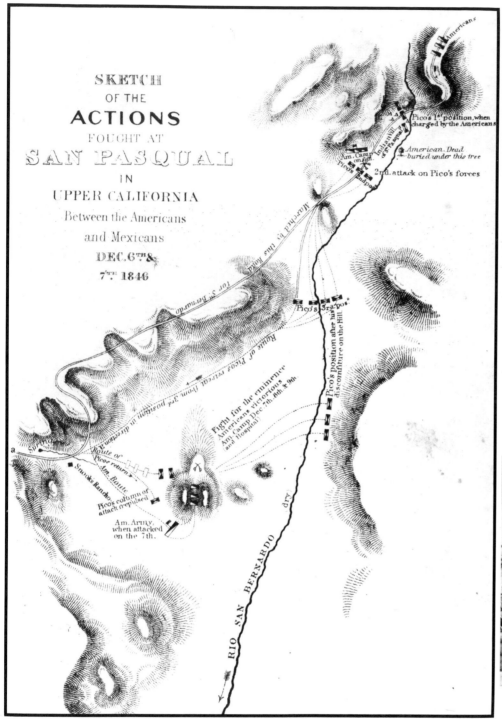

SKETCH
OF THE
ACTIONS
FOUGHT AT
SAN PASQUAL
IN
UPPER CALIFORNIA
Between the Americans
and Mexicans
DEC. 6TH &
7TH 1846

WAR: The conflict between Mexico and America is seen in sketches at San Pasqual (left) and crossing the River San Gabriel (above). Commodore Robert F. Stockton (top) was in charge of the U.S. Pacific Fleet that strengthened the American hold on San Diego against Mexican troops including lancers on horseback (center).

They were not convinced that California's separation from Mexico was inevitable and that a new government would bring protection and stability. The Estudillos remained neutral. When San Diego was left virtually undefended after Fremont's departure, a number of loyal Californians again flew the Mexican flag. Finally, Albert B. Smith, a sailmaker, nailed the Stars and Stripes permanently to the plaza flagpole.

In November 1846, Commodore Robert Stockton of the Pacific Squadron arrived in San Diego aboard the 60-gun *USS Congress* to assure American control. He posted a garrison on the hill near the presidio and called the encampment Fort Stockton. In addition, General Stephen Watts Kearny's Army of the West had been marching overland from Santa Fe to reinforce American troops in California. Guided by Kit Carson, the Kearny column of 110 officers and men reached Warner's Ranch on December 3 after covering some 1,000 miles of rugged terrain since September 25. They rested at Warner's Ranch while messengers were dispatched to Fort Stockton at San Diego. Meanwhile, 200 California lancers under Andres Pico prepared to intercept the American invaders. On the night of December 5, Kearny marched to a position above the San Pasqual Valley. Early on the morning of December 6, he made a premature and disorganized attack on the Californians. This engagement—known as the Battle of San Pasqual—was fought approximately five miles east of present-day Escondido and several hundred yards southeast of today's battlefield marker. The Americans suffered 31 casualties, including eighteen dead, while the Californians escaped unharmed. On December 7, the battered Kearny column camped on a nearby hill. Constantly harassed by the lancers, they were forced to burn their baggage and eat their remaining mules. The campsite became known as Mule Hill. Kit Carson and Navy Lieutenant Edward Fitzgerald Beale finally slipped out of camp and made their way to San Diego to get help. Two hundred United States Marines and sailors arrived from San Diego on December 11 to escort Kearny's column to the southern port. The Californians withdrew and were finally defeated when Fremont returned from the north. Andres Pico capitulated at Cahuenga Pass near Los Angeles on January 13, 1847, and the war in California was essentially over.

As a result of the war with Mexico, San Diego was infiltrated by newcomers from the military forces of the United States. Major William H. Emory, Kearny's chief of staff, wrote that San Diego consisted "of a few adobe houses, two or three of which only have plank floors ... the rain fell in torrents as we entered the town, and it was my singular fate here ... to be quartered in a miserable place of one room." Dr. John Griffin, Kearny's medical officer who spent most of his time caring for the wounded men, lamented that the houses were ill-ventilated and that their first Christmas in California was a solemn affair.

When the Mormon Battalion under Lieutenant Philip St. George Cooke arrived from Fort Leavenworth via a long march from Santa Fe, they were too late to participate in the war for which they had volunteered. Instead, they hired themselves out to the townspeople of San Diego. They made a whitewash and used it to brighten up the houses. They also built a bakery, fired bricks, built log pumps, dug wells, did blacksmithing and repaired carts. The wife of Captain Jesse Hunter of the Mormon group gave birth to the first American child born in San Diego. Called Diego in honor of his birthplace, the boy was cared for by local Mexican women when his mother died a short time later. Captain Hunter served as Indian agent at Mission San Luis Rey; his orders were to protect the Indians from local residents. Lieutenant Robert Clift became San Diego's justice of the peace from June 1847, until March 1848.

General Andres Pico (top) and Brevet Major General Stephen Watts Kearny.

Most of the Latter-day Saints preferred to move on to Salt Lake City, Utah, but Colonel Jonathan D. Stevenson, in command of a regiment of New York volunteers, asked that they stay on in California. Seventy-eight of the Mormons remained at Fort Stockton while others went north. Those staying behind were joined by Company I of Stevenson's men who had made the former San Diego Mission their headquarters and barracks. The soldiers at the mission conducted the first American census and listed 248 white residents, 483 converted Indians, 1,550 wild Indians, three Negroes and three Sandwich Islanders (Hawaiians).

On February 2, 1848, the Treaty of Guadalupe Hidalgo was signed, ending the war between Mexico and the United States. An international boundary commission under John B. Weller and Pedro Garcia Conde was set up to survey the new line from Texas to the Pacific Coast. After some delay, they began to work in San Diego.

To complicate matters, James Marshall's discovery of gold on the American River near Sacramento in late January 1848 had become known

Mormon soldiers, too late to participate in the war, hired themselves out to townspeople to perform needed handyman functions around town.

throughout the state and had touched off the migration of numerous gold-seekers. Many passed through San Diego on their way to northern mining areas. The *Daily Alta California* reported in December 1849 that the port of San Diego had "taken quite a start. Quite a number of Americans have gone down there recently and established themselves in business for the winter. A number of frame houses are in the process of erection and many others are being shipped from this port [of San Francisco]. The town is represented to us as being quite a bustling, lively, little place."

Several military men such as Cave J. Couts, John Bankhead Magruder, Samuel P. Heintzelman, Thomas W. Sweeny, Thomas D. Johns, Edward Murray, Edward H. Fitzgerald and John E. Summers had purchased property in La Playa or near the plaza. Couts married Juan Bandini's daughter Isidora and later acquired Rancho Guajome near former Mission San Luis Rey. Couts also owned the Colorado House (a hotel on the plaza) and took an active part in local affairs. H.M.T. Powell, an artist from New Mexico who had arrived in 1849, made several sketches of the town and port and at Couts' request drew one of the area's first maps.

Powell described the heart of San Diego as a place of bullfighting, gambling and drinking. Although such activities no doubt took place, life around the plaza consisted generally of children playing, families gathering and normal socializing. Washington Plaza, as it was sometimes called, hosted caravans with trade goods and vendors who often sold their wares from stands in the square. A town well (sunk at the eastern end near the Estudillo house) had a windmill for drawing water. The Americans introduced a Fourth of July celebration in 1847 and continued to celebrate that date each year with firecrackers, marching bands, speeches and much singing and dancing.

An Act to Incorporate the City of San Diego was passed on March 27, 1850. The first elections were held on June 16, and Joshua H. Bean, a

OLD TOWN: *Plaza and Cosmopolitan Hotel (center), in the 1860s (top) and county assessor José Estudillo (above).*

former soldier, was chosen as the first mayor. An act had also been passed the previous February 18 dividing California into 28 counties in anticipation of entry into the Union. San Diego's boundaries included all of today's Imperial and much of Riverside and San Bernardino counties. First county officers elected by voters at the two precincts of San Diego and La Playa on April 1 were assemblyman: Oliver S. Witherby; county judge: John Hayes; county clerk: Richard Rust; county recorder: H.C. Matsell; treasurer: Philip Crosthwaite; sheriff: Agoston Haraszthy; assessor: José Antonio Estudillo; district attorney: William C. Ferrell; surveyor: Henry Clayton; coroner: John Brown and county attorney: Thomas W. Sutherland. Also serving as treasurer for a time was Juan Bandini. The first term of the District Court of San Diego was convened on May 6, 1850, with Oliver S. Witherby as presiding judge. The first grand jury included Charles Haraszthy, Ramon Osuna, James Wall, Loreto Amador, Manuel Rocha, J. Emers, Bonifacio Lopez, Holden Alara, Seth B. Blake, Louis Rose, William H. Moon, Cave J. Couts, José de Jesus Moreno, Cristobal Lopez and José Antonio Aguirre. The total population given for the county was 798, with the city listed at 650. Assessment rolls of the city totaled $374,260 divided among Old Town, $264,210; New Town (a settlement by the bay), $80,050 and Middletown, $30,000.

The new arrivals in San Diego helped transform the little Mexican community into a growing commercial center. New businesses were started and more homes were built. One man, however, thought that the town's location was poor for shipping. William Heath Davis — once called "Kanaka Bill" because of his Hawaiian parentage — first saw San Diego in 1833 and never forgot it. In 1850, Boundary Commission surveyor Lieutenant Andrew B. Gray interested him and several others—including Miguel de Pedrorena, José Antonio Aguirre and William C. Ferrell—in investing in 160 acres by the water's edge. Davis laid out a 32-square block area between present-day Broadway and Market streets, purchased lumber, bricks and some prefabricated houses for his New Town, but people did not settle there. Davis gave some land to the U.S. government for an army post and the "San Diego Barracks" served for a number of years as the army supply depot for Southern California. A shaky city began to assemble around a plaza called Pantoja Park, and several stores were opened. Davis spent $60,000 on a wharf, constructed a warehouse and built his own residence on State Street. When the new site failed to develop, it became known as Davis' Folly. As founder of New San Diego, Kanaka Bill was ahead of his time.

Another proposed development called Middletown (a similar bay tract) was laid out between Old Town and New Town at the same time. A grant of 687 acres was made to Davis' brother-in-law José María Estudillo and others including Oliver Witherby, Cave Couts, Agoston Haraszthy and Juan Bandini. This site also failed to attract settlers for many years. So for the first decades of the American period, what is now known as Old Town continued to be the heart of San Diego.

As Easterners and Europeans brought in their ideas of architecture, the town around Washington Plaza began to take on a different appearance. Louis Rose, a native of Germany, arrived in 1850 via New Orleans and entered into several businesses. He opened a tavern on the first floor of the Robinson-Rose Building. During the 1850s, a single-story adobe—built by Juan Rodríguez and called Tienda California—became the Exchange Hotel run by Juan's son-in-law George Tebbetts. In 1855 Maurice and Lewis Franklin, Jewish merchants from Liverpool, England, obtained the property and constructed the first three-story building—the Franklin House. The hotel housed a meeting hall, barber shop, offices and quite a variety of activities. Another structure to experience an American evolution was a four-room, single-story adobe occupied after 1847 by two black Americans, Richard Freeman and Allen B. Light, former fur traders. New proprietors in 1857 covered the adobe with board siding and created

A woman of distinction

María Victoria Domínguez de Estudillo was one of the most gracious and charitable women of early San Diego. Her roots were from Mexico and Spain, and she inherited the concept of *familia* in the fullest sense. Her great uncle, Juan José Domínguez, was one of the soldiers who accompanied Father Junipero Serra to San Diego in 1769. María Victoria was born within the presidio walls in 1805. She married Jose Maria Estudillo, a lieutenant, March 1, 1824. She had five sons — José María, Salvador, José Guadalupe, José Antonio and Francisco — and six daughters — María Antonia, Francisca, Rosario, Concepción, María de los Reyes and Dolores. Although her husband received a grant of Rancho Janal, María Victoria preferred the house in town with her friends and neighbors. In 1851 after her daughter and son-in-law died, she took in their four children. That same year, her widowed sister died, leaving five more children in María Victoria's care. She also adopted several Indian children whose parents were dead. Then, in 1852, her husband died. But her strong will and determination kept the family together. She continued to live in Old Town always caring for others. Five days before she became bedridden with her final illness in October 1873, she visited a sick Mexican woman. She died at the age of 72, still elegant and stately, with a heart always open to the appeal of the poor and needy.

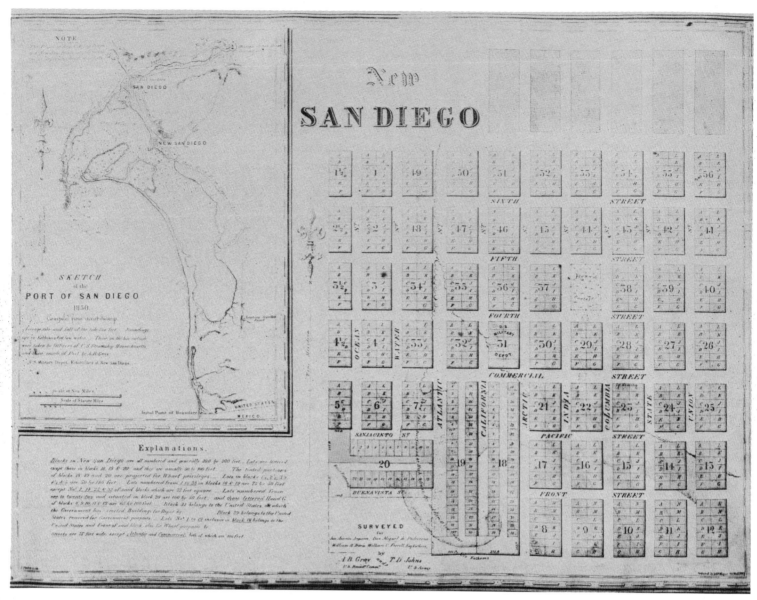

the American Hotel. The building included a saloon, billiards and bowling. María Lorenza Silvas and George Smith were married there in 1860. The newlyweds inherited the Machado-Silvas adobe and retained its original design. Over the years, it served as a home, rooming house, restaurant, art studio and even a community church.

All did not go smoothly in San Diego during the 1850s. Sheriff Haraszthy attempted to collect taxes from the Indians in the back country. In November 1851, Antonio Garra, chief of the Cupeños, incited his people to fight against white settlers. He had the help of some San Diegans but was caught after a few scattered attacks. William Marshall and Juan Verdugo were executed in the Plaza for their part in instigating the Indian uprising. Garra was shot by a firing squad on January 10, 1852. Few other Indians attempted to fight back. Edward F. Beale was appointed Indian agent for San Diego but little provision was made for these native Americans during the next 30 years. Sheriff Haraszthy, a native of Hungary, left San Diego in 1852 when he was elected to the California Legislature. He gained fame later as one of the founders of California's commercial wine industry.

Journalism came to San Diego with John Judson Ames who brought a printing press to Davis' New Town in 1851 to start publication of the weekly San Diego *Herald*. As New Town's prospects temporarily dimmed, Ames moved his press to quarters fronting on Old Town's plaza and

NEW TOWN: map in relation to the port of San Diego (top) and its promoter William Heath Davis (above).

TWO TOWNS: The first American house in New Town was the home of William Heath Davis (above); however, Old Town continued to be the heart of San Diego. In Old Town were the Machado House, American Hotel and Washington House (right) and the Robinson-Rose House (top).

there ran into Army engineer and humorist Lieutenant George Horatio Derby. Although Derby successfully directed construction of a dike to turn the San Diego River into False (later Mission) Bay to halt the silting of the harbor, he is perhaps better remembered for his writings as John Phoenix or the veritable Squibob. Ames, a staunch Democrat, asked Derby to take over the *Herald* while he was in San Francisco for a visit. Derby, a Whig supporter, reversed the paper's politics with a touch of good humor. (Derby's writings have since been reprinted many times.) Ames operated the *Herald* until April 7, 1860, when he closed up shop. More than eight years passed before another paper—the *San Diego Union*—began publication.

With completion of the Gadsden purchase in 1853, talk of a transcontinental railroad was frequently heard in San Diego. Secretary of War Jefferson Davis had ordered a number of cross-country surveys, and a southern route seemed to be the most practical. Residents of Old Town organized the San Diego & Gila, Southern Pacific & Atlantic Railroad Company, but they failed to build a railroad from San Diego to Yuma.

James Birch opened a stage line between San Diego and San Antonio, Texas, in 1857 to provide passenger and mail service. Birch died soon after, but the company lived on for four years as the "Jackass Mail Line". John Butterfield, organizer of the American Express Company, opened a stage route from Tipton, Missouri, to San Francisco, California, on September 16, 1858, providing 25-day service. The Butterfield stage carried passengers and mail along the Birch route from Texas into East County but by-passed San Diego by turning northward through Warner's Ranch. It passed through Carrizo Springs, Vallecito, the San Felipe Valley, Warner's and Oak Grove. Since San Diego was never on the main route of travel, it continued to rely heavily on ships for transportation and communication. The outbreak of the Civil War ended any hope for a transcontinental railroad through the South as plans and surveys were made after 1862 for a northern line.

During the late 1850s, despite the lack of easy communication with the East, San Diego was moving forward. Thomas Whaley, a native of New York, began construction of his two-story brick home and store on May 6, 1856. The spacious Whaley House just off the plaza served for a time as a theater and became the County Courthouse in 1869. The last Whaley to live in the house was Corinne Lillian, youngest of the Whaley's six children. She died in 1953 at the age of 89. A group of San Diegans saved the house from demolition in 1956 and have seen to its complete restoration. Near the Whaley House stands the former home of George Pendleton, a native of Virginia and classmate of Cave J. Couts at West Point. Pendleton, who arrived in 1855, was the nephew of Colonel John Bankhead Magruder, one of the town's first lawyers. Pendleton married Concepción B. Estudillo and served as county clerk and recorder from 1858 to 1870. George Derby stayed in the Pendleton house while temporary editor of the San Diego *Herald.*. The home was moved in 1962 from its original location to the lot adjoining the Whaley House.

José Antonio Aguirre gave an adobe structure to the Catholic Church in 1858 for a chapel. It was located near the Campo Santo cemetery. The walls were covered with board siding and the interior remodeled. Blessed as the Church of the Immaculate Conception, it served as the center for Catholic activities. Certain Protestant denominations used portions of various other buildings around the plaza. Although there had been schools conducted at the presidio and in a number of San Diego homes, the first schoolhouse was not built until 1865 at the corner of Congress and Mason streets. It was moved to make room for a two-story building in 1872, but has now been restored and returned to Old Town as a historic structure. Mary Chase Walker from Manchester, New York, taught there in 1865, but was forced to resign for befriending a black girl. Mary Walker later recalled, "My school was composed mostly of Spanish and

John Judson Ames (top), founder of the San Diego Herald Weekly. George Allen Pendleton (above), county clerk and recorder, and wife.

half-breed children with a few English and several Americans. Many American soldiers and some sailors had come to San Diego in the early days and married pretty señoritas." Walker married Old Town businessman and long-time resident Ephraim Morse shortly afterwards. Morse lamented the fact that the old presidio had fallen into ruin after most of the roofing and tiles had been used in building homes below. Even the church walls had been carried away.

During the 1860s, life in San Diego began to slow down. There was a general drought, and many of the cattle were dying on the nearby ranches. The rancheros made fewer visits to the town center to purchase luxuries. The Civil War had disrupted communication with the East, and the promised railroad had never arrived. Ephraim Morse summed up the state of affairs: "I'm still keeping store here but not making money. There is but little business here, the place not being so large as it was ten years ago ... there are only two men in San Diego that don't occasionally get drunk and they are James McCoy, the sheriff, and myself." (McCoy had one of the most elegant houses in town, just off the plaza and surrounded by a white picket fence.)

One bright spot was the arrival in San Diego of newspaper publisher William Jeff Gatewood from San Andreas. Gatewood had married Philip Crosthwaite's sister and settled in northern California. After the gold rush, Crosthwaite induced the family to move to the southern community and start a paper. Gatewood, with J.N. Briseno and Edward W. Bushyhead, set up their equipment in the frame building owned by José Antonio Altamirano. It was next door to Altamirano's wife's family home, the adobe house of Miguel de Pedrorena. The first *San Diego Union* paper came off the press on October 10, 1868, but Gatewood did not remain long at the helm. By May 1869, he had become president of the San Diego, Gila & Atlantic Railroad Company and had sold out to Bushyhead and Charles P. Taggart. That first newspaper office still stands on its original site, fully restored, with an adjoining historical museum. Soon, however, Old Town would no longer house the newspaper. Times were beginning to change.

Even though the economic situation had contributed to a slowdown of activities around the Plaza, a most significant factor in the decline of Old Town was the arrival of a Connecticut Yankee by the name of Alonzo Horton. Born in 1813 as one of seven children, Alonzo had moved with his family to New York. After running a small shipping business between Oswego, New York, and Canada, Alonzo moved west in 1836 to Milwaukee and speculated in land. At the close of the Mexican War, he founded a small town called Hortonville about 20 miles from Oshkosh. He sold his interests for $7,000 and headed for California in 1851. He returned to the East Coast and

TOWN FOLK: The congregation of the Old Mission Chapel gathers circa 1886, (top left), and Old Town grew (top right). Ephraim W. Morse (center) was a successful Old Town businessman; his wife, Mary Chase Walker Morse (above), was the first teacher in San Diego County.

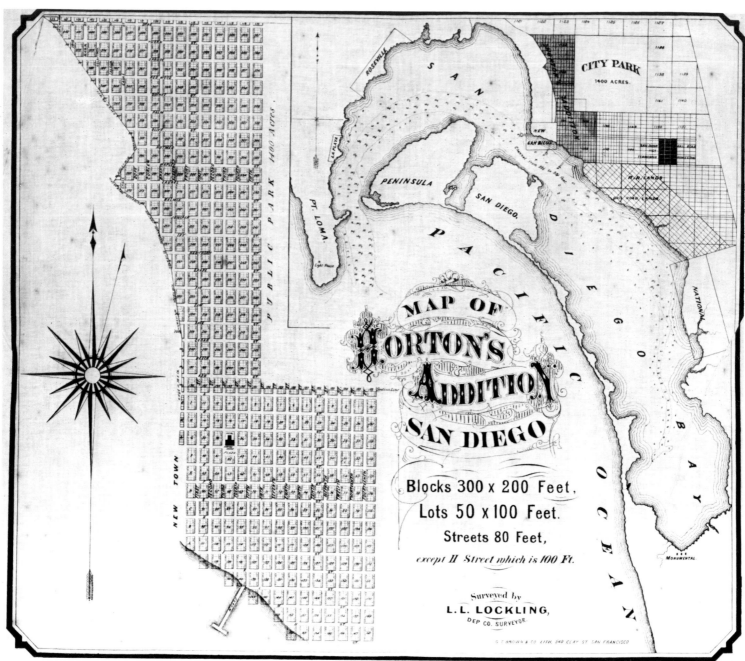

MAP OF
HORTON'S
ADDITION
SAN DIEGO

Blocks 300 x 200 Feet,
Lots 50 x 100 Feet.
Streets 80 Feet,
except II Street which is 100 Ft.

Surveyed by
L. L. LOCKLING,
DEP CO. SURVEYOR

FOUNDING FATHER: Alonzo Horton (right) was the founder of modern-day San Diego. The best known map of Horton's Addition (above) was made by L. L. Locking, deputy county surveyor.

married Sarah Wilson Babe in Jersey City in 1860. After several business ventures, he settled with his wife in San Francisco and opened a store at Sixth and Market streets. One night early in 1867, Horton heard a speaker talk about the wonderful opportunities in San Diego, one of the healthiest places with one of the best harbors in the whole world. He was then 54 years of age — a little beyond what people thought of as "prime" in those days, but the same age Father Serra had been when he received his call to California 100 years before. Just the thought of San Diego's possibilities kept Alonzo Horton awake all night.

On April 15, 1867, the steamer *Pacific* brought Horton and a small group of passengers up the bay to the foot of present-day Market Street. Since nothing but a few pilings remained of Davis' wharf, the passengers were rowed ashore and helped to dry land. While Horton was awaiting a buckboard to take him to the plaza, he looked around at the harbor. He thought it "must be a Heaven on Earth . . . the best spot for building a city he ever saw." But when he saw Old Town, he commented that he would not give five dollars for the whole thing. "It doesn't lie right. Never in the world can you have a city here." Horton knew that even though others like Davis had failed, the harbor site was the only logical choice for building a new town. He contacted George Pendleton, county clerk to see about electing a board of trustees who could sell pueblo lands. He met Ephraim Morse and the two became fast friends. Morse showed him the land that was available, and Horton's Addition soon became a reality. Horton attended church at the Adobe Chapel and struck up an acquaintance with Father Antonio Ubach, the resident priest. Ubach helped the eager newcomer to find appropriate trustees for the land auction. Sheriff James McCoy served as auctioneer on May 10, 1867, and Horton purchased 960 acres for $265 or 27½ cents an acre. The trustees gave Horton a deed to the land on May 11, and he registered as a voter in San Diego. He returned to San Francisco on the next steamer with a promise to be back. And back he came — New Town was born again.

In the meantime, Alfred Seeley, owner of Old Town's Seeley Stables, purchased the house of Juan Bandini, added a story and converted it into the Cosmopolitan Hotel. He remodeled the Franklin House as a stage depot for his San Diego-Los Angeles line. Seeley confidently announced to his fellow residents around the plaza, "Old Town is *the* town, the real San Diego; your mushroom town ... will soon peter out, and all the people who want to travel will have to come to Old Town to take the stage." But even Thomas Whaley and his partner Philip Crosthwaite were selling out cheap for cash. By 1870 the *San Diego Union* reported that they were fitting out the first floor of Horton's Hall for a store. "One by one the leaves are falling from Old Town, and the old place looks desolate. Nothing will be left there in a short time but a few saloons and lawyers."

The final blow came in 1870 when the County Board of Supervisors answered the cry of New San Diego residents and ordered removal of all county records from the Whaley House in Old Town to the Express Building in New San Diego. A posse was organized in Old Town and placed in front of the Whaley House. The *Union* reported: "Old Town has seceded ... They have nailed their flag to the staff in the Plaza ... the watchword is Old Town - Now and Forever - One and Inseparable" Then the *Union* itself moved to its new headquarters downtown. The removal of the records was finally carried out — quietly — in April 1871, and the historic center took second place. A disastrous fire swept through the area in 1872 and sealed Old Town's fate. Nevertheless, a number of residents remained and one observer in 1873 wrote that "Old Town has the finest school house in the Pueblo, with an average attendance of 75 pupils ... The residences of our citizens are generally comfortable even if not of the highest style of architecture."

Old Town cemetery (top), and Father Antonio Ubach (above).

Chapter V

A time of new beginnings

1870-1890

Alonzo Horton may have been blessed with Yankee ingenuity, but a significant key to San Diego's development was its Hispanic heritage — not because of its missions, presidios or ranchos but because of its pueblo lands. When San Diego's Chamber of Commerce was formed by a small group of citizens in January 1870 it could point with pride to some eleven square leagues or 47,324 acres of municipally-owned lands — its inheritance from Spain's practice of preserving ample lands for city purposes and the common benefit of all settlers. Fortunately, Horton (the chamber's first treasurer) and certain Old Town residents knew what they had. With a farsightedness hardly equalled by today's most ardent planners, they set aside 1,400 acres for a public park.

Horton first talked about the idea of a public park in 1867 when he asked trustees Joseph S. Mannassee, Thomas H. Bush and Ephraim Morse to consider two 160-acre tracts as park sites. Some thought a 320-acre park more than sufficient for a town of 2,310 people. Morse — perhaps thinking of his native Boston Common — felt that since the city had 40,000 acres available, they should reserve nine tracts or 1,440 acres. He suggested the land bounded by Sixth, 28th, Ash and Upas. Before the final resolution was passed by new trustees José Guadalupe Estudillo, Marcus Schiller and Joshua Sloane in May 1868, 40 acres to the south between Ash and Date were sold. Strenuous attempts were made to reduce the amount of park land, but trustee Estudillo, joined by James McCoy and Matthew Sherman, requested that the state Legislature approve the transfer of the land to park purposes. It was done on February 4, 1870. The final amended federal survey of San Diego's pueblo grant was not completed until 1872, but the 47,324 acres of the Fitch survey was confirmed by the United States in 1874. Eighteen years later, in 1890, 83 percent of the land was gone, having been conveyed by the city to private interests. The park (a portion of the 8,000 acres still owned by the city) remained a wilderness area covered by dense chaparral and a few patches of yellow, white and blue flowers of wild adenostema, sagebrush, Spanish violets, shooting stars, milulas and white popcorn.

Workmen broke ground on the first day of January 1870, for the grand Horton House Hotel, a magnificent structure planned to grace the heart of the city. The newly-formed Chamber of Commerce had first met at David Felsenheld's store at Sixth and F streets the same month. They elected Aaron Pauley as president and Horton as treasurer. They discussed the need for better transportation to San Diego (especially a railroad) and planned harbor improvements, a new courthouse, a library, schools and churches. Their first brochure reflected the optimism and broad horizons of these early residents when they predicted San Diego would be "the natural commercial center of a vast scope of country, rich in mineral and agricultural wealth" embracing all of the Southwest and northern Mexico. All the city needed was for Congress to approve the building of a railroad to the Pacific so that "the bulk of traffic between the States east of the Mississippi and the Asiatic ports" would pass through San Diego

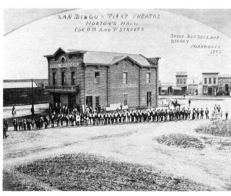

EARLY CHAMBERS: The city continued to flourish with new businesses such as The Berlin House or Deutsches Gasthaus (left top), owned and operated by German immigrants (left bottom). George White Marston (top) arrived in 1870 to begin work as a clerk at the Horton House. Horton's Hall (above) was the city's first theater, located at Sixth and F Streets, near David Felsenheld's store where the newly-formed Chamber of Commerce first met.

The men were wrong about the railroad, but were undaunted in their spirit. On the positive side, a minor rush to the back country had occurred with the discovery of gold by rancher Fred Coleman (thought to be a black who had escaped slavery in the South). He lived with his Indian family north of the Cuyamacas. In February, shortly before Washington's birthday, another major discovery was made of gold-bearing quartz; the George Washington Mine was soon opened. Among those in the area at the time were Drury, James and Frank Bailey and their cousins Mike and Webb Julian, all from Georgia. Drury Bailey had homesteaded much of the land because of its scenic beauty and founded Julian City in honor of his cousin Mike. In August a new discovery was made by Julian's assayer Louis Redman who marked the spot with an American flag. This "banner" gave its name to the spot, now at the foot of Banner grade on Highway 78. A number of other mines were opened, but within a few years the quantity and quality of gold declined. One by one the mines closed, leaving Julian a picturesque but quiet town in the heart of apple country.

By June 1870, residents of San Diego thought a bank would be appropriate since anyone of substance either had to buy a safe, hide his money or ship it to San Francisco. On June 9, the Bank of San Diego was officially formed with a capitalization of $100,000 and officers Alonzo Horton (president), James M. Pierce (vice president) and Bryant Howard (treasurer). The *San Diego Union* hailed the bank's formation and later that same month moved its offices to Fourth and D streets. In less than a year, the paper became a daily with 400 subscribers. Western Union opened a telegraph line in August.

The palatial 100-room Horton House held its gala opening on October 10, 1870. The building — construction was supervised by Horton's brother-in-law W. W. Bowers — was one of the most sumptuous of the times. All rooms were richly carpeted and boasted marble-top tables and washstands. They were connected to the desk by a bell. The 360-degree view from the hotel's observatory was breathtaking. Water from a 55-foot-deep well supplied a 7000-gallon tank that could provide 2,000 gallons of water per hour. The $150,000 hotel took its place beside the Grand in Paris, the Astor in New York, the Cosmopolitan in San Francisco and the Pico in Los Angeles. Horton set aside a half block across the street as a plaza so his guests would have a place to sit in the sun.

The hotel's first clerk was a young man just turned twenty — George White Marston. His family had known the Hortons in Wisconsin and there learned about San Diego. George stayed at the hotel for six months and then went to work in merchandising. In three years, Marston and Charles S. Hamilton bought out Joseph Nash and started a store of their own. San Diego had a sizable Spanish and Mexican population, and Horton House guests included travelers from all parts of the world, American soldiers from Arizona, miners from Lower Caifornia and the usual number of adventurers.

SIGNS OF BUSINESS: The Frary and Foster stage pulls up to the Belle View Hotel (top) and a carriage rolls by the Marston Store, circa 1878 (above). The Horton House (top right) boasted a billiard room, reading room, bridal suite, ladies parlor and saloon, circa 1895 (bottom right). The silver pitcher (inset at right) is from the dining room and the key (below), from room 73. All of the rooms in the hotel were lighted with gas, carpeted, supplied with fresh water and connected to the front office by a bell.

As 1870 closed, prospects for San Diego looked bright. Assessed valuation of real estate in the city was $2.28 million with a population of about 3,000. There were 915 occupied houses and 69 business buildings. New Town and Old Town struggled to see which would become the civic center. When Old Town defender George Pendleton died in March 1871, the board of Supervisors appointed Chalmers Scott to his offices of county clerk and recorder. The board then leased a part of Horton's Express Building at Sixth and G streets and turned the first floor into a courtroom with the clerk's office upstairs. County Judge Thomas Bush had vigorously opposed moving San Diego's records to the new location, but he accepted the inevitable without further protest. On April 14, the South San Diego or New Town post office became the San Diego post office. The fire that devastated Old Town in 1872 further sealed the fate of the city's first center.

With the official move of the county seat, the Board of Supervisors accepted Horton's offer of a site for a new courthouse at D (Broadway) and Front streets. When the cornerstone was laid in August, speaker E. D. French said he "hoped the ill feeling ... between Old and New San Diego might be buried in the stone." The elegant courthouse was completed in June 1872, and (with three additions) served for 90 years as courtroom jail and most county offices. With this building occupied, Horton had succeeded in doing almost all he had set out to do. There was one major exception — no railroad seemed to be on the horizon.

In 1868 Frank and Warren Kimball from New Hampshire had purchased the 26,632 acres of Rancho de la Nacion for $30,000 from a financial firm in San Francisco on behalf of themselves and brother Levi. Hoping that a railroad would soon be coming to San Diego, they cleared and laid out a 100-foot wide thoroughfare six miles long and marked out a town they called National City. The Kimball brothers also built a wharf and competed with San Diego for the terminus of the southern railroad. (The northern transcontinental line had been completed May 10, 1869.) So far the steamer *Orizaba* had brought most newcomers to San Diego. Its Skipper Henry James Johnston purchased 65 acres in what became Mission Hills, and his daughter eventually built Villa Orizaba overlooking the harbor.

In the spring of 1871, Congress passed a bill approving construction of the Texas & Pacific Railroad. Speculation was rife when Colonel Thomas Scott, president of the company, came to the Horton House to check over possible depot sites. The offer of enough open land and town property assured location of the terminus on San Diego Bay. Property values went up accordingly. But the untimely failure of the great railroad speculator Jay Cook on "Black Friday," September 18, 1873, caused the end of Texas

THE LATE 1800S: The old San Diego courthouse, circa 1875 (above); the Pacific Coast Steamship Wharf, 1890 (bottom left); Fifth Street looking north from L. Street, circa 1887 (top right); and the Central Carriage Shop in downtown San Diego, 1887 (bottom right).

SKIPPER, SHIP: The captain of the Steamship Orizaba *(below) was Captain Henry James Johnston (bottom) who was interested in the future of San Diego and purchased 65 acres in what would later become the prime residential area known as Mission Hills.*

1887 BUSINESS: Dodge and Burbeck's Book Store (above) and the San Diego Title and Abstract Company (left).

& Pacific plans. Ten miles of graded road were abandoned, and San Diego was left with a number of jobless—and soon to be homeless—railroad workers.

During this time, a few developments occurred in the large City Park. A fair-sized Indian ranchería remained in the south part near Eighth and Date under the leadership of El Capitan, a Diegueño who claimed ownership of the entire pueblo. The San Diego Water Company, organized in 1872, had obtained permission from the city to drill a well in Pound (Cabrillo) Canyon (named for an animal pound set up by the city for stray cattle and horses). Two reservoirs with 70,000 and 100,000-gallon capacities were built on the mesa flanking the canyon. In 1875 the water company drilled a well at the foot of Sandrock Grade on the river and pumped water up to a reservoir at Fifth and Hawthorne. Unfortunately for San Diego, lack of water was frequently interrupted by floods which swelled the river over its banks. In 1875 Congress appropriated $80,000 to channel the river back into False Bay since silt and sand had washed down until Derby's Dike was no longer functional. Still the park area—high on the mesa—was difficult to supply with water.

The economy had taken a setback in 1873 with the collapse of the railroad, but it seemed to recover year by year. In the back country, agriculture flourished and pioneer beekeeper J.S. Harbison of Harbison Canyon shipped 33 carloads of honey to the East. The Southern Pacific railroad finally connected Los Angeles to San Francisco in 1876, and plans were always being made for a southern connection. A number of Chinese families moved into town after the railroad was completed. They formed the nucleus of Chinatown around Wo Sung & Co.'s importing house on Third Street. By 1879 a new group of businessmen sent Frank Kimball to Boston to encourage the Santa Fe to build a line to San Diego. The residents of California's most southern city also noted the adoption of the state's new constitution in 1879.

Frank Kimball called upon the president of the Atchison, Topeka & Santa Fe and offered to help form a syndicate to accept subsidies from

Program cover for San Diego's 1876 Centennial Celebration, which included a parade, speeches and a fireworks display.

The California Southern Railroad Line and locomotive Number 330 in 1890.

San Diego and National City. In October 1880, the California Southern Railroad was incorporated. Its route would begin at National City and pass through San Diego, Encinitas, Temecula and San Jacinto to Colton, where it would cross the Southern Pacific and join the Atlantic & Pacific at Waterman Junction (Barstow). Problems with the Southern Pacific were finally overcome and tracks were laid to San Bernardino. Then, on February 28, 1884, Southern California suffered a twenty-inch downpour that washed out the tracks from San Luis Rey to Temecula in an avalanche of mud and water. Repairs began immediately, and on November 9, 1885, the California Southern joined the Atchison, Topeka & Santa Fe (which had bought out the Atlantic & Pacific) at Waterman Junction. The first train left the depot at the foot of D Street on November 15 amid praises from both Horton and Kimball. The first train from the East — two coaches, a mail and baggage car — arrived on November 21 in a driving rain but with great excitement. The speculation about things to come set off what would soon be called the "Boom of the Eighties." Passengers could get from coast to coast in a week, and agricultural products such as honey, oranges, lemons, potatoes, salt, fish, butter and wool could be shipped to new markets.

Commercial Bank, 1872-75

BANK OF ESCONDIDO: Founded in 1887, this bank was the only one in San Diego County to stay open continuously during the panic of 1893. Brick for its construction was manufactured in Escondido and lumber was hauled in by team and wagon from Graham, a railroad siding located on the coast south of Carlsbad.

The decade of the eighties was definitely innovative. The first county fair was held in National City in September 1880, and visitors were impressed by the variety of fruits. Apples, grapes, raisins, peaches, pears, figs, apricots, berries, olives and citrus fruits were the major crops in fertile valleys south and east of San Diego proper. The El Cajon Valley was blooming with vineyards.

Downtown, the San Diego Gas & Oil Company turned on the first street lights the night of June 4, 1881. During 1882, George Marston helped organize the YMCA and the Public Library. The San Diego Telephone Company began with thirteen subscribers in June 1882, and a year later the Bank of Southern California was formed with Jacob Gruendike as president. It joined the Consolidated Bank of San Diego, a merger of the Bank of San Diego and the Commerical Bank. Gruendike's bank became the First National Bank in 1885.

Helen Hunt Jackson arrived in San Diego in 1883 to gather the material for *Ramona,* a novel set in California during the Mexican period. Jackson (author of *Century of Dishonor*) was concerned about the treatment of Indians and made friends with Father Antonio Ubach, sponsor of an Indian school. Father Ubach had moved to New Town and established St. Joseph's Catholic Church on some lots at Third and Beech streets donated by Horton for the church in 1875. Father Ubach became a

The San Diego Union Telephone Company advertised "one of 1,000 social uses of the telephone."

CITYSCAPES, SCHOOL: San Diego, looking up Fifth Street from K, resembles a typical Western town, circa 1878 (top left); ten years later (top right), it had taken on a different look. With civilization came teachers (above), including horticulturist Kate Sessions (second from left), and Old Russ High School (below).

model for Jackson's Father Gaspara. In later years, the story that Ramona's marriage place was in Old Town's Estudillo House was circulated by San Diego promoters. Jackson spent some time with Isadora Bandini Couts at Rancho Guajome and studied Indian conditions in the county.

On August 8, 1881, the board of trustees set aside five acres at the south-central edge of City Park for San Diego High School. Joseph Russ, a lumberman, donated wood to build the school; it was completed in 1883. Some dedicated citizens cleared the scraggly ground cover of sagebrush and chaparral to put some plants in the park's hard dry soil. They irrigated the area from the reservoirs there, and soon the land began to bloom. In December 1884, eleven persons, including George Marston, Melville Klauber and Charles Hamilton, petitioned the trustees to allow them to plant—at their own expense—some eucalyptus trees along a rough road in the park and make some further improvements. New park questions arose as it was officially surveyed in 1885.

The U. S. Army offered to trade its downtown San Diego barracks site for a park location in December 1886, but opponents of the exchange won out. Supporters pointed out that the cost of improving the land was far beyond the means of San Diego. Instead, it should be sold in stages until only a reasonable 640 acres remained. On December 2, 1887, city trustees granted Bryant Howard and E. W. Morse 100 acres on the promontory between Cabrillo and Florida canyons to build an orphan's home, industrial school and other charitable institutions. The money came from the J. M. Pierce estate and gifts from Judge Oliver Witherby and others including Howard himself. The trustees also granted five acres for a home for indigent women. Some of the city fathers began to question incursions into the park, and George Marston asked the city not to confirm the grant. It was done nevertheless, and in 1890 Howard planted the grounds of the "Charities Tract" with more than ten thousand trees—mainly blue and sugar gums, acacias, pepper trees, fan palms and cypresses. Irrigation pipes and roads were laid out to the new Orphan's Home and Women's Home. In 1889 the Ladies Annex of the San Diego Chamber of Commerce had raised $514 and planted trees and bushes on fourteen acres between Juniper and Palm streets on the west. Under the guidance of pioneer horticulturist Kate Sessions (a graduate of the University of California at Berkeley), the women planted some 700 trees and shrubs. Sessions had tried her hand at teaching at San Diego High School but preferred plants to students. Water was a continual problem, so the women began to take water from the fire hydrants near the park. The water company complained but allowed the practice to go on. Residents of the nearby Golden Hill area, led by Leroy Wright and Matt Heller, planted trees, laid out a nine-hole golf course—the city's first—and kept the area as green as possible. When Bryant Howard lost his fortune in the panic of 1893, he could no longer maintain or improve the 100-acre Charities Tract as stipulated in his deed from the city, so the property reverted to the grantor. Soon the Women's Home burned down.

1887 LAND BOOM: Coronado lots for sale (top), Morena auction sale of lots (right center) and La Presa lots (right bottom). Lawyer and businessman Levi Chase (above) was reportedly the first buyer when land went up for sale in Coronado: after holding on to the property for less than twelve hours, he resold it for twice the price.

While the boom of the '80s was in full swing, some key buildings were constructed. Among these were W. W. Bowers' beautiful Florence Hotel at Fourth and Fir and the four-story St. James Hotel between Sixth and Seventh on F. But the most exciting hotel of all was that incredible edifice dreamed up by Elisha S. Babcock, a railroad man from Indiana, and H. L. Story, a piano manufacturer from Chicago. One of their pastimes was to row across San Diego Bay and shoot rabbits. So they purchased the entire peninsula in December 1885, for $100,000 and incorporated under the name of Coronado Beach Company. They promised to build the largest hotel in the world—one that would be "too gorgeous to be true." They auctioned off a million dollars worth of land in a short time and decided that Coronado should be *dry* except for the hotel which would have a monopoly on drinks. Babcock and Story built a wharf and organized the Coronado Ferry Company. They also organized the San Diego Street Car Company which had lines around the city and up to the park. Babcock and Story continued to promote construction of their magnificent hotel that boasted 399 rooms, most with a fireplace and wall safe. The breathtaking circular dining room remained unobstructed by a single pillar, and thousands of guests could move freely about the room. The grand ballroom, conveniently terraced, also provided a spectacular open feeling. The workmen were mostly Chinese from San Francisco, and the hotel staff came from Boston. The Hotel del Coronado, landscaped by Kate Sessions, opened on Saint Valentine's Day 1888 — just as the land boom began to collapse around it.

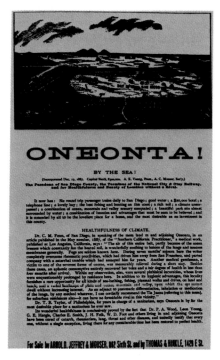

FOR SALE: San Diego was "For Sale" everywhere when the bottom fell out (below) of the dramatic boom of the 1880s (above).

Hotel del Coronado

A GRAND HOTEL: The 399-room Hotel del Coronado (above) and its circular dining room (left). Sporting activities at the hotel included rabbit hunting (top right) and ocean fishing (bottom right).

ONE AFTERNOONS SPORT AT CORONADO CALIF. DEC. 1905.

WATER SPORTS: Cuyamaca Club members in September 1889 (top); a rowing team on the water (above); and members of the San Diego Rowing Club take a New Year's Day swim in 1906 (right).

The water seekers had been busy during this time finding new sources for the growing number of residents. John D. Spreckels — a sugar-refining magnate and son of Claus Spreckels of Hawaii and San Francisco — purchased a half interest in the Otay Water Company in 1885. Under the new name of the Southern California Mountain Water Company, they supplied the city with most of its water and built a large dam. The San Diego Flume Company was organized that same year to bring water from the upper reaches of the San Diego River to the heart of the city. The company built the Cuyamaca Dam, and when its wooden flume was completed in February 1889, a number of dignitaries including Governor Robert Waterman rode down the flume at breakneck speed. A giant celebration was staged in San Diego with fountains of water 125 feet high streaming out of nozzles on street corners. No longer would the city be dependent upon exhaustible wells. (The actual flume water had been held up but no matter — they celebrated with water from wells and soon the "real" water arrived.)

Spreckels went on to invest in other businesses, primarily a warehouse on the waterfront called Spreckels Brothers Commercial Company. He was an economic survivor. He eventually took over most of the Babcock and Story interests as their fortunes collapsed with falling land prices. In 1903 Spreckels assumed complete ownership of the luxurious Coronado Hotel, all unsold lots on Coronado, the Silver Strand and North Island. He also bought up various street car lines as they too failed.

There were other firsts of the decade — the Cuyamaca Club founded in 1887 for purely social purposes; the County Medical and Dental Societies (73 physicians and eleven dentists) and the San Diego Rowing Club. These activities offset the 71 saloons and alleged 120 houses of prostitution.

The Fourth of July, 1888, brought fireworks, a brass band and a special celebration featuring an oration by Clara Shortridge Foltz, the first woman admitted to the practice of law in California. In 1888 her residence and office was on Seventh and F streets. She edited a daily newspaper, the *Bee*, along with her other activities. The *Bee* merged with the *Union* in 1889, and Foltz became a deputy district attorney in

WATER FLUME: Dignitaries took a ride down the flume (bottom) on its opening day, Feb. 22, 1889. John D. Spreckels (below) also promoted water projects.

VILLA MONTEZUMA: Built in 1887 by Jesse Shepard (left), the villa's ornate interior (top right) included a variety of stained glass work (top left). The picture above may be the oldest known photograph of the Villa. The house was later preserved by the city and restored by the San Diego Historical Society.

Unidentified school group on the beach in the 1880s.

Los Angeles. She ran for governor in 1930. The year 1889 also saw the founding of the San Diego Savings Bank.

Another famous resident of San Diego was the mysterious Benjamin Henry Jesse Francis Shepard, a slender man with a handlebar mustache. He arrived in town at the age of 38 with the trappings of great wealth. He built a beautiful home at the corner of 20th and K streets and called it the Villa Montezuma. Shepard was quite a singer with an impressive range — four octaves from low to high C. Concerts and seances were held at the Villa, and some said Shepard was in tune with the spirit world. Father Ubach encouraged him to give up spiritualism, and in 1889 he joined the Catholic Church. (Just after that, he moved to Los Angeles, but his magnificent villa has been preserved by the city and restored by the San Diego Historical Society. It is a showplace of stained glass windows, hand-carved fireplaces and other Victorian features such as a gabled roof with cupolas and towers. The interior features Spanish cedar, redwood and Douglas fir. It would be difficult to exaggerate the beauty of this historic house.)

Mission Bay was known as False Bay until Harr Wagner, a San Francisco publisher, came to town and produced a literary journal called the *Golden Era*. He ran a contest to rename the bay since he thought it was a miniature of San Diego Bay. Rose Hartwick Thorpe won the contest with the name Mission and *Golden Era* ran a poem which spoke of the "peaceful waters of fair Mission Bay — now blue, now gray." Pacific Beach — hoping to gain settlers for its new subdivision — advertised the establishment of the San Diego College of Letters at Lamont and Garnet streets. La Jolla was also promoting itself as an ideal beach town with fascinating caves and popular picnic spots along its shores. Frank T. Botsford and George W. Heald, the first subdividers, planted more than 1,000 trees on the barren cliffs above the ocean. Many trees died from lack of water, but those that survived enhance La Jolla today.

LA JOLLA: Frank A. Botsford (bottom) was regarded as the "Father of La Jolla," a popular area of San Diego with its 80-room La Jolla Park Hotel (below); the hotel did not offically open until January 1, 1893, due to litigation caused by the collapse of the San Diego land boom.

Ocean Beach was promoted by William (Billy) Carlson and Frank J. Higgins. They changed the name from Mussel Beach, so given by Old Towners who gathered mussels there for Sunday picnics. They called Ocean Beach the greatest seaside resort in southern California and opened the Cliff House Hotel in 1888. The promised rail connection from Old Town through Roseville and over the hill (Point Loma) to Ocean Beach failed because of mud slides, and the hotel burned down in 1894.

Carlson and Higgins also promoted Monument City at the southwest corner of the United States. They

promised a beautiful hotel, but it suffered the same fate as other developments in the area such as Oneanta by the Sea (a health resort in the Tia Juana River Valley); Tia Juana City (five miles inland) and Otay ("The Magic City" ten miles southeast of San Diego). When the boom of the '80s burst, these cities remained paper promotions. Santiago Arguello's huge rancho near the border area remained essentially as it was during the Mexican period. A survivor of the boom was the luxurious Lakeside Inn, a three-story hotel with 89 rooms on Lindo Lake. Built in 1887, it was a popular stage stop after a four-hour ride from San Diego. The opening of a railroad in 1889 made the trip much easier.

Some key developments took place in city government during the final year of the decade. Voters prohibited further sale of the remaining pueblo lands and reserved 369 acres to preserve the Torrey Pines. A new charter made San Diego a fourth-class city and provided for the election of a mayor. The state Legislature approved the new charter on March 16. Douglas Gunn became the first elected mayor in 37 years, and the new form of government — including a paid fire department under a board of fire commissioners and a board of harbor commissioners — went into operation in May. It came into being just as city and county assessments dropped seriously — from $40 million in 1888 to $25 million in 1890.

The collapse of the boom was disastrous to a number of land speculators and especially to New San Diego's prime mover Alonzo Horton. He was then 75 and living in his white mansion on First Street. In 1889 his wife Sarah was tragically killed in a carriage accident. During the next few years, he lost some of his remaining properties because of delinquent taxes, but kept his hand in San Diego's development. As the 1890s dawned, the population of the city had leveled off to around 16,000. Although it was a large drop from previous years, it seemed stable. Much would happen during the next few decades, but events could hardly equal those of the 20 years just passed.

AROUND TOWN: The nearby community of Otay, ten miles southeast of San Diego, was promoted as the "Magic City" and advertised its watch company (top left). The bay and harbour (bottom left) was pictured in Frank Leslie's Illustrated News on March 23, 1889. Downtown, the Larson and Loring Book and Toy Store (top right). The three-story Lakeside Inn (bottom right) opened in 1887 and was advertised at a cost of $50,000. Designed to attract land buyers to the community of Lakeside, it was torn down in the 1920s.

Wyatt Earp — capitalist

Wyatt Earp, famous marshal of the Old West who brought law (if not order) to such frontier towns as Dodge City, Kansas, and Tombstone, Arizona, lived for a few relatively quiet years in San Diego as a substantial property owner. Perhaps the survivor of the gunfight at the OK Corral saw the growing coastal town as a haven from the gun-slinging bandits of his past.

Earp arrived in San Diego during the late 1880s and acquired the first of his thoroughbred racehorses that occupied his interest in later years. He purchased and operated three gambling houses featuring faro, blackjack, poker, keno and other games of chance. The city directory of 1887-1888 lists Mrs. Wyatt Earp as residing at the Belle View Hotel at Fourth and G streets while the directory for the following year shows Wyatt Earp — capitalist — living at 946 Third Avenue.

His most exciting activity in his new hometown seems to have been to referee a prize fight at a fiesta south of the border. During his stay in San Diego, he caught the land boom fever and purchased two lots from the Bandini family on the northwest corner of Ash and Columbia. For a time he also owned the northeast corner of the same cross-streets, the northeast corner of Beech and Union and four lots at First and Lewis streets. With the waning of the boom, the Earps sold all their properties and moved on with their racehorses to tracks in San Francisco and the East. By 1896, Wyatt Earp was just a memory in San Diego.

Chapter VI

From panic to progress

1890-1910

San Diego County, as seen by about nine-tenths of those who have heretofore visited it, is anything but inviting to the settler or tourist," wrote Theodore S. Van Dyke in Wallace Elliott's 1883 illustrated history of the region. "Hard, gravelly table-lands, either barren or clad with a dreary black brush, rolling hills of gravel bristling with cactus and cobble-stones, stony slopes scarred with gullies and washes, no trees, no streams, no springs, the general barrenness relieved only by a few choice little valleys and a few tracts of good table-land all held at high prices, such is the picture that strikes most glaringly all who approach by way of the coast."

But, continued Van Dyke, San Diego's natural resources could not readily be seen by the casual visitor since the good land lay "scattered in a thousand shapes all over a tract about a hundred miles long and seventy miles wide, the greater part miles away from the coast." The Valle de las Viejas, Julian, Mesa Grande, Bear Valley, Fallbrook and Santa Margarita produced a fair crop of grain even when other southern California areas failed.

The boom of the '80s, however, had not depended upon the agricultural productivity of the back country. It grew from land speculation involving hundreds of urban lots in the center of town and along the coast. And these lots were useful only for permanent homes, vacation cottages or businesses — all of which depended upon an influx of people. When the dreamed-of thousands of newcomers turned around and went home — or failed to come at all, — the many lots from Carlsbad, through Del Mar, La Jolla and southward to Monument City went begging. The sunshine and healthful climate attracted some, but even "immunity from lightning, tornadoes and storms of any kind, from hydrophobia, yellow fever, cholera and other things" could not stop the panic of 1893 from hitting the county. Nevertheless, permanent and postive gains were made.

As the decade of the 1890s began, San Diego was still not on any main railroad line and began to feel the pinch of rivalry with Los Angeles. Passengers bound for San Diego were warned there was no good drinking water in the southern city and were told to buy jugs of water if they insisted upon going. John D. Spreckels, who purchased the *San Diego Union* in 1890, combatted such bad publicity by promoting positive aspects of the city. Spreckels kept his Coronado interests definitely separate, however, since he favored Coronado's withdrawal from San Diego by municipal election in 1890. Even though Coronado was incorporated separately in 1891, Spreckels remained tied to San Diego through ownership of the street-car line and promotion of a railroad to the East.

A little-known failure of the early 1890s was a branch campus of the University of Southern California that gave its name to University Avenue. In June 1886, the College Hill Land Association of San Diego (largely through efforts of the Reverend Edwin S. Chase of the San

RECREATION: An early-day beach party took a Baptist Church group to La Jolla (top left) and a smaller group for a drive along Ocean Beach (inset), circa 1907. Also at La Jolla, a group of Wheelmen cycled to the beach (right bottom), circa 1900. Another form of recreation could be found in the Stingaree ("red light" district) where messenger boys (above) were used to deliver clothing, food, liquor and other necessities from stores which were out of bounds for the girls. In November 1912, the district was raided and Union headlines read, "138 Women Are Arrested in Stingaree Raid/136 Promise To Leave City; Two Agree to Reform."

Diego Methodist Church) donated 450 acres of land north and east of the city for purchase of a building and endowment of a branch of USC. Plans and specifications for the San Diego College of Fine Arts were secured from a New York architect, excavation completed, foundation constructed and cornerstone laid. Some houses were built in the University Heights tract west of Park Boulevard, but a lack of funds caused work on the college to be stopped. Classes were held in the San Diego Bank of Commerce building until further financial setbacks forced USC to discontinue its San Diego branch. In 1896 the directors reconveyed the original site and unfinished foundation to the land company with the provision that it be donated to the state for a normal school. An Escondido seminary built by USC at a cost of $40,000 also had to be abandoned and the land was sold to the Escondido School District. The College Hill Land Association offered eleven acres at Normal and El Cajon Boulevard for the state school. A magnificent white building with Doric columns was dedicated on May 1, 1899, with Alonzo Horton as honored guest. University Heights grammar school was opened at University and Vermont.

As a result of the financial panic of 1893, five of the eight San Diego banks failed, leaving only the First National Bank, Bank of Commerce and San Diego Savings Bank. Even though times were difficult, some early businesses, such as Marston's, remained solvent, and some new ones began. Joseph Jessop opened a jewelry store in 1890, and Matt Heller started a cash-and-carry grocery store (later absorbed by Safeway). The Chinese cornered the laundry and produce business. Ulysses S. Grant Jr., came to San Diego in 1892, bought the Horton House in 1895 and made plans to build the U. S. Grant Hotel. The Fisher Opera House also opened its doors in 1892, but it did not remain self-sustaining long. To the dismay of local opera fans, it was sold to theosophist Katherine Tingley for her dramatic productions.

One bright light amidst the financial failures of 1892 was the 350th anniversary of Juan Rodríguez Cabrillo's landing on California shores. Mayor Matthew Sherman sent out engraved invitations to the festivities to be held on the wharf at the foot of D Street. Manuel Cabral, a Portuguese fisherman, dressed in a velvet suit and plumed hat, was scheduled to arrive at high tide in a ship representing the *San Salvador*. He missed the high tide mark and the ship stuck in the mud 300 feet from dry land. The awaiting crowd surged to the railing to get a better look, but the rickety wooden structure gave way, and many dignitaries, including Mayor Sherman, fell into the mud. Cabral nevertheless unfurled the Spanish flag and took possession of the area in the name of Spain. Marching military bands, including one from Mexico City, took part in the parade up D Street to Horton Plaza. Father Ubach brought a group of Indians from San Luis Rey to perform their native dances. The three-day celebration cost the city $5,000 but began a tradition continuing until the present day.

VENTURES: State Normal School and El Cajon Boulevard (bottom left); Jessop's first jewelry store at 1317 F Street (above); M. F. Heller's cash grocery on the northwest corner of Eleventh and F Streets, 1892 (top right); and the 1894 celebration of Cabrillo's landing (bottom right).

As a result of the financial panic of 1893, five of the eight San Diego banks failed, leaving only the First National Bank, Bank of Commerce and San Diego Savings Bank.

Other "historic" traditions included a half-day excursion to the "Old Spanish Lighthouse" by Reuben the Guide. Reuben dressed as a Mexican and told stories about the Point Loma lighthouse which had actually been built in 1854 by the United States government. Robert D. Israel and his family lived on the point and tended the light from 1871 to 1891. The Israels delighted in visits by tourists who made the long trek out to see the lighthouse. (Later, in 1913, Hispanic and American traditions were combined in the Cabrillo National Monument built to commemorate San Diego's maritime heritage.)

Reuben the Guide dressed as a Mexican (top) and led half-day excursions to the lighthouse on Point Loma (above), built in 1854 by the U. S. government.

In 1892, Kate Sessions leased 30 acres of City Park land at Sixth and Upas for a plant nursery in exchange for setting out 100 park trees per year and giving the city another 300 trees. She introduced the cork oak from Spain, camphor from Asia, rubber trees from the tropics and several kinds of eucalyptus from Australia. She cultivated seeds from Baja California, South America and elsewhere to earn the name "Mother of Balboa Park." But the greatest impetus to park development came in 1902 when the San Diego Chamber of Commerce formed a Park Improvement Committee to develop a master plan and solicit funds. At the urging of Sessions, horticulturist Mary Coulston, Julius Wangenheim and others on the Chamber committee, George Marston offered to bring in a professional landscape artist to design the park. He hired Samuel Parsons Jr., president of the American Society of Landscape Architects and former superintendent of New York's Central Park. Parsons, who had studied seventeenth and eighteenth century picturesque parks in England and France, arrived in San Diego in 1902. He was not put off by the rocky, barren terrain. To him, it formed a "great natural picture" with its "rugged, picturesque canyons" and "spreading mesas." He staked out all tentative park roads, proposed the main trees and sketched the overall design. From 1902-1904, Marston paid out more than $20,000 (in addition to the original $10,000 paid for the Parsons Plan), and the park began to take shape. On March 17, 1904, 2,500 school children celebrated Arbor Day by planting 60 pines and cypresses on the west edge of Cabrillo Canyon. President Theodore Roosevelt sent a telegram of congratulations saying, "Your love of trees now will make you as men and women, lovers of forests, both for their natural beauty and economic value." From 1904-1906, some 14,000 more trees and shrubs were planted in an effort to create a "natural" setting.

The park was heartily supported by civic leaders, and exemplified the City Beautiful movement begun in Chicago in 1893. E.W. Scripps, owner of the San Diego *Sun* since 1891, thought that a rose garden supplying free roses "would give the plain people of the city the idea that their interest and pleasure was as much considered by the Park Commission as that of the people who rode in carriages and autos." In 1909 G. Aubrey Davidson, president of the Chamber of Commerce, suggested that San Diego hold an exposition to celebrate the opening of the Panama Canal in 1915. The Panama-California Exposition Company, formed in September 1909, supported a private subscription and city bond issue that raised $2 million. Park commissioners Thomas O'Halloran, M.A. Luce and Leroy Wright adopted the name "Balboa Park" offered by Harriet Phillips of the San Diego Pioneer Society. Since Vasco Nuñez de Balboa discovered the Pacific Ocean and claimed the entire west coast of the Americas for Spain on September 29, 1513, it seemed appropriate to honor the Spanish explorer. Besides tying the park to Panama, the celebration could be combined with Cabrillo's September 28th arrival. The hiring of project architect Bertram G. Goodhue brought rich decoration, exotic architecture and multiple uses to the park. Goodhue's central complex of stuccoed spanish colonial buildings forever set aside the Parsons Plan for a natural picturesque park free of man-made obstructions.

The Varied Industries Building (below) from the Panama-California Exposition at Balboa Park, 1915.

San Diego County in 1888: a different picture

In 1888, the county of San Diego included parts of present-day Imperial County and Riverside County. Fifty-eight small towns were listed:

Agua Tibia	Cota	Glamis	Menefie	Perris	Terra Cotta
Alpine	Del Mar	Helix	Murrieta	Potrero	Tia Juana
Anon	De Luz	Holabird	National City	Poway	Valley Center
Ballena	Descanso	Howe	Nellie	Radec	Viejas
Banner	Dulzura	Jamul	North San Diego	San Diego	Vineyard
Bernardo	El Cajon	Julian	Nuevo	San Luis Rey	West Fallbrook
Buena	Elsinore	Lakeside	Oceanside	San Pasqual	Wildomar
Campo	Encinitas	La Presa	Olivenhain	South San Diego	Winchester
Carlsbad	Escondido	Leucadia	Otay	Stratton	
Coronado	Fallbrook	Linda Vista	Pala	Temecula	

Helix Post Office and Store, 1895

Robinson Hotel in Julian, circa 1910

El Cajon Valley Knox Hotel, the 1890s

In addition to park planning, the Chamber of Commerce hired John Nolen, a city planner from Cambridge, Massachusetts, to do a master improvement plan for the city in general. The Nolen Report of 1908 recommended the construction of a wide landscaped walkway called The Paseo descending twelve blocks between Date and Elm streets from the park to the bay. In the best Hispanic tradition, the Paseo would have been a unique and beautiful treelined promenade in the heart of the city. San Diegans missed a great opportunity to enhance the downtown area when they failed to implement the plan.

Newspaper competition was fairly strong during the late nineteenth century. The *San Diego Union* experienced its greatest growth under Spreckels' ownership. The installation of a Linotype in 1895 enhanced the eight-page daily, and in 1896 the *Union* outbid four rival newspapers — *Sun, Vidette, Record* and *Tribune* — for the county tax list. James D. MacMullen, managing editor of Spreckels' San Francisco *Call,* joined the staff in 1899 and served as editor-manager until his death in 1933. Soon after MacMullen's arrival, the competition lessened. The *Union* purchased the plant of the *Morning Call* (formerly the *Vidette*) in 1900, and took over the *Tribune* (started in 1895) in September 1901. The combined papers moved into the Horton Bank Building at Third and Broadway in December 1901 and in less than six years built a new six-story structure, complete with a sixteen-page press.

FOURTH ESTATE: The San Diego Sun *building (top) and the* San Diego Union *and* Evening Tribune *building (above).*

Despite publishing rival newspapers, Spreckels and E.W. Scripps, owner of Miramar Ranch, had common interests. With A.G. Spalding of sporting goods fame — they had purchased 7,000 acres of the Fanita Ranch in Santee in 1898. Scripps eventually bought the others out and added the Fanita Ranch to his Miramar holdings as a horse breeding farm. In 1907, Spreckels, Scripps and Spalding joined George Marston and Charles Kelly to protect and finally purchase the site of the ruined San Diego presidio. After publication of William E. Smythe's *History of San Diego* in 1908, the public began to take an interest in the hill behind Old Town as the "Plymouth Rock" of the Pacific Coast. Spreckels and Scripps also joined Spalding on the county road commission created by the board of supervisors in 1909 to provide roads into the back country. Auto roads were laid out or graded from San Diego to El Cajon, north to Santee, Lakeside, Ramona and Julian; from Julian to Cuyamaca, through Green Valley to Descanso and Pine Valley; from Fallbrook to Pala, Rincon, Warner's Hot Springs, Santa Ysabel and Escondido, which in turn connected Escondido to Vista and Oceanside on the coast. Scripps'

sister, Ellen Browning Scripps, also cooperated in city interests by helping to sponsor an institution for marine biological research in La Jolla under Dr. William Ritter in 1905 and by protecting Torrey pines on land adjacent to Torrey Pines reserve.

Historian William E. Smythe had come to San Diego from Massachusetts and run unsuccessfully for Congress in 1902. He claimed San Diego was ridden with monopolies and corruption. With George P. Hall, he promoted a cooperative farming community with a campaign of "a little land and a living" south of San Diego. The "Little Landers" purchased 550 acres in the Tia Juana River Valley and sold one-acre plots from $350 to $550 and lots at $250. On opening day January 11, 1909, twelve families bought lots, and the colony began. The "farmers" consisted mostly of professional people who attempted to survive by growing their own food and sharing their profits. Many had to work outside the area to sustain the experiment.

Another cooperative effort on a much larger scale was the theosophical movement promoted by Katherine Tingley on 132 acres of choice Point Loma land. An attractive, thrice-married, childless matron from Massachusetts, Madame Tingley had successfully taken over leadership of a group of theosophists whose origins were in the East. Theosophy — a word derived from *theos* (God) and *sophia* (wisdom) — can be defined as speculative thought about God and the universe arising from either mystical insight or from a comparison of the teachings of various religions. Inspiration for the Point Loma community came indirectly through Helena Petrovna Blavatsky (1831-1891), a controversial Russian woman who had a great interest in spiritualism and the teachings of Indian mahatmas. Upon Blavatsky's death, several successors struggled for leadership in theosophical thinking, but Katherine Tingley had the

NEW MOVEMENT: *Katherine A. Tingley (above), founder of the Universal Theosophical Society, brought to San Diego a unique experiment in living. The gateway to Point Loma's Theosophical Society (top) gave visitors and residents a feeling they were entering another world. Visible through the arch is the exquisite glass-domed Temple of Peace.*

wisdom and foresight to win control of a major branch of followers. She proposed the founding of a School for the Revival of Lost Mysteries of Antiquity in 1896 after the aged General John Fremont in New York confirmed her dream about a place where she could build a "white city in a golden land by the sundown sea." Fremont told her of Point Loma. Without further investigation, she had her agents purchase the tract in 1896: The cornerstone for the first building was laid on February 24, 1897.

Following Tingley's leadership, theosophists from the Boston society formed the Universal Brotherhood of Theosophists in 1900 at Point Loma. After the original School of Antiquity was completed, the Isis Conservatory of Music and Drama, the Lotus Home for refugee Cuban children and the glass-domed Temple of Peace appeared on the landscape. A Greek theater overlooked the Pacific Ocean, and eventually there were 50 buildings on the grounds. The personal magnetism of Katherine Tingley inspired converts from all walks of life and included A.G. Spalding. Visitors frequently commented on the orderly, almost military, atmosphere where uniforms were common and children sat rigidly at dining tables, observing a rule of silence. Formal classroom instruction at the Raja Yoga school was never more than three hours a day, but the students excelled in spelling, arithmetic, music and other subjects. They also learned gardening and various useful crafts. Harrison Gray Otis, owner-publisher of the *Los Angeles Times,* criticized the community in an article called "Startling Tales from Tingley" and alleged improper conduct. Tingley sued for libel and won $7,500 in damages. She was less successful, however, in a later suit filed by an unhappy wife of a loyal resident. Tingley's fortunes rose and fell, but she was able during her life-time to maintain the utopian community as a prosperous experiment. She died in 1929 at the age of 82 and was succeeded by Gottfried de Purucker, a supporter from the beginning in 1896. (When de Purucker died in 1942, the theosophists left Point Loma. The site became the home of California Western University after World War II. Today it is Point Loma College. Several of the original buildings grace the campus of this institution of higher learning.)

Blochman Banking Company, circa 1895 (top); and President Benjamin Harrison visits Hotel del Coronado, 1891 (above). The Horton House (lower right) was demolished in 1905 to allow construction of the U.S. Grant Hotel, 1906 (top right).

The turn of the century had seen San Diego embark upon a new era. In addition to already active businessmen, a group of newcomers with equal vision took the lead. Louis J. Wilde, who arrived in 1903, organized four new banks — the Citizens Savings Bank, the American National Bank, the United States National Bank and the First National Bank of Escondido. He built the Pickwick Theatre in 1904, the Louis J. Wilde Building and the ten-story American National Bank building at Fifth and D streets soon after. In 1908, when the U.S. Grant Hotel suffered financial setbacks and looked as if it would not open, Wilde raised enough money to complete it and joined U.S. Grant Jr. as a partner. The luxury hotel, opened in 1910, cost more than $1 million and featured an exotic fountain designed by noted architect Irving Gill. The fountain — illuminated by electric lights with fifteen color effects — fittingly contained the portraits of Juan Rodríguez Cabrillo, Junípero Serra and Alonzo Horton. Louis Wilde urged changing D Street to Broadway in 1914.

Other city builders were D.C. Collier, a promoter of Ocean Beach and O.W. Cotton, developer of Pacific Beach and East San Diego. Ed Fletcher, a young produce merchant from Littleton, Massachusetts, thought that water to develop coastal regions could be obtained from the San Luis Rey River and other sources in the back country. He and his partner Frank Salmons worked for the South Coast Land Company which bought up lands and existing water rights along the San Luis Rey River. It obtained all of the original settlement of Del Mar, more than 800 acres in Leucadia, 1,400 acres of

Agua Hedionda, nearly all of Carlsbad and large holdings in Oceanside. Salmons meanwhile discovered a gemstone (Kunzite) mine in Pala while Ed Fletcher worked on water development.

John D. Spreckels — whose successes and power were feared by some — had retained his home in San Francisco until failing health and the great earthquake and fire of 1906 drove him to San Diego. Since his health took an immediate turn for the better, he built a mansion, complete with pipe organ, in Coronado across from his hotel. After his permanent move to San Diego, Spreckels began to promote the railroad to Yuma in earnest. After solving a series of problems involving the Southern Pacific Railroad, he and his partners surveyed the proposed route that would go through National City, the Carrizo Gorge, 44 miles

PROPERTIES: Ed Fletcher (above, on far right) in front of the Ed Fletcher Company on D Street near Sixth Avenue, circa 1909. At one time, the South Coast Land Company owned most of Carlsbad (left) where mineral water was the attraction advertised on a railroad platform.

A dog called Bum

Every town should have an historic pet as well suited to the role as Bum. Bum was a bedraggled, friendly, lame St. Bernard who came to be loved by most San Diegans during the late 1880s and 1890s. He was born in San Francisco in July, 1886 and stowed away aboard the Pacific Coast Steamship Company's *Santa Rosa* bound for San Diego shortly afterwards. His mother had died for lack of a tag. Bum walked down the gangplank of the southern port during the boom of the '80s and took up with James Edward Friend, an itinerant journalist who liked to be called "Captain." Friend wrote a biographical sketch of Bum's life for *The Weekly Drift*. We assume he checked his facts. Apparently Bum's first provider in San Diego was a Chinese fisherman named Ah Wo Sue who had trouble keeping Bum in one place. One day in August 1887 while Bum was loafing around the Santa Fe Railroad yards, he got into a fight with a bulldog. The dogs rolled under the wheels of a passing engine. The bulldog was

killed; Bum lost his right forefoot and suffered a gash in the stomach. Ah Wo Sue nursed Bum back to health, but the dog preferred the life of a wanderer. He even took the train to Los Angeles for a short visit.

Bum's favorite activities were following parades and funerals and visiting local saloons for a handout — food or drink. Often he could be seen staggering along the street or sleeping it off in some downtown corner. But some well meaning reformers complained about the drifter. So Captain Friend applied to the city council for a license. Bum's dog tax receipt — complete with picture — was issued on August 29, 1891.

Except for the usual scuffles, Bum lived a good life in and out of various shops in the downtown area. His second bad experience came in May 1894, when he got too close to a nervous horse behind George Magwood's store. Bum was kicked and his left hind-leg broken. Dr. John Stone was called in by Friend, and the fractured leg was promptly set. Bum remained at the Magwoods for some time after the operation.

Although Friend and his dog were inseparable, Bum still belonged to the town. He was everybody's pal. One restaurant even displayed a sign, "Bum eats here." In March 1898, Friend died. He had already written Bum's final story. "When Bum dies and I should 'not be at home' his obituary is ready written. The newsboys will see that both of us have decent funerals and the band will be present." A few months after Friend's death, Bum became crippled with rheumatism and was retired to the County Hospital. He died in November 1898, not to be forgotten by an entire community.

Bum under the Surgeons care. 643

BUM WAS HERE: A dog tax receipt, complete with a picture of the dog named Bum (inset) was issued on August 29, 1891. Several years later, the San Diego pet St. Bernard was kicked by a horse and a surgeon was called in (left) for repairs. Although he belonged to itinerant journalist James Friend, Bum was everybody's pal - including Juanita and Helen Leffert (above).

of territory in Baja California (to avoid the rugged Laguna mountains) and across newly-created Imperial County. Spreckels personally obtained the right-of-way from Mexico, and Mayor John F. Forward Jr. turned the first sod on ground-breaking day, September 9, 1907. Honored guests were Alonzo Horton and Frank Kimball who must have imagined their dreams finally coming true. Because of problems of the Mexican Revolution after 1910, flooding of the Imperial Valley, World War I and the need for 21 tunnels, the line was not completed until 1919. It cost $18 million and was an important link with Arizona. (The line was partly destroyed by flash flooding from Hurricane Kathleen in 1976 but was repaired in 1980.)

San Diego made national headlines as a result of the *USS Bennington* disaster on July 21, 1905. The Navy gunboat was anchored in the harbor when observers heard a deafening noise. Boilers had exploded below decks, killing 60 men and injuring 46. Dr. W.L. Kneedler, Army surgeon at Fort Rosecrans, helped in rescue operations, and all San Diego physicians were called for assistance. Open wagons carried injured men to hospitals. Funeral services and a mass burial were held on July 23 at the post cemetery at Fort Rosecrans. The last rites were conducted by the Reverend J.A.M. Richey, rector of St. Paul's and by Father Antonio Ubach of St. Joseph's. On a different note, President Theodore Roosevelt sent the Navy's Great White Fleet on a world tour in December 1907, to impress Japan and other potential rivals with America's determination to play a significant role in economic and political affairs. Sixteen battleships, seven destroyers and four auxiliary ships under the command of Rear Admiral R.D. Evans stayed four days in the San Diego harbor. Sixteen thousand sailors visited the city. Curiously, the San Francisco earthquake of 1906, coupled with anti-Japanese legislation in the northern city, had precipitated a move by many Japanese families to San Diego. The nucleus of a Japanese business community around Fifth and Market streets were on hand to greet the Great White Fleet on April 14, 1908.

Santa Fe depot (top), 1887; mass grave for the Bennington victims, 1905 (center); and the Great White Fleet off Coronado, 1908 (above).

EQUAL RIGHTS: A Labor Day parade in 1910 included a decorated wagon of women (top right) asking "Equal pay for equal work regardless of sex." Women also worked in the Old Mission Olive Factory (below right) and in the home, such as the Noeltner's family residence (far right) at 640 17th Street.

By the end of the decade, San Diego's progress could easily be measured. The population had nearly reached 40,000, and the influx of people had brought business stability. Headway had also been made in solving the problem of an adequate water supply. Since an average rainfall of ten inches per year was insufficient, private companies had developed the mountain reservoirs and were selling water to the city on a contract basis. From 1887 to 1897, these companies constructed six major dams in the county. Two large private concerns fought over who could best serve the city. The San Diego Flume Company was successful for a few years, but an eleven-year drought between 1895 and 1905 dried up the Flume's reservoir and forced it to pump brackish San Diego River water. The Southern California Mountain Water Company, organized by Elisha Babcock and taken over by John Spreckels, had built the Upper and Lower Otay and Morena Dams. In 1906 the company agreed to deliver a maximum of nearly eight million gallons of water daily to the city at a stipulated low price for ten years. Finally, in 1913, the city — which had already purchased the San Diego Water Company in 1901 — added the facilities of the Southern California Mountain Water Company and boasted a wholly-owned municipal water system.

Certain key figures of New San Diego had died, but a new generation was taking over the reins of government. Ephraim W. Morse died in 1906, Father Antonio Ubach in 1907 and both William Heath Davis and Alonzo Horton in 1909. Lydia Knapp Horton, an attractive widow whom Alonzo had married in 1890, summed up her husband's feelings at the end of his life. He had a broad vision and faith in San Diego, she said, and he "was never surprised at any of the great improvements that were made here in his later years." Nor was he sorry when the Horton House was torn down. On the contrary, he was glad to see the fine new building go up. Lydia Horton and others would see even greater changes during the next few decades.

The building of Lake Wohlford, 1894-95 (top); sporting goods merchant A. G. Spalding and his wife (above) motoring on Point Loma. Coronado Tent City, circa 1904 (top right) drew early-day sun seekers, though some stayed inside the tents (bottom right).

Chapter VII

Birth of a metropolis

1910-1930

San Diego in 1910 was an optimistic, progressive metropolis of almost 40,000 people. By the end of the decade its population would reach 75,000 — a number that would again nearly double by 1930. The official program at the groundbreaking for the Panama-California Exposition on July 19, 1911, boasted: "The fourth epoch of California begins with the rebuilding of San Diego ... the marvelous progressive movement in Southern California and the awakening of imperial enterprise throughout the Southwest; closing with the completion of the Panama Canal and the San Diego & Arizona Railway, thus concentrating the traffic of a continent and the commerce of a great ocean in the harbor of San Diego ... the first port of call in American territory north of the canal." The ceremony, attended by many notables, was highlighted at 4 p.m. when President William Howard Taft pressed an electric button in the East Room of the White House (7 p.m. EST) and unfurled an American flag at the site. Bishop Thomas J. Conaty from Los Angeles celebrated the first pontifical military mass in San Diego since Father Serra's arrival in 1769.

Despite the Bennington disaster of 1905, San Diego — with Chamber of Commerce help — was destined to become a major naval base. In 1918, the Chamber raised $280,000 to purchase tidelands at the foot of 32nd street for the Navy's first principal facility in the city, later to become a large destroyer base.

Transportation and communication by sea and land were seen as keys to the future when the Pacific Navigation Company's steamship *Yale* arrived with 400 excursionists on March 4, 1911. The ship's officers and passengers were driven around the city in automobiles decked with Yale and Harvard pennants representing the company's two new steamships. San Diegans had received 325 new cars in 1910, and road building commanded great priority. When the *Yale* departed, the pilot of an airplane from the Curtiss Flying School bombarded it with oranges to

NEW ADVENTURES: Broadway Pier at San Diego Harbor, April 1927 (bottom left); on the coldest day to date — Jan. 7, 1913 — a boy stands on ice almost an inch thick in the Horton Plaza fountain (below); ground breaking of the Panama-California Exposition (left).

symbolize California agriculture and a new hope for the future — aviation.

John J. Montgomery had made the first controlled wing flight south of San Diego in 1883, but the Wright Brothers with their immortal powered flight at Kittyhawk, North Carolina, in 1903 had made flying a national pastime for many and a commercial venture for an enterprising few. Californians soon held aviation meets, formed aero clubs and watched barnstorming spectaculars. In 1908, Glenn Hammond Curtiss from Hammondsport, New York, built his first airplane and a year later won the Gordon Bennett Cup race in the *Golden Flyer*. In 1911, the Spreckels-owned Coronado Beach Company offered Curtiss the use of North Island for three years to run a flying school. On January 26, 1911, Curtiss made aviation history as he took off from the mile-long waters of Spanish Bight (now filled in) between Coronado and North Island in the world's first successful seaplane. Curtiss invited the military to provide the first students for his flying school, and Lieutenant Theodore G. Ellyson became the first pupil and Navy Pilot Number One. Three Army lieutenants — Paul W. Beck, G.E.M. Kelly and John C. Walker — and three civilians — Charles Witmer, Robert St. Henry and Lincoln Beachey — also joined the class of 1911. Curtiss and his two associates, Hugh Robinson and Eugene B. Ely, performed numerous aerial stunts at a meet sponsored by D.C. Collier's San Diego Aero Club on January 26 and 27, 1911.

William Kettner, a charter member of the Aero Club and long a city promoter, was elected to Congress in 1912 and began to promote San Diego's ideal location for the military. The U.S. Army Signal Corps Training School temporarily moved to North Island in 1913. It became known as Rockwell Field in 1914. Since the Coronado Beach Company had allowed Curtiss and the Army to use the land free, while they paid $50,000 in taxes, they wanted the premises vacated. Kettner framed a bill for federal takeover of the property, and in 1917 sponsored an act authorizing the United States to take possession of North Island as a permanent Army and Navy aviation school. The act also appropriated the necessary money to compensate the owners. In 1922 the Navy completed its hospital in Balboa Park, and San Diego was named headquarters for the Eleventh Naval District. With Fort Rosecrans and the Marine base established in 1919, the military was destined to become a significant factor in the city's growth.

San Diego had readily taken to the air. The first airmail service was inaugurated in 1918 and in 1922 North Island Army Air Service Lieutenants Oakley Kelly and John Macready set a sustained flight record of 35 hours and 18 minutes. Lieutenant James H. Doolittle then set a coast-to-coast record of 21 hours and 19 minutes from Jacksonville, Florida, to San Diego. Kelly and Macready made the first non-stop transcontinental flight from New York to San Diego in May 1923 and were greeted upon their arrival by T. Claude Ryan, a young Army reserve pilot from Parsons, Kansas. Ryan — a graduate of the cadet school at March Field (Riverside) and Mather Field (Sacramento) — had come to San Diego in 1922 and decided there was a future in commercial aviation. He convinced San Diego's harbor master to let him use a small dirt landing strip on the tidelands at the foot of Broadway and bought a war surplus bi-plane for $400. By 1925 he had purchased more planes and moved to Dutch Flats opposite the Marine base. With partner B. Franklin Mahoney, the two organized Ryan Airlines and began an air service between San Diego and Los Angeles, the first regularly scheduled year-round passenger airline in the United States. Ryan soon became dissatisfied with available airplanes and designed a high-wing monoplane — the M-1. It was produced in 90 days and tested on February 1, 1926. Later it flew more than 1,100 miles from Vancouver Field, Washington, to Los Angeles in just under ten hours.

BY LAND, SEA AND AIR: A 1911 advertisement for Curtiss School of Aviation (top) claims "90 percent of the aeroplane exhibitions throughout the U.S. are given by Curtiss aviators"; the first refueling in mid-air took place over San Diego, circa 1923 (above); the main gate of the U. S. Naval training station entrance (bottom right) at Barnett Avenue and Lytton Street in the 1920s; the U. S. Naval repair base for destroyers, 1927 (far right); trans-Atlantic air hero Charles Lindbergh (center) in San Diego on May 9, 1927; the group that built "The Spirit of St. Louis" (far right center), with Lindbergh seventh from left, 1927; group of Curtiss students with an early "flying machine" (top right) in 1912 at Curtiss camp of aviation on North Island.

Students   Curtiss Camp   San Diego. Cal. 1912   1359

KEEP OUT
OF THE WATER

He did!
OFFICIAL PHOTO
BY ERICKSON.

"We Built the Ryan New York to Paris Plane"

STATION

U.S. NAV.

13697

Meanwhile, across the country on a night flight between St. Louis and Chicago in the fall of 1926, a young airmail pilot was thinking of the $25,000 offered as a prize for the first non-stop trans-Atlantic flight. Charles A. Lindbergh had obtained the financial backing of his employers and other businessmen in St. Louis but could not find the proper airplane. When he read about Ryan's M-1, he felt that, with modifications, it would be right. The company was then working on a larger plane for speed flyer Frank Hawks. Ryan, who had sold his interest in Ryan Airlines but was still manager of the company, responded to Lindbergh's request for a plane by offering in 60 days a plane that could cross from New York to Paris non-stop. Lindbergh came to San Diego to inspect the M-1. He signed a contract on February 28, 1927, for a plane to meet his requirements. When all tests were completed, the *Spirit of St. Louis* — costing just over $10,000 — exceeded expectations. Lindbergh left Rockwell Field for St. Louis and completed his historic 33½-hour flight from New York to Paris on May 21. His success brought honor and prestige to the Ryan organization and presaged the aviation industry's move into the space age. That same year, the harbor was dredged to provide a turning basin for the *USS Lexington* and *Saratoga,* the nation's first major aircraft carriers. The dredged material became the fill for Lindbergh field, dedicated on August 16, 1928.

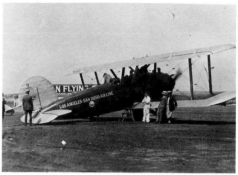

Industrial Workers of the World riot, 1912 (top); Los Angeles to San Diego airline (above).

San Diego's otherwise peaceful existence was interrupted by the outbreak of the Mexican Revolution in 1910. A number of conspirators, led by Ricardo Flores Magon, began slipping arms across the border into Baja California. They were members of the Marxist Liberal Party, not the mainstream revolutionaries that had overthrown Mexico's long-time dictator Porfirio Diaz. In Los Angeles they received help from members of the Industrial Workers of the World (I.W.W.) who had come to California to organize agricultural workers. Magon had dispatched a tiny army to the Imperial Valley. These men joined Mexicans across the border. The rebels captured Mexicali, Tecate and pressed on toward Tijuana. In San Diego, support for the rebel cause was urged by anarchist Emma Goldman who felt that American troops patrolling the border should be removed. Other IWW members arrived in San Diego and began openly recruiting rebels. Tijuana was finally captured, and a red flag hoisted with the slogan *"tierra y libertad."* ("land and liberty").

Many IWW members remained in San Diego and began calling for the overthrow of capitalism. A confrontation with local merchants led to the passing of a city ordinance banning streetcorner speaking in certain downtown areas. On February 9, 1912, police arrested 41 men for violating the anti-speech ordinance and gave impetus to the free speech movement. In March a mob of some 5,000 people gathered near the city jail but were dispersed by fire hoses. A vigilante committee of local citizens succeeded in running most IWW members out of town in April. On May 8, European-born socialist Joseph Mikolasek was shot during an encounter with police; riots exploded in the downtown area. When Emma Goldman tried to speak in the city a week later, she too was taken by the vigilantes and placed on a train heading out of the city. This ended the IWW movement in San Diego, but the Mexican Revolution continued. The effects north of the California border were thereafter minor. Mexican problems began to take second place as San Diego responded to the news of Archduke Franz Ferdinand's assassination on June 28, 1914 and threats of an impending global conflict.

The spark that set off World War I was overshadowed in San Diego by the opening of the Panama-California Exposition in Balboa Park at midnight, January 1, 1915. Bertram Goodhue's completed buildings represented the Spanish colonial style that he had studied and enjoyed on a visit to Mexico. Since his first assistant architect Irving Gill had had

Soldiers marching Mexican rebels at Fort Rosecrans, 1911 (above); amateur photographers on an outing, 1912 (top); San Diego Gas and Electric Company Station "B", circa 1918 (right).

something else in mind, Goodhue hired Carleton M. Winslow of New York to help carry out the Hispanic theme. Frank P. Allen, a veteran of Seattle's World's Fair, became chief engineer and John P. Morley left Los Angeles to become superintendent of parks. Since San Francisco was planning a world's fair at the same time, San Diego decided to keep its exposition regional in character. The Santa Fe Railroad built an Indian village similar to the Pueblo of Taos although the plan as a whole — with its baroque buildings, tree-shaded prado and open plazas — suggested a typical Spanish city of the seventeenth century. The magnificent approach via Cabrillo Canyon Bridge presented such a breathtaking view that, years later, visitors would still be impressed by Goodhue's feeling of Spain with its Mediterranean and Moorish counterparts.

President Woodrow Wilson at the White House touched an electric button that turned on a light suspended by a balloon to open the exposition. The guns at Fort Rosecrans and those on the ships in the harbor fired in unison to signal the event. A fireworks display at the Spreckels Organ Pavilion portrayed a replica of the Panama Canal from which the prow of a ship labeled "1915" emerged. The phrase "The land divided — the world united — San Diego the first port of call" was outlined in flame. Mayor Charles O'Neall commented with pride that the future of San Diego — metropolis of the West — seemed assured. Governor Hiram Johnson presented the California Building and California Tower to G. Aubrey Davidson, president of the exposition, for the people of San Diego. Secretary of the Treasury William Gibbs McAdoo represented President Wilson, and the Conde del Valle de Salazar appeared for King Alfonso XIII of Spain at the opening. Balboa Stadium

COVER CELEBRATION: Opening of the Southwest depicted on the January 1, 1913 cover of the San Diego Union (bottom left); the Panama Canal heralded on the January 1, 1914 cover of the San Diego Union (bottom right); and the builders of San Diego's fair honored by the Union, 1915 (below).

1915 EXPOSITION: The Panama-California Exposition (top); Balboa Park, Cabrillo Bridge and the California Tower (above); William Howard Taft and G. Aubrey Davidson (right), president of the exposition.

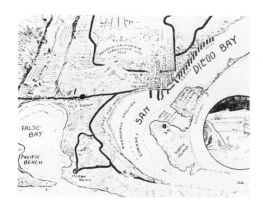

in the park was hailed as the world's largest municipal structure. Other famous visitors were Vice President Thomas R. Marshall, Theodore Roosevelt (who complimented himself for making completion of the canal possible), William Jennings Bryan and Secretary of the Navy Franklin D. Roosevelt. Because of its success, the exposition was held open for another year.

To stimulate interest in driving to the fair, Ed Fletcher, William Gross (an actor for whom Grossmont was named) and Wilbur Hall (a magazine writer), left for Washington, D.C. on November 2, 1915, with driver Harry Taylor. They traveled the plank road to Yuma and over the new bridge spanning the Colorado River. The car — minus a few passengers — reached the Capitol after 23½ days without difficulty. San Diego had a direct automobile link with the East, but the drive presented quite a challenge to the casual visitor. The fair officially closed on December 31, 1916. At 11:59 p.m., taps was sounded from the Plaza de Panama, and at midnight Madame Schumann-Heink sang a tearful "Auld Lang Syne" at the Organ Pavilion. A fireworks display spelled out "World's Peace, 1917."

With the closing of the fair, opinions were divided about San Diego's future course. Louis Wilde promoted industrial development, while George Marston preferred city beautification. Indicative of the time, "smokestacks" won out over "geraniums," and Wilde was elected mayor in April 1917.

One of the most permanent and significant results of the Panama-California Exposition was the San Diego Zoo formed around the menagerie of creatures brought together for the occasion. Since the animals' future seemed uncertain during the fair's second year, Dr. Harry Wegeforth and his brother Dr. Paul Wegeforth advertised in the *San Diego Union* of September 27, 1916, for interested parties to join with them and Drs. J.C. Thompson and Fred Baker in forming a zoological garden. The four physicians convinced naturalist Frank Stephens of the Natural History Society to join them as director. Kate Stephens, also a naturalist, was curator of mollusks at the Museum of Natural History. The first meeting of the official board of directors was held at Dr. Baker's home. His hobby was conchology, and he helped found the Marine Biological Institution which became Scripps Institution of Oceanography in 1925. His wife Charlotte, also a leading physician, encouraged the zoo's development. Dr. Thompson, a neurosurgeon assigned to the Navy Hospital, was involved in planning the zoo's educational program but had to leave the board in April 1917, for government duty. Joseph Sefton Jr. replaced him and contributed a great deal of time and money to the project. Carl H. Heilbron and D.C. Collier helped purchase the first group of animals from nearby Ocean Beach Wonderland. The few bears and other animals were kept in cages along Park Boulevard until 1922

EXPOSITION ACTIVITY: The 1915 site, according to the San Diego Union (far left); annual pass of $10 to the San Diego Panama-California Exposition (left); the California Tower (below); Balboa Park on the Isthmus, home of the Cawston Ostrich Farm (left center); selling tours to the 1915 exposition (bottom). Ellen Scripps (top left) and D. C. Collier (above) helped a zoo get started in San Diego.

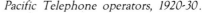

Pacific Telephone operators, 1920-30.

when the zoo moved to its present location. Dr. Harry Wegeforth worked hard from 1916 to 1922 to attract interest and money in the zoo and received help from Ellen Browning Scripps, John D. Spreckels, George W. Marston, John Burnham, Ralph Granger and Frank C. Spalding. Money, nevertheless, was difficult to raise. In 1921 the San Diego City Council agreed to appropriate $5,000 for maintenance and improvements and approved the zoo's current site by city ordinance. The zoo slowly grew from a meager exhibit of wild animals to an institution, but its future was never secure until the mid-1930s when the city took over support. Mrs. Belle Jennings Benchley, who became bookkeeper at the zoo in 1925, gradually assumed more responsibilities until she became the first full-time director after only a year and seven months. She ran the zoo successfully through a combination of studied competence, patient determination, a love of animals and what she liked to call "animal instinct." Belle Benchley — then the only woman zoo director in the United States — remained at the helm until her retirement in 1953.

Other park developments included the building in 1926 of the Fine Arts Gallery (now the San Diego Museum of Art) designed by architect William Templeton Johnson. A native of New York, Johnson had spent considerable time in Mexico absorbing the influence of Spanish colonial art forms. He patterned the entrance to the gallery after that of the University of Salamanca in Spanish Renaissance style. His later Natural History Museum building emphasized the classical revival mode with Mediterranean features. In 1926 Johnson was chosen from a group of six architectural contestants to design the three American buildings of the Iberian-American Exposition in Seville, Spain.

Because of his excellent reputation, Johnson was selected by Joseph W. Sefton Jr. (son of the founder of the San Diego Trust and Savings Bank) to design a new bank building at Sixth and Broadway. Sefton had served as director of publicity for the Panama-California Exposition and had a deep interest in construction and design. The bank had purchased the 100-by-500-foot lot in 1924 for $600,000 and demolished the Hotel Beacon. The new building was completed in April 1928, and remains today as a prime example of early Renaissance Revival style. Its arcaded tower and penthouse are a prominent feature of San Diego's skyline. Other buildings designed by Johnson included the Lion Clothing Store, Francis W. Parker School and the Serra Museum.

Scripps Institution of Oceanography, La Jolla, circa 1928 (top left); San Diego Trust and Savings, 1928 (top right); architect William Templeton Johnson (above); Pioneer Truck Company, 1920 (top right); street car on Broadway, 1924 (bottom right).

The problem of water continued to occupy the minds of San Diego's civic leaders. Each crisis was met with equanimity until the city fathers began to talk about a possible shortage toward the end of 1915. Rainfall that year had been reasonably good — 13.62 inches compared with an annual average of 9.25 during the previous five years. Nevertheless, Morena Reservoir had not been filled since its construction in 1897 and was holding only five billion of its fifteen-billion-gallon capacity. Other reservoirs had not been filled, and the city's demands were increasing monthly. Water rights were much discussed since City Attorney Terence B. Cosgrove, an expert in water matters, had opined that a grant from the King of Spain allowed San Diego to proceed against ranch owners upstream on the San Diego River who had appropriated much of the water. Los Angeles had made good a similar claim on the Los Angeles river and, although there was never such a grant, the courts had held that somehow a Spanish "pueblo" had a right to all the waters it needed from the river on which it was founded. This gave city inhabitants rights over upstream farmers who conceivably could obstruct the city's supply. Los Angeles had added to its local water rights by building the Los Angeles aqueduct to bring water more than 200 miles from the Owens River. San Diego would also need to make plans to bring water from distant places.

Into this atmosphere of impending drought stepped a rainmaker of some repute — Charles Mallory Hatfield. The Hatfields had moved to San Diego from Fort Scott, Kansas, in 1886 and worked in the sewing machine business while trading property throughout southern California. In 1902 they lived on a ranch in Gopher Canyon in Bonsall where Charley began experimenting in rainmaking operations. With the help of brother Paul, he set up a number of towers and apparently induced some rain in dry areas. Hatfield enjoyed several "successes" between 1903 and

As the successor to a Mexican pueblo, San Diego prevailed against ranch owners upstream on the San Diego River who had appropriated much of the water.

THE RAINS CAME: Remains of the concrete bridge at Old Town after the flood, Jan. 28, 1916 (bottom); Charles Hatfield, the rainmaker from Kansas (center left), conjures up a cloudburst; years later, rainmaker Hatfield looks back (center) on newspaper headlines, "Water Supply Assured" in the San Diego Union, Jan. 23, 1916; the Hatfield rainmaking towers, 1916 (top left); and the Lower Otay Dam (below) after the weather breaks Jan. 27, 1916.

1912 in the Southwest and as far north as Alaska. San Diego realtor Fred Binney suggested Hatfield to the city council as early as 1912, but the time was not right. In December 1915, Charley offered his services to the city on a "no rain — no pay" basis. He agreed to fill Morena Reservoir free to four-fifths capacity and charge only for the 40th to 50th inch at $1,000 per inch. Cosgrove said the contract would be legal, and his assistant Shelley Higgins began to prepare the draft. Hatfield started operations at Morena Dam on the first of January, and by the fifth it began to rain. A heavier rain fell on January 10 and on the 14th it reached torrential proportions. The San Diego River overflowed its banks on the 17th, and the Tia Juana River destroyed the "Little Lander's" homes and gardens on the 18th. The *San Diego Union* headlined "Is Rainmaker at Work?" "Hatfield's scheme was on almost every tongue yesterday," the paper reported. "Many were inclined to jest, but all agreed that things were going his way." But the rain did not stop. During the next few days, it washed away roads and bridges. The back country was isolated, and a veritable river rushed out of the canyons of Balboa Park. Lower Otay Dam gave way on January 27, causing untold damage and injuring a large number of Japanese farmers living in Otay Valley. Hatfield appeared at city hall to collect his $10,000 but was blamed for the flood damage. He finally sued the city but gave up any hope of payment when Cosgrove insisted upon his being liable for all flood claims against the city. The city decided to plan for future water resources in a more realistic manner.

As early as 1917, San Diego led the formation of the League of the Southwest to promote the Boulder Canyon project on the Colorado River. This water supply could ensure San Diego's dreams of becoming a major port and industrial center. The city went ahead with other plans and in 1922 completed Barrett Dam on Cottonwood Creek; in 1924 voters approved a bond issue for construction of El Capitan Dam. San Diego also purchased the San Dieguito Water System and won its case against upstream Cuyamaca Water Company, asserting its right as a "pueblo" to all San Diego River water. Because of its early interest in the Colorado River, the city applied to the California Division of Water Resources in 1926 for the right to 112,000-acre-feet (100 million gallons) of water a day from that source. The right was granted and later extended to include the

IN THE SUBURBS: Mission Beach, 1922 (top); cottage for author Owen Wister (above); Grape Day parade in Escondido, 1914 (top right); Oceanside's Mission Avenue, circa 1917 (bottom right).

Lakeside Auto Speedway, circa 1912 (left); Pickwick Hotel at First and Broadway, May 1927 (below); and the San Diego Athletic Club 1930 (bottom).

county. By 1928, the fight for Boulder Dam and the All-American Canal in the Imperial Valley was ending. Despite protests from Arizona, Congressman Phil Swing finally maneuvered the Swing-Johnson Bill to the floor of the House, where it passed on May 25, and Hiram Johnson fought it through the Senate. When Johnson agreed to limit California's share, the bill passed on December 14. San Diego, hoping to construct its own facilities through the mountains, did not at this time join the Metropolitan Water District formed by Los Angeles and other cities for distribution of Colorado River water to southern California.

Both city builders John D. Spreckels and E. W. Scripps died in 1926, but their activities were carried forward. The Spreckels interests in the *San Diego Union* and *Evening Tribune* were purchased in early 1928 by Colonel Ira C. Copley of Aurora, Illinois. The Colonel's parents had established residence in San Diego in 1890, and Ira had joined the Cuyamaca Club in 1907. A rival newspaper, the *Independent* — founded by George Marston, Ed Fletcher and others to oppose Spreckels — went out of business. Copley also bought Spreckels' 20-room mansion in Coronado and appointed William Wheeler president of the Union-Tribune Publishing Company.

San Diegans organized their first historical society on January 24, 1880, "for the diffusion of a general knowledge of natural and civil history" and for the collection of a cabinet of curiosities. When interest in the society waned in the late 1880s, other organizations such as the Native Sons and Native Daughters of the Golden West took its place. Finally, the Pioneer Society of San Diego, incorporated in 1911, began collecting documents, books and a few artifacts to form the nucleus of a small museum and library. On December 13, 1928, George W. Marston as founder and first president, incorporated the San Diego Historical Society as a nonprofit, cultural and educational institution. He was assisted by his close friend Julius Wangenheim and society Vice President Leroy Wright. Marston had been acquiring land on Presidio Hill since 1907. By 1928 he had twenty acres. The Chamber, which observed its 50th anniversary in 1920, hired city planner John Nolen to develop and landscape a park. Marston employed architect William Templeton Johnson to design a building appropriate for the Pioneer Society collections and to honor Father Serra. Johnson chose the simple yet imposing Mission Revival style with its stark, clean lines and graceful arches. The dedication ceremonies were held on July 16, 1929, the Mission's 160th birthday. The city accepted Marston's gift reluctantly and agreed only to provide water for the park. Marston continued to pay other expenses for maintenance and improvement for nearly a decade. The Serra Museum — with its commanding view of city, bay, ocean and mountains — stands atop Presidio Hill as a monument to the Hispanic heritage of San Diego and the generosity of George White Marston. Its grassy slopes and rolling mounds are pleasing to the eye and protect the archeological evidence of an earlier time. Future plans include restoration of the original presidio chapel, birthplace of California.

BY THE BEAUTIFUL SEA: Women pause from play on Moonlight Beach (top) at Encinitas; woman bather prepares for a 1920 dive (left); women don roller skates at Mission Beach, 1926 (above).

Chapter VIII

A time of courage

1930-1950

San Diego, like the rest of the nation, was riding the crest of prosperity during the late 1920s. Lindbergh's successful flight, completion of the "Broadway of America" coast-to-coast automobile route, assurance of water from the Colorado River and the opening of Mexico's multi-million dollar Agua Caliente gambling resort — all brought publicity to California's southwestern corner. Areas throughout the county immodestly promoted the wonders of their natural setting.

When the Santa Fe Railroad found eucalyptus wood too soft for railroad ties, they converted their land in Rancho Santa Fe into luxury estates graced by tall eucalyptus groves. The company sold 80 percent of the land in five to 50-acre lots to wealthy motion picture stars and executives from around the country. Carlsbad had meanwhile become the "Avocado Capital of the World" while Encinitas was the "Home of the Mid-Winter Flower Show." La Mesa ("Jewel of the Hills") competed with Chula Vista ("Truly California at its Best") and National City ("Where Rail and Water Meet"). Escondido became the "Sunkist Vale" with its flourishing citrus industry while Ramona called itself the "Turkey Capital." In downtown San Diego, the Gildred Brothers — Philip and Theodore — covered a full block bounded by A, B, Seventh and Eighth streets with a ten-floor garage, a four-story department store and the third largest theater (the Fox) on the Pacific Coast. San Diego was variously called "the playground of America" and "the capital of the Southland's empire of amusement." The city's population reached nearly 150,000.

It took a few months for the effects of the stock market crash of October 29, 1929, to be generally felt in San Diego — and for people to realize its permanence. Land promotions collapsed, building permits dropped by half and bankruptcies ran high. Fortunately, certain federal and state projects eased unemployment — the $10 million appropriation for Boulder Dam, highway monies to build through Rose Canyon (to substitute the Torrey Pines grade for Sorrento Valley's winding road) and

The Bonham Brothers Mortuary Marching Boys' Band, circa 1935 (bottom left), in front of the old courthouse; Chula Vista police force, 1931 (below); and Agua Caliente gambling resort (right) in Mexico.

Lindbergh Field, mid-1930s (left); Hodges Dam, 1937 (bottom right); San Diego State College (top right), dedicated in May 1931 now San Diego State University.

funds to dredge the harbor and enlarge Lindbergh Field. Some gains were made in air-related industries. Pacific Air Transport — soon a part of United Air Lines — extended its Seattle-Los Angeles service to San Diego. American Airways, predecessor of American Air Lines, added San Diego to its Phoenix connection. Edmund Price of Solar Aircraft took his wife and three children on a cross-country flight from San Diego to New Bedford, Massachusetts, to attract business in 1931. They received great publicity but sold no airplanes.

The mild climate in San Diego made standing in breadlines at least more comfortable. A city bond issue provided $300,000 for recreational projects including a golf course and tennis courts in Balboa Park. A new city charter approved in April 1931, initiated a clear-cut city manager plan. Appointed by the council, the city manager would have authority over fire, police, health and other city departments, but not over the harbor, city attorney, city clerk, auditor and controller or civil service. The six-member city council would be nominated by districts and elected at large. The mayor — nominated and elected at large as a seventh and presiding member of the City Council — would be ceremonial chief of the city. The charter also provided for a hydraulic engineer, a water department and an accounting system to determine water costs. The sum of $150,000 a year was allocated for harbor work. Bond money of $3.6 million to construct El Capitan Dam was approved by voters in December 1931, and the La Mesa, Lemon Grove and Spring Valley (later Helix) Irrigation District received the right to appropriate two million gallons of water daily.

The new San Diego State College campus ten miles east of downtown was dedicated in a three-day ceremony on May 1, 2 and 3, 1931. The Spanish-style buildings (in keeping with the city's heritage) accommodated 2,000 students enrolled and a curriculum of 200 courses. Partial restoration of Mission San Diego was also completed in the fall of that year. In the presidential election, Franklin D. Roosevelt led Herbert Hoover by 10,000 votes in San Diego County although at the local level Republican George Burnham defeated Phil Swing for the House seat. Swing, an attorney, continued his work with water by representing the Imperial Valley Irrigation District in Washington, D.C., to gain approval for the All-American Canal. It was approved as an emergency project of the Public Works Administration in October. At the end of 1933, four national and six state banks were operating successfully in San Diego.

Because of the increased interest in developing the Imperial Valley, certain persons in San Diego wanted to ensure preservation of a portion

The mild climate in San Diego made standing in Depression bread lines at least more comfortable.

of the Anza-Borrego Desert as a park. Frederick Law Olmstead, a well-known landscape architect, had surveyed park possibilities in California in 1928 and emphasized the fragile nature of the deserts. Clinton G. Abbott, director of San Diego's Museum of Natural History and Guy L. Fleming of La Jolla (guardian of the rare Torrey Pines), submitted plans for a park in the Anza-Borrego area. Since voters rejected a bond to match state funds, George Marston personally purchased 2,320 acres in or near Borrego Palm Canyon, deeded them to the state and induced others to sell 5,500 more acres for state acquisition. With the backing of Marston and the State Park Commission, a second Swing-Johnson Act transferred 200,000 acres of federal land to Borrego State Park in March 1933.

By 1934, the Depression seemed to have reached its full effect in San Diego, but a number of measures encouraged recovery. Prohibition of liquor — the eighteenth amendment — was repealed in 1933 and legal sales resumed. The Navy spent $1.4 million and the Army $1.8 million on construction projects. Price's Solar Aircraft stayed alive with Fred Rohr, formerly with Ryan Airlines, as plant manager. Major Reuben H. Fleet, president of Consolidated Aircraft Corporation in Buffalo, New York, made a most far-reaching decision when he decided to move his plant with 800 employees and $9 million in orders to San Diego. Fleet had learned to fly at Rockwell Field with the Army Signal Corps during World War I. He had examined a number of locations and found San Diego to have everything he needed — a good airport, a publicly-owned waterfront, an excellent harbor, a city large enough to furnish labor and materials and a proper climate for test flying and deliveries. Consolidated began operating in San Diego in October 1935. This move almost single-handedly assured San Diego's future as an industrial center. In retail sales, another significant move was made when R.M. Walker joined George A. Scott in signing a 20-year lease on a downtown building to begin the San Diego-based Walker-Scott chain.

HOT AND COLD: The rugged Anza-Borrego Desert State Park (above), which encompasses more than 480,000 acres; a hot fudge sundae (right inset) from the Ingersoll Candy Company (top right); and Crystal Pier (bottom right) with cottages, cafe and fountain lunch.

The highlight of the mid-1930s was the planning of a second major exposition — San Diego's first World's Fair. Promoter Frank Drugan returned from Chicago with pictures of that city's Century of Progress and promised that exhibits would be available to San Diego. The Chamber of Commerce directors discussed the pros and cons of such an ambitious undertaking amidst the financial panic of the time. With characteristic optimism, they approved the concept, called it the California Pacific International Exposition and appointed attorney Walter Ames to organize a nonprofit corporation. Unlike other times, no corporations had any profits to make "tax deductible gift giving" attractive, so some contributions were in the form of loans. G. Aubrey Davidson, president of the 1915-1916 exposition, became chairman of the board of directors and young Frank G. Belcher of the Spreckels Companies, president. Oscar W. Cotton agreed to chair the campaign to raise $500,000 — a tough assignment. Cotton and his committee convinced the people of San Diego that they could certainly better the record of 40,000 people who had pledged $1 million in 1915. After all, the benefits of the exposition would far outweigh the cost, and San Diego could celebrate completion of the Metropolitan Aqueduct from Boulder Dam and other federal projects. By the end of September, the fund drive topped its goal at $700,000, and Richard S. Requa became director of architecture. In his book *Inside Lights on the Building of San Diego's Exposition: 1935,* Requa explained that he wanted to provide examples of all styles used during the Spanish period in America, including the prehistoric and Indian architecture of the American Southwest, central Mexico and Yucatan. The new area would be laid out around a spacious plaza southwest of the Spreckels Organ Pavilion. Just four months before the scheduled opening, Edsel Ford (who had visited the 1915-1916 fair on his honeymoon) decided to participate and brought other industries in at the last minute. Congress passed a bill appropriating funds for a permanent federal building copied from the Mayan Palace of Governors in Uxmal, Yucatan.

Three internationally famous gardens were selected for reappearance in Balboa Park — one from the Moorish section of Ronda, Spain; another from a patio garden in Guadalajara, Mexico and the third duplicating that adjoining the Alcázar in Seville, Spain. The original 1915-1916 buildings — as well as the newer Fine Arts Gallery and Natural History Museum — were incorporated into the grand plan. Other new structures included the Old Globe Shakespearean Theater, a Spanish village and a series of small cottages housing representatives of the Latin American countries. New outdoor lighting enhanced the nighttime view. The exposition officially opened on May 29, 1935, at 11 a.m. with a United States Marine color guard leading a parade across Cabrillo Bridge into the Plaza del Pacifico. That night at eight, President Franklin Roosevelt telephoned a signal for the lights to go on and congratulated the people of San Diego for their courage and confidence in putting on the fair. The first day's attendance was 60,000. Operating expenses were higher than anticipated, but managing director Philip Gildred kept it going successfully. President Roosevelt stayed at the Hotel del Coronado and

> *The Chamber of Commerce directors discussed the pros and cons of a major exposition amidst the financial panic of the time. With characteristic optimism, they approved the concept.*

Pass bearer and family into America's Exposition, May 29 through Nov. 11, 1935 (above).

RARE PICTURE: In a never-before-published photograph (above) a group of early San Diego artists pose at Leslie Lee's studio and home, Hollow of the Hills near Alpine, in 1930. They include (standing, left to right) artist Charles Reiffel; architect William Templeton Johnson; (seated, left to right) unknown; unknown, painter Lela Titus; muralist Belle Baranccanu; director of San Diego Fine Arts Gallery Reginald Poland; sculptor Donal Hord; wife of artist Maynard Dixon, Edith Hamlin; wife of artist Everett G. Jackson, Eileen Jackson; artist Jackson; unknown; artist Leslie Lee; photographer Sherman Trease, who took the picture; and (seated on ground, left to right) artist Thurston Field; writer Milicent Humason Lee; potter Blasa Quevedo; artist Dixon; and artist Aime Titus. JADE MASTERPIECE: Considered by many authorities to be Donal Hord's masterpiece, "Thunder" (left) is one of the largest jade sculptures known in the world, weighing 104 pounds and standing 21 inches high.

1935 EXPOSITION: Lagoon (below) and the Southern Countries Building in Balboa Park (right).

SIGHTS TO SEE: Boy Scouts visit the 1935 Exposition's Indian Village (top); California Building Scientific Library (left); and souvenir ticket from the exposition (above).

personally visited the park in October. He saw the exposition as a sign that the country's economic future was indeed brighter.

The closing of Mexico's $10 million gambling and racetrack resort at Agua Caliente came as a shock to many when President Lázaro Cárdenas banned games of chance on July 21, 1935. Economic repercussions were felt on both sides of the border. Fortunately, President Roosevelt had inaugurated the Works Progress Administration in the summer of 1935 with a number of massive projects earmarked for San Diego. The year closed with the groundbreaking for the new Civic Center made possible through federal relief financing. City builders George Marston, G. Aubrey Davidson, Julius Wangenheim and others — including Ralph E. Jenney, a San Diegan directing the California Relief Commission — had obtained $300,000 for a combined city and county building on the tidelands. Several sketches were submitted for the waterfront edifice. President Roosevelt dedicated the completed $2 million structure on July 16, 1938. Other WPA projects included $5 million for construction of a racetrack and county fairgrounds at Del Mar, additions to the San Diego Zoo, enlargement of Lindbergh Field and the building of a stadium at San Diego State College.

President Roosevelt had inaugurated the Works Progress Administration in the summer of 1935 with a number of massive projects earmarked for San Diego.

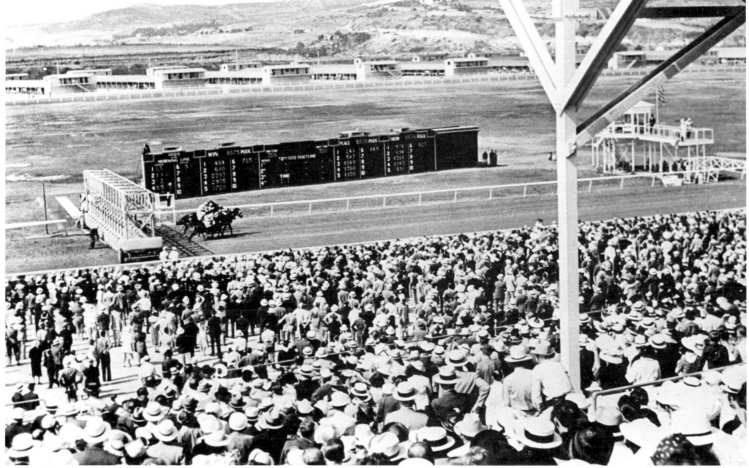

WORLD WAR II: The sign in an aircraft
production center (top left) read "Navy
pilots are waiting for these Ryan planes!"
Meanwhile, pilot training at Ryan (bottom
left) continued. The war brought
relocation of all persons of Japanese
ancestry (above), removed by federal order
to centers in the desert.

By the end of the decade, the nation's economy had responded
to the threat of war in Europe. Germany's invasion of Poland
in September 1939, brought increased contracts for aircraft
industries and naval facilities. Fred H. Rohr set up his own
company to provide special airplane components. He started in a garage,
moved to a warehouse and then built a new plant in Chula Vista.
Consolidated Aircraft increased its employees to 9,000 during 1940 while
eight navy and marine establishments occupied nearly 4,000 acres with
634 buildings — an investment of $51 million.

San Diego's fishing industry contributed a large share to the city's
growing economy. The 1939 tuna catch was for the first time over 100
million pounds. The fleet of tuna clippers had increased in value to $10
million, and the harbor had become the leading tuna port of the Pacific.
During World War II, many of the clippers were pressed into wartime
service. The bulk of fishing was divided between the Portuguese residents
of Point Loma and the Italians of the Middletown area near India and
Columbia streets. The Portuguese colony of San Diego — many originally
from the Azores and Madeira Islands — operated a large fleet of boats as
early as the 1920s. St. Agnes Church (so significant in the annual blessing
of the fleet) became a noted religious and cultural center. Portuguese
women and children formed a close-knit group in the absence of their
husbands at sea. The Italians, almost as numerous as the Portuguese, came
mainly from Sicily or northern Italy in the Genoa area. Our Lady of the
Rosary Church, built in 1925, with its beautiful stained-glass windows and
magnificent murals by Venetian painter Fausto Tasca, formed
the nucleus of their community. Prominent Italians of the early decades
included the DeFalcos in the grocery business and the Ghios of
Anthony's restaurant fame.

San Diego's black community numbered about 4,500 during the
mid-1930s and had settled mainly in the region between K Street and
Logan Avenue with a business center at 30th and Imperial Avenue. By

TUNA TRADE: A fishing boat, "Glory of the Seas," (below) docked at Campbell's yard, May 1944; many of the fishermen's wives worked at tuna canneries (left).

1937 they had built nine churches and were active in local community affairs. The Oriental population remained relatively small — about 500 — with Chinese merchants still active in the area from Fourth Avenue and Market Street to the waterfront. About 1,000 Japanese residents divided their efforts among the fishing industry, landscaping and vegetable growing south and east of the city. Wives of fishermen worked in the canneries. Long subjected to discriminatory laws along with the Chinese, a near death blow came to the Japanese community with the outbreak of World War II. All persons of Japanese ancestry were removed by federal order in April 1942, to relocation centers in the desert. After the war ended, most returned to their native San Diego to pick up the pieces of their lives. Their success in doing so is a story of courage and hard work.

CULTURAL CENTER: The nucleus of the Italian community was Our Lady of the Rosary (above), built in 1925 complete with magnificent murals by Venetian painter Fausto Tasca and sculptures by Carlos Romanelli.

The native-born residents of Mexican descent continued to live in or near Old Town, many working in the restaurant business. Mexican immigrants arriving generally between 1917 and 1930 settled principally in the Logan Heights area and found work on the railroads, in building activities or in agriculture. As the Depression hit California during the early 1930s, a number of families returned to Mexico. By the early 1940s, however, the demands of war provided employment for a new group of immigrants who crossed the border to work in war-related industries. The areas of San Ysidro, Chula Vista and National City could boast a large Mexican population with cultural ties on both sides of the border. The Church of the Immaculate Conception in Old Town and Our Lady of Guadalupe near Crosby Street serve as popular religious centers for the Mexican community.

With the purchase of Scripps' *San Diego Sun* by the Copley interests in 1939, San Diego's news was reported by its two main daily papers — the *Union* and *Evening Tribune* — and several smaller publications such as the *Southwestern Jewish Review* (later *Heritage*) published for a sizable Jewish community, the *Southern Cross,* official journal of the San Diego Roman Catholic Diocese, the *Sud-California Deutsche Zeitung,* a German weekly and the monthly *Zoonooz.* Two radio stations — KGB and KFSD — were based in San Diego while seven Tijuana stations broadcast throughout the area.

The federal census of 1940 showed that San Diego's population had grown to more than 200,000 and that of the county was nearing 300,000. With the outbreak of World War II, the rate of San Diego's growth increased tremendously. Local aircraft plants attracted workers from other states. All existing military establishments were expanded and new facilities were acquired as San Diego became a center for pilot training. Camp Callan for Army artillerymen occupied a five-mile stretch of land along Torrey Pines Mesa, an amphibious base was developed by the Navy on Coronado Strand along with Brown Field on Otay Mesa, Ream Field in Imperial Beach and Miramar Naval Air Station. The Marines acquired more than 123,000 acres of historic Rancho Santa Margarita to build Camp Pendleton, the world's largest military base. They also set up Camp Elliott on Kearny Mesa. Since the added population needed an assured water supply, the federal government worked with the city and county to determine the most feasible method for obtaining additional sources.

The federal census of 1940 showed that San Diego's population had grown to more than 200,000 and that the county was nearing 300,000.

San Diego had hoped, because of wartime demands, to obtain federal funds to build its own connection to the Colorado River. It could then take advantage of its 1926 right to 112,000-acre-feet of water annually. The San Diego County Water Authority, with nine member agencies, was organized on June 9, 1944, for the express purpose of importing this water. Fred Heilbron chaired the Authority and Phil Swing, general counsel, served on a committee appointed by President Roosevelt to work with the Metropolitan Water District and the Navy for an emergency pipeline. A serious drought, the end of World War II and successful negotiations finally led San Diego to seek annexation to MWD. This involved merging its precious water right with those of the larger agency in exchange for a connection with the existing aqueduct system and participation as a separate member agency in MWD. Annexation occurred in April 1946, and construction plans went forward immediately. The new aqueduct began operating December 11, 1947. Without it, San Diego could not have met the water needs of its nearly 600,000 people in 1948. Because of prevailing drought conditions and population increases, San Diego exceeded its original right within ten years. (By 1980 it would be using four times its original right.)

World War II brought San Diego a new prosperity. Many members of the military decided to bring their families from the Midwest and East and live permanently by the blue Pacific. In 1945, San Diego voters approved a bond issue of $2 million to begin development of a magnificent aquatic playground in Mission Bay. John Spreckels' $4 million amusement center built in the 1920s had passed to the city, and many thought the region comparable to Newport Beach. Glenn C. Rick, San Diego's planning director, first suggested the Mission Bay concept in 1935. After the war, Rick, Mayor Harley Knox and others continued the planning with recreation as a major goal. Roscoe E. Hazard sold 500 acres he had purchased in the early 1920s to the city for $300 per acre — the same price he had paid. Dredging operations were proposed to divert the San Diego River directly into the ocean through a series of rock jetties at Mission Bay to prevent further silting. The fill would be used to create small islands. The city's work — well underway by the end of the decade

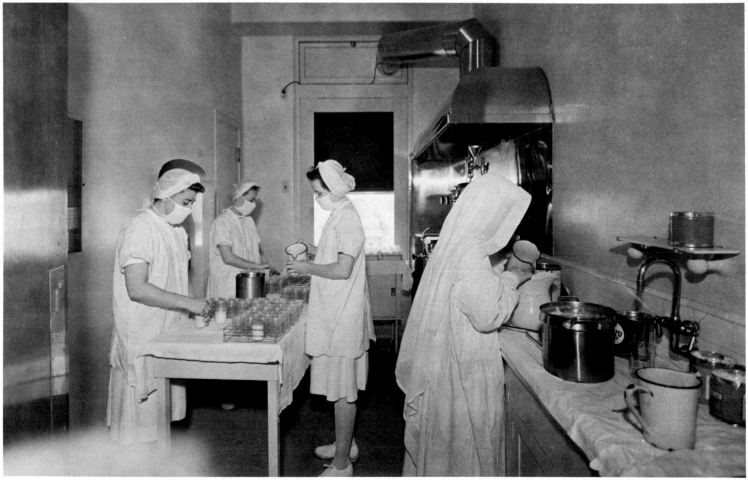

MOUNT PALOMAR: Bird's eye view taken in April 1948, and the installation of the observatory's 200-inch lens (bottom).

HILLS, VALLEY: The Most Reverend
Charles F. Buddy (above), bishop of San
Diego and founder of the University of
San Diego which overlooks Mission
Valley; and Mission Hills residence (top),
1900 block of Titus Street.

— allowed the first phase of Mission Bay Park to be dedicated in 1949.
San Diego's climate and natural advantages dictated that recreation would
be a major trend in the city's future growth. There already were 200
baseball teams on local fields, and the San Diego Padres (a popular minor
league baseball club) commanded a steady attendance at Lane Field on
the waterfront.

In 1949, the Most Reverend Charles Buddy, bishop of the Catholic
diocese of San Diego, saw the realization of a dream he had conceived
upon his arrival in 1937. He and the Reverend Mother Rosalie Hill of the
Religious Order of the Sacred Heart in San Francisco had planned an
institution of higher learning to be built in Spanish Renaissance
architecture. A charter was granted, and construction began on the Linda
Vista mesa overlooking Mission Valley. The San Diego College for
Women opened in 1952 as the first phase of a Catholic university
complex. At the same time a private methodist-related university
was being planned for the grounds of Katherine Tingley's theosophical
institute. California Western University — an outgrowth of Balboa
College in the downtown area — received permission to relocate on
Point Loma. The next few decades would witness a phenomenal growth
in San Diego's institutions of higher education.

New leaders of San Diego's future would emerge in the post war years.
San Diegans mourned the deaths of city fathers Julius Wangenheim in
1942 and George White Marston in 1946. A younger generation, with
new goals and interests, would take the lead. Solutions to problems of
growth would not come easily and the ideal way between dreams and
reality would sometimes be impossible to reach. No longer would San
Diego be held together in its aims by promotion of New Town, planning
a world's fair, fighting the Depression or stepping up production for
wartime needs. The next decades would witness a strain between
developing a civic and business center downtown and the desirability of
moving to the suburbs. Voters had rejected the grouping of public
buildings on Cedar Street mall in 1947 and looked outward to areas
east, south and north. Shopping centers and freeways — the wave of the
'50s — would cause public and private interests to clash on numerous
occasions. One of the major areas of controversy would be the
development of Mission Valley.

Chapter IX

The automobile age

1950-1970

The automobile affected almost every major decision regarding the growth and direction of San Diego during the post-World War II decades. Not the least among its effects was the changing pattern of retail shopping — self-contained business centers in regions remote from downtown. San Diego did not face this phenomenon alone. The rise of the automobile and expansion of highways led to a flight from the center of American cities. The result was the collapse of all but a few mass transportation systems in the United States. It was a circular process — increasing reliance on automobiles made less money available for public transportation which therefore became less efficient and less desirable. On the other hand, greater mobility encouraged cities everywhere to consolidate a larger geographical area and more people under a single autonomous government. Large city departments run by experts were favored over neighborhood agencies. This policy, which also widened the city's tax base, led to annexation of surrounding areas. San Diego grew from 99 square miles in 1950 to some 307 square miles in 1970. The idea that "bigger is better" prevailed until well into the 1960s when citizens began to feel detached and voiced concern over their lack of effective control of local issues. Urban historian Kenneth T. Jackson summarized the problem: "These two generally opposite tendencies are simply recent manifestations of a dilemma that has confronted the residents of American cities for two hundred years. On the one hand, democracy seems to call for government to remain small and close to the people; on the other, efficiency and the regional character of many contemporary problems point to the necessity of government's becoming metropolitan in authority and planning."

From the time of its founding, San Diegans had looked for ways to promote growth because people meant prosperity. These were the days before the third member of the trio — pollution — appeared. Because there was available land to accommodate more people, those in city government sought to achieve a balance between downtown control and neighborhood integrity. Not only did San Diego face decisions about growth, nearly every incorporated area in the county experienced this

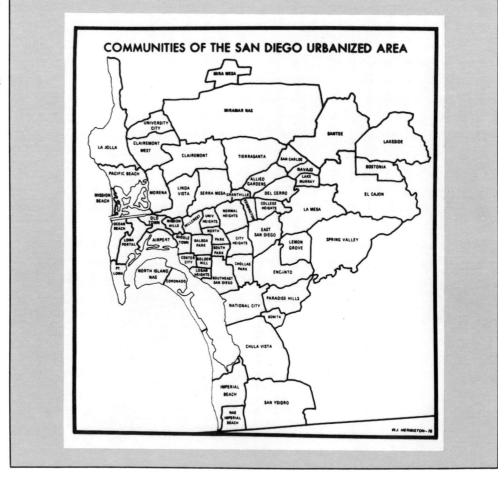

URBAN SPRAWL: Map (below) of the communities of San Diego's growing urbanized area; freeways (right) connect Mission Valley with other suburbs.

COMMUNITIES OF THE SAN DIEGO URBANIZED AREA

IN THE BAY: Shelter Island (top) and the U. S. Pacific Fleet's Naval Air Force headquarters (bottom) on North Island.

same postwar expansion. From 1950 to 1970, El Cajon grew from 5,600 to 52,273; Escondido from 6,544 to 36,792; Chula Vista from 15,927 to 67,901 and Oceanside from 12,881 to 40,494. San Diego's population doubled from 334,387 to 696,769. An alternative to central city annexation that still allowed for efficiency in certain areas of government was the creation of special service districts. This type of legal institution — first used as early as 1790 by Philadelphia to administer schools, prisons, public health and the port — gave an agency limited powers to meet specific educational, medical, water, sewer or other regional needs.

One advantage of San Diego's downtown area was its relatively young age. Its original commitment to wide streets prevented the crowding and decay that had occurred in older Eastern cities. But the preference for single-family dwellings in outlying areas, the lack of a scenic promenade along the waterfront and the absence of high-rise residential units precluded the development of a large core of permanent residents in the city's center. The failure of the Nolen Plan and the Cedar Street Mall temporarily delayed further downtown projects. Even though the San Diego Symphony had been founded in 1927 and San Diegans supported other musical and theatrical performances, construction of a decent auditorium and civic center did not follow easily. The Harbor Department did make one concession to Nolen by assigning the lee side of Point Loma to recreation. Creation of Shelter Island through dredging operations provided the city with a valuable and scenic piece of real estate. Anderson Borthwick, Harbor Commission chairman, met the opposition of Point Loma residents by assuring them that the island would be devoted to fine hotels, private marinas and a public park. A second recreational island would be created off Harbor Drive during the 1960s.

Although cutbacks had been made in military spending, the outbreak of the Korean War in 1950 brought new life to San Diego's aircraft industries. Convair received new contracts and began work on the Atlas missile. Ryan Aeronautical, which had been producing the high-performance Navion, returned to manufacturing components. Since the city failed to act upon its right to use the Miramar air field, the Navy — which had used it before and during World War II — kept possession of the area for use as the world's largest Naval Air Station.

A controversial highway was planned through Balboa Park connecting Mission Valley with downtown. Park defenders opposed the move. But others said that so large a park had been a mistake — smaller parks more strategically located would have served a greater number of people. Those who did not want to abandon downtown saw the park as an obstacle choking off the life-support system to the city's heart. The compromise was a seven-mile divided state highway through Cabrillo Canyon with a large green belt in the middle zone. The State Division of Highways set out 500,000 plants and trees — 28 varieties — to beautify the parkway. Further attempts to remove the trees or widen the highway were blocked, giving downtown commuters (many unable to spend time in the park) an opportunity to view one of the most luxuriant freeway settings in California.

Controversy also arose over developments inside Balboa Park. During World War II, virtually all park facilities except the zoo had been turned over to the Navy as a giant hospital complex. Museum collections were moved out and beds moved in — 960 in the Museum of Natural History, 759 in the Museum of Man and 423 in the Fine Arts Gallery. The House of Hospitality became the nurses' dormitory and the Ford Building an aircraft training school. The park was temporarily named Camp Kidd after Admiral Isaac Kidd. The Navy returned the buildings after the war and paid out nearly $1 million for damages. The Balboa Park Protective Association, formed in 1950, opposed further encroachments in the park, including the proposed Switzer and Maple Canyon freeways. The Balboa Park Citizens Committee in 1956 led by Dr.

One advantage of San Diego's downtown area was its relatively young age. Its original commitment to wide streets prevented the crowding and decay that had occurred in older Eastern cities.

Douglas McElfresh worked hard to develop satisfactory park guidelines. The City Council followed up the committee's report by hiring Harland Bartholomew & Associates, a firm of landscape architects and city planners, to prepare a master plan. The Bartholomew Report, adopted in 1961, is today's basic document for park development. Much of it has been implemented, especially in the museum area. A major problem was the traffic pattern — competition between pedestrians and automobiles and open spaces versus parking spaces.

Four lanes in Mission Valley.

Mayor Harley Knox had guided the city through several trials, but failing health prompted his decision not to run again in 1951. Attorney John D. Butler won the election to become the first native son to serve in the city's highest office. The 1950s witnessed a setback in the grouping of public buildings around a central mall when the historic Andrew Carnegie Public Library and the County Courthouse were torn down. In 1956, when only three cities over 250,000 population were without a public auditorium (San Diego numbered more than 500,000), an $8.5 million general obligation bond issue was placed on the ballot. Because of location problems, the Civic Theater and Convention Hall failed to receive the required two-thirds majority. In the late 1950s, Mayor Charles C. Dail still had little success in promoting the center. The El Cortez Hotel with its outside elevator sparked interest in downtown but not enough. George A. Scott continued his plans for a major shopping center at the junction of Federal Boulevard and College Avenue, but he had no plans for Walker-Scott to abandon downtown. He was only following the successful experience of other cities. A Fiesta del Pacífico was promoted during four summers (1956 to 1959). It presented an elaborate state pageant entitled the "California Story". Although the pageant was well done, it did not receive the overall support originally expected.

One of the turning points in the pattern of San Diego's growth was the decision by the May Company of Los Angeles in 1957 to build a shopping center in Mission Valley near the junction of U.S. Highways 80 and 395 (now Interstate 8 and State 163). This meant rezoning agricultural and residential land to commercial use. Some stores grouped around large parking areas had already been built in Linda Vista and at South Bay Plaza. In Mission Valley, rezoning had permitted a new baseball park for the minor league Padres, and some hotels were under construction. Charles H. Brown's Atlas Hotels helped bring tourists into the area with the Town & Country Hotel built in 1953 (its convention center was added in 1970). Brown envisioned ranch-type facilities with swimming pools and tennis courts. He later expanded Hotel Circle with the Hanalei Hotel and others. Although flooding of the valley did not occur during the 1950s, the May Company and others were warned of the potential. The May Company executives assured the City Council that all structures in the shopping center would rest on nine-foot fill — higher than any flooding ever recorded. The City Planning department, however, had been working on a master plan for the valley that provided for flood control and envisioned recreational development. They argued: "Mission Valley is the gateway to potentially the finest recreational area in the world. It will develop into an area complementing Mission Bay, offering accommodations and entertainment to visitors and residents. It would be possible for some future generation to tie Mission Valley, Old San Diego and Mission Bay Park together by a motor-boat canal, scenic roadway, bridle trails, and a scenic railway — futher enhancing our position as a tourist center." Harry Haelsig, city planning director, felt that the May Company's proposal was not in keeping with the city's long-range planning. City staff members feared that once Mission Valley was paved with commercial enterprises, it would be lost forever to the community as an open area. The Planning Commission overruled its staff, three to two, and a formal hearing was set by the City Council in June 1958. The May Company threatened to go elsewhere if it could not build on the proposed site. Downtown merchants who opposed the center were accused of not wanting competition, but George Scott insisted their concern was future flooding and the cost of appropriate protection. Arthur Hamilton Marston, grandson of George White Marston and his successor in retail merchandising, pleaded with the Council to consider the consequences of opening the door to rezoning. He agreed that shopping centers were "a fact of mid-twentieth century American life" but asked that the city analyze how they fit into the pattern of residential, recreational, commercial, industrial and administrative land use. Arthur Jessop asked that the Council consider all future possibilities for the valley because if it did not, it might "as well tatoo on the Council walls: 'Thus died planning in San Diego.'" Guilford Whitney feared a new central city just four minutes from downtown would cause a slum business district in the original area. Others supported the concept of a conveniently-located shopping center and were afraid the May Company might change its mind. But the May Company pledged cooperation and friendship and agreed to pay its fair share of community services. The Council adopted the zone change unanimously. Opponents felt the city had lost an opportunity to make Mission Valley a unique area with a proper blending of hotels, recreational facilities and shopping. Flood control was still a part of the city's overall plan.

Soon other shopping centers became a reality. Broadway-Hale department stores acquired a site in Chula Vista while The Marston Company joined in the planning of Grossmont Center, built by Del Webb of Phoenix. George Scott's College Grove opened in July 1960 and Mission Valley Center in February 1961. Broadway-Hale bought out Marston's, the oldest name in San Diego merchandising, to open in Grossmont Center in the fall of 1961. El Cajon's Parkway Plaza and

City staff members feared that once Mission Valley was paved with commercial enterprises, it would be lost forever to the community as an open area.

others throughout the county were not far behind. New suburban
shopping clusters also grew with the birth of such communities as
Clairemont, Kearny Mesa, University City, Del Cerro and Allied Gardens
filling in the gaps between San Diego and neighboring cities.

In the meantime, Mission Bay planners were experiencing problems. A
basic question arose over who was to enjoy the facilities — local residents
who could come for the day or tourists wanting to stay in large
convention-like hotels and take advantage of the sun and beach. There
were also major environmental concerns. Glenn Rick resisted a too-rigid
master plan to allow for greater flexibility. Commitments had already been
made to the state for a wildlife preserve on the northern half of the
eastern bay area. Seventy-seven acres of sanctuary were made a part of
the master plan in 1958 although scientists warned that the ecological
balance would never be the same. The slowness in reaching any
agreement created numerous problems. The federal government
contributed $10 million, the city $19 million and the state $3.5 million for
initial dredging, development and flood control. No plan could be totally
successful, but the bay began to unfold as a tremendous aquatic
playground with almost 2,000 acres of navigable water, more than 2,000
acres of parkland and almost 32 miles of shoreline. Areas were designated
for boat launchings, picnic and playgrounds, hotels and motels and
beaches. Of the available land, 25 percent was for commercial purposes to
make the park self-supporting.

The master plan was opposed by some members of the Mission Bay
Commission, but it passed the City Council unanimously in 1958. In
early 1960, the Department of Parks and Recreation took over direction
of Mission Bay development. All hotels and facilities had to meet certain
standards. The year 1964 witnessed the opening of Sea World, one of the
most successful marine-life parks in the United States. Not only did it
give Mission Bay a popular focal point with its outdoor exhibits and

SEA WORLD: Trainers take a ride on dolphins (left) and Shamu, (above) a three-ton killer whale, goes to college in his show at the marine amusement park in Mission Bay.

marine life, it provided an exotic fish collection and educational displays depicting man's relationship with the sea. It also included a 300-foot observation tower with a revolving elevator.

San Diego Bay's problems were very different from those of Mission Bay. Because the bay was used primarily for commercial and military purposes and not for swimming or water-skiing, people were less concerned about its quality. Prior to 1943, the city let raw sewage into the bay through twenty outfalls. By 1948, waste from National City, Lemon Grove, La Mesa and North Island poured into the bay. Voters refused to approve a sewer bond issue of $16 million in 1954 to correct the problem. A more elaborate plan for a treatment plant and ocean outfall at Point Loma was estimated at $26 million with all metropolitan area users sharing costs. It was finally approved by the city and built in 1963 at an eventual cost of $51 million. It contained 27 miles of drains. The federal government added a connection with the sewer system of Tijuana for emergency conditions to prevent emptying of sewage through the Tia Juana River bed and pollution of beaches.

Residents of Imperial Beach, Chula Vista, National City and Coronado

San Diego Bay's problems were very different from those in Mission Bay.

also have had a large stake with San Diego in port development. In 1953 the Chamber of Commerce sponsored a study about creating a San Diego Unified Port District. Later, state Senator Hugo Fisher and Assemblyman James Mills sponsored an act creating the district. It was approved in 1962 by city officials of all but Coronado. Many South Bay residents favored a second entrance into the bay at Imperial Beach for marina access.

The second pipeline for the first San Diego Aqueduct was completed in October 1954 during a prolonged drought. Almost immediately additional water supplies were needed. Voters approved bonds of $35 million for the San Diego County Water Authority to construct a second aqueduct. The first pipeline of the new facility, completed in 1960, barely kept ahead of the demand. The Authority continued its constant and systematic planning under the leadership of Fred Heilbron and guidance of General Counsel William H. Jennings, also a member of the State Water Commission. Population growth, increased agricultural needs and less-than-average rainfall pointed toward a potential shortage. By the end of the decade, 22 member agencies belonged to the Authority. These were the Fallbrook Public Utility District; the five cities of Del Mar, Escondido, National City, Oceanside and San Diego; the irrigation districts of Helix, San Dieguito, Santa Fe and South Bay; and the municipal water districts of Bueno Colorado, Carlsbad, De Luz Heights, Olivenhain, Otay, Poway, Rainbow, Ramona, Rincon del Diablo, Padre Dam, Valley Center and Yuima. The second pipeline for the second aqueduct was completed in 1973.

The All-American Canal (above) serves water, the Imperial Valley.

During the late 1950s, San Diegans, spearheaded by City Councilman George Kerrigan, fully supported the State Water Project plan on the Feather River, the largest tributary of the Sacramento. The 730-foot high Oroville Dam was the first step toward developing a great untapped source of hydroelectric power and water. With the endorsement of Governor Edmund G. "Pat" Brown and the overwhelming support of San Diego, the largest state bond issue in history — $1.75 billion — was approved in 1960. The fight to complete the state project continued into the 1970s as the north fought its completion. Nevertheless, the California Aqueduct crossed the Tehachapis in 1971 to relieve the pressure on Colorado River users. By 1980, the Peripheral Canal — an important link around the Sacramento/San Joaquin Delta to protect water rights, recreation, fish and wildlife and water quality — was authorized by the California State Legislature.

Higher education expanded significantly in San Diego during the mid-1950s. The University of San Diego and California Western University both opened their doors in 1952. San Diego State College had an enrollment of 4,134 students that year. Community colleges included San Diego Junior (now City) College and Vocational School. The board of regents of the University of California system considered a move to San Diego. John Jay Hopkins, chairman of Convair and General Dynamics Corporation, urged the location of a scientific and technical campus in the La Jolla area. If this were done, he would provide a grant of $1 million and build his own research center estimated at $10 million. The new campus would be highly specialized and tie into Scripps Institution of Oceanography. On July 10, 1956, Hopkins dedicated a site for the new university on Torrey Pines Mesa, former pueblo lands that had been voted by the people for a new atomic research center. The Chamber of Commerce's University of California Committee chaired by Chamber Director Robert H. Biron, won the state Legislature's approval of University of California San Diego (UCSD), then led the successful city ballot campaign. Dr. Roger Revelle, director of Scripps Institution, emphasized the graduate nature of the new campus, although the board of regents believed an undergraduate training program essential. The university as proposed would be built on 1,000 acres and serve 10,000

Higher education expanded significantly in San Diego during the mid 1950s.

COLLEGE CAMPUSES: University of San Diego (top and inset); San Diego State University (left); and the University of California, San Diego, in La Jolla (above).

students by 1970. (Actual figures showed UCSD with 4,400 students and 1,900 acres for its three colleges in 1970.)

From its inception, UCSD attracted scholars from throughout the United States. Dr. Herbert York, former U.S. director of defense research and engineering, became the university's first chancellor. Revelle left San Diego to head Harvard's Center for Population Studies but returned to UCSD in 1975. Within a short time, the reputation of UCSD, in conjuction with Scripps, became distinguished worldwide.

The Salk Institute for Biological Research was founded in 1963 in La Jolla by Dr. Jonas Salk, developer of polio vaccine. The institute has provided research facilities for scientists from throughout the nation. La Jolla, long known for its scenic beauty, emerged in the 1960s as a burgeoning center of education and research. The La Jolla Museum of Contemporary Art emphasizes the twentieth century in its excellent collection of paintings, sculptures and graphic arts. The outstanding writer of children's books, Theodor Geisel, better know as "Dr. Suess," is an often-honored La Jolla resident.

The revitalization of the downtown area began in the 1960s with a wave of high-rise construction. Fortunately, downtown had never actually been neglected, even with construction of outlying shopping centers. The Chamber of Commerce and the San Diego Convention & Visitors Bureau had been attracting businesses and promoting tourism; in the 1960s the Economic Development Corporation was launched to spur industrial growth. The first new skyscraper housed the offices of Home Federal Savings & Loan Association, headed by Charles K. Fletcher, son of pioneer developer Ed Fletcher. The younger Fletchers all would play active roles in San Diego's business community. A second skyscraper was

WONDERS OF THE SEA: Aerial view (above) of the University of California's Scripps Institution of Oceanography which operates the Thomas Wayland Vaughan Aquarium-Museum (inset.) "The Cat in the Hat" (below), a creation of La Jolla resident Theodor Geisel, better known as "Dr. Suess."

130

completed at Second and Broadway to house C. Arnholt Smith's United States National Bank. Irvin Kahn's 24-story First and C Building also enhanced the skyline. A new organization called San Diegans, Inc. headed by Joseph Jessop Sr. grew out of the Downtown Association and began work with the city planning department. The City Council finally authorized a master plan for downtown and came up with a proposal for a new city hall, convention center and auditorium, a civic theater and parking garage at a total cost of $15 million. Financing would come from the county's purchase of the city's half of the Civic Center for $3.5 million, $8.5 million borrowed from the City Employees Retirement Fund and $2 million from capital outlay. The remainder would be raised by private contributions. Guilford Whitney led the fund-raising campaign

JEWEL CITY: North of downtown San Diego, La Jolla (Spanish for "the jewel") is known for its resort shops, beaches and spectacular homes as well as the Salk Institute for Biological Studies and Scripps Institution of Oceanography.

and received tremendous backing from many including James S. Copley (publisher of the *San Diego Union* and *Evening Tribune*), Morley H. Golden (a general contractor active with San Diegans, Inc.), First National Bank of San Diego (now California First), Bank of America, Home Federal Savings, San Diego Federal Savings, U.S. Grant Hotel, San Diego Gas & Electric Company and others. The new and modern Charles Dail Community Concourse was dedicated on September 16, 1964, and the magnificent 3,000-seat Civic Theater, designed by Lloyd Ruocco, opened in January 1965. This first grouping of public buildings achieved by San Diego won the city a designation as an All-American City by the National Municipal League. Even though an economic recession during the 1960s threatened the future of some institutions, more high-rise buildings continued to appear against the horizon.

The decade of the 1960s brought a significant change to the city of Coronado. Local residents had known for several years that the delay in crossing the bay by ferry was beginning to out-weigh the advantages of insularity. The Coronado City Council asked as early as 1952 for a feasibility study of a bridge. John Alessio, who purchased the Hotel del Coronado in 1960, spent more than $2 million refurbishing the interior. He approached the City Council for immediate approval of the bridge to speed access to the hotel. The Council voted it down, three to two, but the San Diego Unified Port District gave the necessary approval. As the bridge came closer to reality, a number of residents who wanted to protect Coronado from excessive traffic opposed it. Alessio sold the "Hotel del" in 1963 to Larry Lawrence who continued to work for the bridge in political circles. Lawrence enlarged the hotel with a seven-story addition and made a number of improvements. Other areas earmarked for development at that time included Coronado Shores (ten high-rise condominium units on 22 acres of land southwest of the hotel), and the bayshore community of Coronado Cays further south on the Silver Strand.

The Navy did not object to the bridge as long as it stood 200 feet above the water to permit ship and aircraft operations in the bay. The Army Corps of Engineers approved the design and location. The California Toll Bridge Authority, of which Governor Edmund G. Brown was a member, voted to build it with revenue bonds. Sadly, the historic

The Navy did not object to the building of a bay bridge as long as it stood 200 feet above the water to permit ship and aircraft operations in the bay.

Coronado Ferry Company was purchased and, like similar ferry companies throughout California, went out of business. Appropriate points of entry and exit and new traffic patterns were finally decided by the state. The San Diego-Coronado Bay Bridge — an awesome structure designed by Robert Mosher of La Jolla — presented a graceful curve across the water on the day of its opening August 3, 1969. Dr. W. Paul Vetter, mayor of Coronado and long-time member of the planning commission, officiated at the ceremony with the state's new governor, Ronald Reagan.

BAY BRIDGE: The San Diego-Coronado Bay Bridge at night (top); shortly after the bridge's last link went in (above), the ferry companies went out of business.

San Diego is proud of its athletes. Individual champions honored throughout the years include swimmers Florence Chambers and her famous pupil Florence Chadwick who swam the English Channel in 1950 in thirteen hours and 20 minutes, breaking the 1926 record of Gertrude Ederle. Boxer Archie Moore won the light-heavyweight title in 1952, and Bobby Valdes was a successful featherweight boxer of the late 1960s. Maureen Connolly — Little Mo — won her first Forest Hills crown in tennis at the age of sixteen in 1952, and Karen Hantze, winner of ten national championships as a teenager, won at Wimbledon in 1962. San Diego also produced its share of college stars.

The Pacific Coast League San Diego Padres were a popular and successful baseball team, winning pennants in 1962, 1964 and 1967. When the National League expanded in 1969, San Diego received a major league franchise. The name Padres was retained, and Buzzie Bavasi (long associated with the Dodgers) became part owner with C. Arnholt Smith. They would share San Diego's new stadium with professional and college football. In 1958, just three years after the Padres had moved into Westgate Park — their home field in Mission Valley — Barron Hilton, owner of the newly formed American Football League's Los Angeles Chargers, indicated his desire to move to San Diego. The City Council agreed to renovate Balboa Stadium and increase its seating capacity from 23,000 to 34,500, but the Chargers were definitely a part of the planning

BALL PLAYERS: Hamilton's Hardware Store baseball team (top) of the 1890s; San Diego Padres' pitcher Rollie Fingers (left) and right fielder Dave Winfield (above).

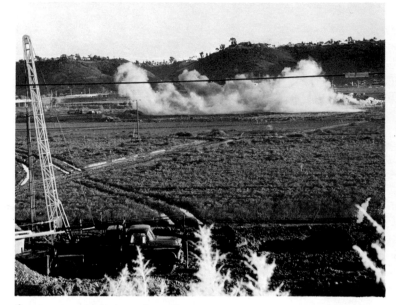

for a new municipal stadium in Mission Valley. The architectural and engineering firm of Frank L. Hope & Associates selected the site and designed the $27.6 million ultra-modern structure seating more than 50,000 spectators. Voters enthusiastically approved the stadium bonds in November 1965. It was opened and ready for use in August 1967. The Chargers won four division championships during the 1960s. Under head coach Sid Gillman, formerly of the Rams, the team boasted such popular and effective players as John Hadl, Lance Alworth, Ron Mix, Paul Lowe, Keith Lincoln, Speedy Duncan, Gary Garrison, Walt Sweeney, Ernie Ladd and Earl Faison. Barron Hilton sold the cinderella Chargers to a group headed by Eugene Klein and Samuel Shulman in August 1966, for $10 million. The Hiltons retained a minor interest. After 1969, the AFL merged with the NFL, and the Chargers suffered some rough times. Old time fans would look back longingly to 1961 and the very first game in Balboa Stadium when the Chargers defeated the Oakland Raiders, 44-0. Instead, the most exciting team using the new stadium during the late 1960s was Don Coryell's San Diego State Aztecs.

The city also promoted construction of the International Sports Arena in November 1966. Costing $6.5 million, it was designed to seat 13,000 spectators for hockey and 13,700 for basketball and other public events. The Sports Arena was built on city-owned land through private investors led by Robert Breitbard. In 1966, Breitbard obtained a franchise in the Western Hockey League, the Gulls, and in 1967 obtained a franchise for a National Basketball Association expansion team he called the Rockets. Both teams were popular but short-lived. The Rockets were sold to Houston interests, and the Gulls disbanded in order to make room for the Mariners, a World Hockey Association franchise.

San Diego's numerous golf courses — nearly 70 — attracted tourists as well as local residents. The first San Diegans to win national acclaim were Gene Littler (1953 U.S. Amateur, 1961 U.S. Open and other major competitions totaling 29 by 1980); and Billy Casper (1959 and 1966 U.S. Open, plus a record of 51 tour wins). Woman golfer Mickey Wright had won six national titles by 1969 and started a strong tradition for women in golf. Junior golfers Lon Hinkle, Craig Stadler, Jack Renner, Sharon Barret and Tim Robinson also enhanced San Diego's reputation for fine golf. The Wickes Andy Williams San Diego Open is a major tournament held each January at Torrey Pines. It received national acclaim during the 1970s and attracts many movie and television personalities along with top professionals.

Sailboat racing was another popular sport, and San Diegans captured the prestigious Star-boat world title on several occasions. The first was

The city also promoted construction of the International Sports Arena in November 1966.

Milt Wegeforth (1938) followed by Gerald Driscoll (1944), Malin Burnham (1945), four-time winner Lowell North (1957, 1959, 1960, 1973) and Dennis Conner, 1980 America's Cup winner, (1971, 1977).

The advent of television in the late 1940s brought about a change in the social pattern of American life perhaps as great as the invention of the automobile. Its overall effects would just be more difficult to assess. Cities everywhere in the United States competed for FCC licensing. San Diego was no exception. KFMB, on the radio since 1943, beamed its first television broadcast from the Continental Room of the Hotel San Diego at 8:01 p.m. on Monday, May 16, 1949. Its transmitter was located on Mount Soledad. San Diego became the 36th American city (63rd license issued) with its own channel. The station cost owner Jack Gross $300,000 to build. As early as 1950, there were 25,000 television sets in San Diego County, although many families were still gathering in front of appliance stores to capture a glimpse of a nine-inch black-and-white screen. KFMB-TV, channel 8, under new ownership, moved briefly to 1375 Pacific Highway. Such local programs as "Smokey Rogers" (with his three-hour daily show), "Monty Hall," "Tiny Town Ranch" and "People in the News" attracted a large audience. Channel 8 was purchased by John A. Kennedy of West Virginia, owner of the short-lived *San Diego Daily Journal.* He moved that station into the former newspaper headquarters at Fifth and Ash. Howard Chernoff, general manager of the *Journal,* took over management of the television and radio stations. Channel 8 broadcast all three major network programs until NBC went with the new channel 10 in 1953 and ABC affiliated with channel 6 in 1955. Channel 8, which remained with CBS, featured such local personalities as Harold Keen and Ray Wilson in news broadcasting and Bob Dale with the Payday Movie. Helen Alvarez {Smith} and Jack Wrather, owners of a Tulsa, Oklahoma, channel, purchased KFMB in 1953. Channel 8 became a part of Trans-Continent Broadcasting in 1959 and was sold in 1964 to Midwest Television with August C. Meyer, president. Under General Manager Robert L. Myers, channel 8 moved into modern new studios in Kearny Mesa in 1977 and with its affiliates KFMB-AM and FM, remained highly competitive.

San Diego's second television station — XETV, channel 6—was conceived in 1950 by Al Flanagan of channel 8. Because of a freeze on new television licenses begun in late 1948, Flanagan met with Mexican television executives George Rivera and Emilio Azcarraga, with whom he purchased television equipment in New York for a transmitter and studios in Tijuana atop Mount San Antonio. The station was licensed in Mexico and began broadcasting on January 29, 1953. Julian Kaufman, a young executive working in Phoenix television, joined XETV as general manager after its first seven months. He successfully overcame some of the prejudices against the Mexican station. Channel 6 carried both English and Spanish programs until the mid-1950s when channel 12, XEWT, began operating entirely in Spanish. Fear that a lack of FCC restrictions would allow channel 6 to recklessly beam unwanted programs into San Diego proved unfounded. XETV affiliated with ABC from 1955 until 1973 when it again became independent. In the early years, channel 6 brought such children's programs as "Johnny Jet," "Ranger Hal" and "Oakie Bob" to San Diego, along with Johnny Downs, Lynn Taylor and a young newscaster named Lionel Van Deerlin. The first offices were on Park Boulevard, but channel 6 built a modern facility with a Mexican architectural theme in Kearny Mesa and moved there in 1976. In 1980 Kaufman spoke with pride of the cooperation between his San Diego employees and the Mexican engineers and technicians in the Tijuana studios. Present owner of the station is Emilio Azcarraga Milmo.

TIME FOR TV: Live show in the kitchen of Channel 8 (top); ground breaking for Channel 10 (center); ABC comes to San Diego (above). Channel 6 headquarters (bottom).

KGTV, Channel 10, like Channel 8, also grew out of radio. Licensed originally in 1925, its call letters became KFSD in 1926. Programs were

broadcast from the U.S. Grant Hotel with a flattop antenna from 1933 to 1948 when its transmitter was moved to Emerald Hills. The station could not get a television license during the freeze, but owner-applicant Thomas E. Sharp received one of the earliest-allotted after it was lifted. Channel 10's first program as KFSD-TV was aired on September 13, 1953, with its transmitter located on Mount Soledad. The station — an NBC affiliate — was sold by Sharp's Airfan Radio Corporation in 1954 to Fox, Wells & Rogers, who built the new TV-AM-FM studios at 47th street and Highway 94 in 1958. The 43,000-square-foot building designed by Herluf Brydegaard and Lloyd Ruocco housed the most modern equipment available at the time. William E. Goetze became general manager in 1954 and remained through its expansion era. The television station call letters were changed in 1961 from KFSD to KOGO, and it soon after was sold to Time-Life Broadcast, Inc. Goetze was replaced in 1963 by Clayton Brace, manager of a television operation, partially owned by Time-Life, in Beirut, Lebanon. When McGraw-Hill bought the station in June 1971, channel 10 was forced to give up its radio affiliation with KOGO-AM and KFSD-FM. The call letters were changed from KOGO-TV to KGTV, and in 1977 channel 10 joined ABC.

The youngest commercial television station in San Diego is KCST, UHF channel 39. It got off to a shaky start as KAAR-TV in 1966 under the ownership of Atlas Hotel magnate Charles H. Brown. During the first year of broadcasting, Brown was heavily involved in problems with the Hanalei Hotel and could not devote attention to the station. His sudden death in 1967 left son Terry Brown with multiple responsibilities, and the station went off the air. It was purchased by Bass Brothers Broadcasting and returned to the air on January 28, 1968, with an emphasis on sports. The early staff included Mike Smith, Bill Fouch and Dave Walker, all of whom were still with the station in 1980. In order to capture a young audience, channel 39 covered every sporting event possible from Little League baseball to major league basketball. Bill Fox, formerly with channel 8, joined the station as general manager in 1971. Channel 39 affiliated with ABC in April 1973. Storer Broadcasting bought the station in 1974, built a new transmitter on Mount San Miguel and expanded news coverage. In 1977, it affiliated with NBC; it continues its active competition for audience ratings with the three VHF channels.

San Diego's public broadcasting station KPBS (UHF Channel 15) has studios on the campus of San Diego State University. It was founded in 1967 with its transmitter on Mount San Miguel. Like other public channels, its programs are publicly or privately funded and offer an alternative to commercial shows. They include educational workshops, cultural affairs, sporting events and public information programs. Especially popular are children's shows such as "Sesame Street."

SPORTS: The infamous San Diego Chicken (top) hams it up for the baseball crowd; the gold-shirted San Diego Sockers (top left); and quarterback Dan Fouts (above) of football's Chargers. Golf course greens, with Hotel del Coronado in the background (top right), and at Rancho Santa Fe, July 1929 (inset). West meets East when the Chargers (bottom right), in light jerseys, battle the Buffalo Bills.

137

Visiting the zoo is a popular outdoor activity enjoyed by more than three million people per year. Celebrating its 50th birthday in 1966, the San Diego Zoo had achieved fame throughout the country for the world's largest wild animal collection of more than 5,000 specimens of 1,664 species and subspecies. Dr. Charles Schroeder—zoo director since Belle Benchley's retirement in 1953—had been successful and innovative. He realized that more space would be needed if the zoo were to continue to expand. Clayburn LaForce, farm manager for the city, suggested that land in the San Pasqual Valley that had been contemplated for a reservoir be used as an annex. Norman Roberts, chairman of the San Pasqual Study Committee, and Anderson Borthwick, president of the Zoological Society, promoted the concept of a large, open Wild Animal Park of 1,800 acres—larger than all of Balboa Park. It was completed in 1972 and essentially duplicates wildlife areas throughout the world. It features a 45-minute electric monorail tour for visitors to view the animals at close but safe range. A seventeen-acre Nairobi Village features animal and bird shows, exhibits and an animal nursery.

In 1964, State Assemblyman James Mills, because of his former position as curator with the San Diego Historical Society and his long-abiding interest in local history, introduced a resolution to determine the feasibility of creating a State Historic Park at Old Town. Some building restoration for San Diego's Bicentennial celebration was also proposed. The study, completed in 1966, recommended that Old Town—an area architecturally and historically significant to California as well as to the nation—be made a state park. Even before that time, however, other efforts to preserve the history of Old Town had taken place. The *San Diego Union* had restored its first home near the plaza and built a small museum. Outside the park, the Historic Shrine Foundation had saved the Whaley House, the George Pendleton Home and the Mason Street School while the city restored the Adobe Chapel. The Casa de Lopez candle shop—located in the path of Interstate 5—was faithfully rebuilt on a new location with private funds. Those who opposed park control by the state believed that local city and county government could better direct the project. Nevertheless, Mills was successful, and in 1965 the State Board of Park Commissioners designated nineteen structures for restoration. Initial property acquisition began in 1967. As the master plan for the park developed, it was decided that the interpretive period would be 1821 to 1872 allowing a blend of both Mexican and American structures and cultures. The University of San Diego carried out archeological investigations of the sites.

While the state began work on the Estudillo and Machado-Stewart houses, San Diego proceeded to plan its 1969 Bicentennial program. Although much of Old Town's land was purchased by the state by the beginning of the year, little restoration was actually completed. A number of temporary buildings and booths were put up to capture an atmosphere of the Spanish and Mexican periods. Charles E. Cordell, president, and Hugh A. Hall, celebration director, met with the Chamber of Commerce and the Convention and Visitors Bureau to plan events for the entire year. City residents decorated their houses with gold lights, and Mayor Frank Curran officiated at the opening ceremonies. A delegation from San Diego visited Father Serra's birthplace in Petra, Mallorca and established ties with that Spanish town. Special activities were held at Old Town, and even though visitors were fewer than hoped for during 1969, it brought new interest to San Diego's historic center. The decade of the 1970s witnessed a phenomenal increase in the number of persons touring Old Town. The city and county also experienced a remarkable growth in the number of people everywhere.

AT THE ZOO: Entrance (top) and elephants (center) at the San Diego Zoo; a gigantic bird cage (above) was donated to the zoo by Ellen Scripps in 1923.

A ghost for all seasons

HAUNTED HOUSE: Thomas Whaley, a native of New York, began construction of a two-story brick home and store in Old Town on May 6, 1856; the last Whaley to live in the house was Corinne Lillian who died in 1953 at the age of 89.

It is said — and evidence seems to prove — that the Whaley House in Old Town is inhabited by at least four, perhaps five, fairly active spirits. Their activities have been noted by a dozen or more people — docents working in the house, visitors, professional psychics, actors using the theater, and June Reading, curator of the Whaley House museum and archives.

The ghosts include Thomas Whaley, who built the house in 1856. It was a beautiful and spacious brick structure complete with wall-to-wall carpeting — something little seen in southern California. The north room was originally a granary but was extensively remodelled for a county courthouse in August 1869. Just two years later, promoters of Alonzo Horton's New Town wanted to move the county records and courthouse to Sixth and G streets. There was a hearing on the county's obligation to Whaley, but before it was fully settled, the newly-appointed county clerk and recorder, and a few helpers forcefully removed the records one night and took them to the downtown location. Whaley lost the fight for their return but insisted the county should pay rent on the courthouse or compensate his loss. The county never got around to paying Whaley, and he never forgot. He officially died in 1890. Some say

he still stalks around muttering about the unfairness of it all.

Yankee Jim Robinson is another prominent ghost. Robinson was hanged on the premises in August 1852, for stealing a boat. The scaffold stood somewhere between the parlor and the music room. The ghost of Yankee Jim began making his presence felt with noisy footsteps and other creaks when a theater group decided in the early 1960s to put on a play "The Ballad of Yankee Jim" based upon the execution. Apparently Robinson has good reason to haunt the place. He was wounded during his capture and left unconscious during most of his trial. Even the scaffold was poorly constructed, and he strangled for fifteen minutes before actually dying.

Then there is Mrs. Anna De Lannay Whaley who married Thomas in New York in 1853. She lived in the house most of her married life and was active in the community affairs of San Diego until her death in 1913. Her ghost likes to sit in the kitchen and has, on one occasion, run her fingers through a guest's hair.

The Whaleys had five children. Thomas Jr. died in 1858 at the age of seventeen months. The youngest daughter Corinne Lillian (Lilly) lived in the house until 1953. Anna Whaley took in some other children, and one of the

more frequent ghosts is a little red-haired girl. She indicated to those who communicated with her that four other ghosts occupied the house besides herself, one of which was a baby boy. There is also the ghost of a little spotted dog that can sometimes be seen scurrying by.

Most of the time, however, it is not a spirit but signs that are seen — chairs rocking, tables tilting, chandeliers swinging, curtains blowing from a sudden chilly wind. Windows are unexplainably opened, items are slightly moved, cigar smoke wafts through the air. There are voices, music, singing, footsteps and doors closing.

Daughter Lilly finally moved her bed downstairs, when one ghost continually obstructed the stairs with its body pressure. The identity of the ghost on the stairs has not been established.

Another ghost became upset when the George Pendleton house — about to be demolished — was moved onto the Whaley property.

The ghost of Sheriff James McCoy (a heavy cigar smoker) has also been reported.

The Whaley House has been seriously investigated and has passed many tests for psychic emanations. Apparently the ghosts get along well and are not particularly concerned about the crowded conditions. And visitors — they just ignore them.

Chapter X

The past as prologue

1970-1980

The San Diego Chamber of Commerce celebrated its 100th birthday in January 1970. Chamber President Clayton Brace and those most concerned with the city's economic and cultural well-being pointed with pride to many areas of progress. Experts predicted that even though a slight recession was probable for the decade of the 1970s, San Diego would be only slightly affected. They were right. The region's growth was steady and permanent. The city moved from fourteenth largest in the nation to number nine in 1980. San Diego passed San Francisco to become second largest in California. The population boom in the southern part of the state brought with it problems of growth faced for the first time. Fortunately, long-range water planning carried the region through a major drought of the mid-1970s, but it could not prevent the serious damage caused by flooding during periods of intense rainfall from 1978 through 1980 when Mission Valley, the Tia Juana River Valley and other valleys in the county returned to floodplain conditions.

Pressures of urbanization drove land and housings costs up and greatly lessened the amount of acreage in agricultural production—often erasing the boundaries between urban and rural areas. As farmers looked at increased labor costs and the ordinary expenses of growing crops, they were lured by the extraordinary profits of converting land into housing developments. The rolling hills and pastures of Rancho {San} Bernardo and Rancho Los Peñasquitos became multi-million-dollar urbanized centers. To the south and east, remote areas like Rancho Jamacha became the planned community of Rancho San Diego, and Viejas Valley Ranch (now Palo Verde) in Alpine was transformed into two and three-acre estates commanding top prices. Closer to the heart of the city, houses in Mira Mesa and Tierrasanta stretched across the landscape at a rate hardly imagined in San Diego's history. Light to dark-brown condominiums filled up hills and canyons throughout the county as alternatives to expensive

BAY WATERS: *Mission Valley flood water, 1980 (bottom left); San Diego Bay at sunset (below); Santa Fe Wharf, 1890 (far right); naval ship and skyline (right).*

single-family dwellings. Property along the beach fronts skyrocketed in value. The price of an average house in the county increased from $26,900 in 1970 to $102,400 in 1979. Inflation hit all areas, but San Diego's personal per capita income of $8,300 in 1979 was above the national average of $7,836.

San Diego's politics during the 1970s witnessed the forceful enthusiasm of its hard-working mayor Pete Wilson, a former state assemblyman who decided to direct his energies toward the local scene. Elected in 1971, Mayor Wilson emerged as a vital, dominant factor in controlling economic policy and determining patterns of growth. In 1972, when the Republican National Convention pulled out of San Diego for Miami, Wilson quipped that San Diego was an "unconventional city" and decided to use the convention week to promote San Diego as "America's Finest City." Among Wilson's top priorities for improving the quality of life was revitalizing the downtown area. With Chamber of Commerce backing, the City Council established the Centre City Development Corporation (CCDC) in 1975 as the agency to administer redevelopment of 1,200 acres encompassing the Horton Plaza, Marina and Columbia redevelopment projects. The mayor worked closely with planners to create a complex that would be a "dynamic renaissance" of the city's heartland, giving it an entirely new lifestyle as envisioned by Alonzo Horton and John Nolen. Some controversy developed over selecting which buildings should or should not be preserved and restored as historic sites. But all agreed that downtown was a viable part of the community and a key to future city growth.

Horton Plaza — a 41.5-acre project — incorporated fifteen city blocks from Broadway to G Street between Union and Fourth. It provides commercial, retail, office, residential, hotel, recreational and entertainment facilities with sufficient parking areas. It incorporated the historic landmarks of the Spreckels Building, Balboa Theatre, Golden West Hotel and Horton Plaza Park. The Marina Project was the first truly urban residential development planned since the turn of the century. It included Horton House, a fourteen-story tower providing 150 apartments for senior citizens, some of whom were residents of other downtown hotels. A 500-slip marina and ocean-oriented park is currently being developed by the San Diego Port District to fully utilize the waterfront acreage. The Columbia Redevelopment Project is the connecting link between the central business district and the Embarcadero along the bay. A major convention complex with at least two prime hotels is planned between Pacific Highway and Union Street bounded by Ash and Broadway. The 56-acre project also accommodates office and residential areas surrounding the restored Santa Fe Railway Depot. Altogether the plans include 2,000 housing units — garden apartments, townhouses and condominiums — with a waterfront theme.

A privately financed and culturally rewarding project close to the city's heart is the historic Gaslamp Quarter, a 38-acre project covering sixteen blocks from Broadway to Market Street between Fourth and Sixth streets. The people in the Gaslamp District were aided in 1977 by the State Historic Building Code that allowed greater latitude for those restoring old buildings than if the construction were new. Supported by the City Council in the form of a Planned District Ordinance adopted in 1976, the concept differs from redevelopment because its primary objective is the preservation of landmarks of historic, architectural and cultural value that provide continuity with the past. By 1980 the major restored buildings in the Gaslamp Quarter included the Jewelers Exchange Building constructed by Nathan Watts in 1912; The Lester Hotel, a post-Victorian hotel housing the offices of Marilyn Marx's *Gaslamp Gazette*; a two-story Victorian-era storefront hotel at Fifth and Market streets restored by Drs. Antonia Pantoja and Wilhelmina Perry; and the 1880's Grand Pacific Hotel restored by Shirley Bernard. The successful Old

SEAPORT SENTINEL: *The handmade brass and copper weathervane (above) topping Seaport Village's Pier Building (top) is an example of the intricate detailing which is a hallmark of the new Seaport Village.*

Spaghetti Factory restaurant chain chose the Gaslamp Quarter as the site of its San Diego branch. The Francis Family Antique Warehouse was one of the earliest rehabilitation projects and other antique shops have since opened in the district. A recent innovation has been the introduction of trolley-vans offering free rides in the area. Charles Tyson bought San Diego's oldest City Hall, later known as the Crystal Theater at Fifth and G and plans commercial or restaurant uses for the historic building.

Another private development adjoining the city's redevelopment project is Seaport Village — a series of shops, walkways, open plazas and restaurants fronting on the harbor. The 22-acre site, formerly the old Coronado Ferry Station, has been leased from the San Diego Port District. It features an antique carousel and complements both the Gaslamp Quarter and Horton Plaza with a marine atmosphere. It is a short walk along the bay from the *Star of India* and other ships making up San Diego's maritime museum. With a number of seafood specialty stores and restaurants, San Diego's waterfront competes favorably with those of other bay cities. Proceeding north, visitors pass the tuna fleet with its giant purse seiners, historic Lubach's restaurant and catch a glimpse of the *Reuben E. Lee* moored at Harbor Island.

The Save Our Heritage Organization (SOHO) became a significant force in historic preservation during the 1970s. From inauspicious beginnings (a

DOWNTOWN REDEVELOPMENT: San Diego's Centre City encompasses 1,200 acres of the metropolitan downtown area. Approved redevelopment projects are primarily south and west of the high-rise structures that comprise the downtown financial and governmental district and adjacent to tidelands and Embarcadero area.

RESTORATION PROJECTS: Train depot (left) and the "new" Santa Fe Depot of 1914 (inset); the gaslamp District (above); and Temple Beth Israel (below) in Heritage Park.

sign pinned to the Sherman Gilbert House in 1968 by Robert Miles Parker saying "Save This House" and giving his telephone number), it grew by 1979 to a membership of 500 civic-minded citizens. Its first project — the saving of the Victorian house built by John Sherman in 1887 and later occupied by the Gilbert sisters—mushroomed into the larger concept of a seven-acre site in Old Town to become known as Heritage Park. The Sherman/Gilbert House was moved to the site at the end of April 1971, and restoration was begun. Guided by SOHO recommendations and the Cultural Heritage Committee, the Heritage Park package became San Diego County's Bicentennial project. It was funded by the county, matching grants and private donations. Dr. William Winter, owner of the Christian House and Burton House originally located on Third Avenue, offered them to the county for the park. These joined the Bushyhead House from Cedar Street, already saved from demolition. The three houses arrived at the site during the last week in August 1976 to make the Bicentennial project a reality. Two more structures—the Senlis Cottage donated by Will Hippen and the original home of Temple Beth Israel—took their places alongside the others in 1978 to form the nucleus of a nineteenth century "town." The Senlis Cottage serves as headquarters for SOHO and houses its research library. The Temple building was moved to the park with the support of the Beth Israel congregation and will be used by all faiths. The broad green lawn and general landscaping give the houses an attractive setting.

STAR OF INDIA: The oldest iron merchant ship afloat, first launched in November 1863, graces San Diego's waterfront.

The Star of India: a star for San Diego

Today the 205-foot bark *Star of India* graces San Diego's waterfront. It is the oldest iron merchant ship afloat.

She was first launched at Ramsey, Isle of Man, on November 14, 1863, as the *Euterpe*. The full-rigged ship was intended for cargo and limited passenger service between England and India. Her early sailing years out of Liverpool were fraught with disaster — a collision with a Spanish brig, the loss of all three masts in a hurricane off Madras and the death of her captain from a tropical fever. In 1871 she was acquired by Shaw Savill & Albion and put on the run from Liverpool to New Zealand and Australia. She made the around-the-world voyage by way of the Cape of Good Hope and across the Indian Ocean to Auckland or Wellington. She then caught the prevailing winds across the Pacific, headed around Cape Horn and into the Atlantic for home. The opening of the Suez Canal in 1869 gave steamers a place in world trade so the *Euterpe* was sold to the Pacific Colonial Ship Company of San Francisco and placed under Hawaiian registry. When Hawaii became a U. S. territory, she too became American.

As an American, the *Euterpe* carried timber out of Puget Sound to Australia, coal from Australian ports to Honolulu and sugar from the islands back to the West Coast. She was sold in 1902 to the Alaska Packers Association of San Francisco. They changed her name in 1906 to *Star of India* to match her step-sisters known around the world as Corry's Irish Stars — the Belfast-built ship *Star of Bengal, Star of Italy, Star of France* and *Star of Russia*. From then on it was up to Alaska in the spring and back to San Francisco in late summer with fishermen (mostly Sicilian) and Chinese cannery workers. The packers reduced her from a full-rigged ship to a bark. She made her last voyage to Alaska in 1923 and was headed for the scrappers. But she was rescued by James Wood Coffroth, representing a group of San Diegans. She was donated to the San Diego Zoological Society as a floating aquarium and museum. Unfortunately the onset of the Great Depression prevented plans for restoration. During World War II she sat neglected, her paint cracking and her decks rotting. Her once heavy cordage burned away in the bright sun. The U. S. Navy declared her a menace to aerial navigation and sent a work-party aboard to send down her yards and upper masts. In the late 1940s the Zoological Society gave her to the newly organized Maritime Museum Association of San Diego. With the help of local sail enthusiasts, writer Jerry MacMullen and maritime historian Captain Alan Villiers, restoration efforts were begun. The *Star of India*'s finest hour came on July 4, 1976, when she sailed out of San Diego Bay and into the Pacific Ocean. She is now joined by two other historic vessels — the *Berkeley,* an 1898 ferry boat and the *Medea,* a Scottish steam yacht. They are all moored along North Harbor Drive near Ash Street.

Since San Diego had been a part of the Spanish empire in 1776, another observance of the nation's Bicentennial was designed to enhance San Diego's ties with Mexico, under whose jurisdiction the city had once been. The University of California, San Diego and the city of San Diego, embarked upon a project called "Fronteras 1976" to foster positive border relationships in cultural, economic, environmental and educational areas. "Fronteras 1976" was headed by Arthur Hamilton Marston with Lucy Killea as executive secretary. The group expanded its directors to include representatives from San Diego State University, the University of San Diego, the county of San Diego and the Chicano Federation. During the Bicentennial year and afterwards, Fronteras sponsored a number of conferences to explore problems of mutual concern and identify areas of interaction with Tijuana and other areas of Mexico. Because of its success, the group was reorganized as Fronteras de las Californias, a permanent institution to pursue its original objectives. The Chicano Federation, long active in local affairs affecting Hispanic groups, encourages the participation of persons of Mexican descent in San Diego's political life. State Assemblyman Pete Chacon has promoted bilingual education for Spanish-speaking individuals.

Republican Clair W. Burgener, only San Diegan to hold office at all three levels of government.

San Diego's black community made considerable gains during the 1970s through the activities of business, educational and religious leaders. The Reverend George Walker Smith served four terms on the San Diego Board of Education from 1963 through 1979. He was a prime mover in upgrading educational facilities for all students in predominantly minority areas. Leon L. Williams became San Diego's first black councilman in 1969 and was re-elected in 1971, 1975, and 1979. Williams has been active in the Economic Opportunity Commission, the Neighborhood House Association and numerous youth groups.

In 1979 Judge Louis Welsh approved a plan for integration of the San Diego school system without mandatory busing in *Carlin v. San Diego Board of Education*, a lawsuit commenced in December 1967. San Diego — eighth largest school district in the nation with a student population of 110,000 — thus became one of the few major cities to have avoided court-ordered busing. A citizens task force headed by San Diego Police Chief William Kolender was established by Judge Welsh to monitor the school's voluntary integration efforts. Although controversy still exists, progress has been made in programs of voluntary ethnic transfers, magnet schools and part-time learning center exchanges.

At the national level, Republican Congressman Clair W. Burgener became a member of the powerful House Committee on Appropriations and its Subcommittee on Energy and Water Development in 1975. Burgener — the only San Diegan to hold office at all three levels of government — was a member of the City Council from 1953 to 1957, a California assemblyman from 1963 to 1966 and a state senator from 1967 to 1972. Elected to Congress that year, Burgener represented San Diego and part of Orange County. In 1975 the 43rd District was redrawn to include Imperial County. Fellow Republican Bob Wilson, a long-time supporter of Navy interests in San Diego and minority ranking member of the prestigious House Armed Services Committee, was elected to Congress in 1952 and served a record fourteen consecutive terms before retirement in 1980. Lionel Van Deerlin, a Democrat, began his first term in Congress in 1962. He became chairman of the House Subcommittee on Communications, a part of the Interstate and Foreign Communications Committee, in 1975.

James Mills, state senator since 1966 and responsible for legislation creating the port district and Old Town State Historic Park while in the assembly, became president pro tempore of the senate in 1970. Called "a quiet powerhouse" on the political scene, Mills, an author of scholarly works, has strongly supported measures that he believes will benefit San Diego. His bill providing for the use of state gasoline tax revenues to

Although controversy still exists, progress has been made in programs of voluntary ethnic transfers, magnet schools and part-time learning center exchanges.

finance light-rail transit systems has had far-reaching effects.

The state's Old Town project felt some repercussions from the county's Heritage Park nearby. The two areas competed for parking spaces along with private interests. John F. Borchers, the Chamber's executive vice president from 1954 to 1975, and staff member Lucille Mortimer worked with the state in planning for additional parking below the freeway and elsewhere. By the mid-1970s several Old Town buildings were completed. These included reconstruction of the Seeley Stables to house the Roscoe Hazard collection of Western Americana and a new Mission Playhouse. Concessionaire Geoff Mogilner turned the house originally built by Juan Rodriguez during the 1830s into the Tobacco Shop of Racine & Laramie, popular during the 1860s for its various wares. The Machado Silvas adobe was faithfully rebuilt and the interiors of the Casa de Estudillo and Machado Stewart adobe were enhanced, especially with the help of Mary Farrell and the Colonial Dames of America. Old Town's general development plan, introduced to the San Diego public in 1977, temporarily caused quite a stir when it was believed that the Old Town Plaza was to become barren and treeless. The state reassured local residents that only old eucalyptus trees threatening to fall on visitors were earmarked for removal. In the meantime, former Foodmaker Corporation executive Richard Silberman and Diane Powers, of Design Center Interiors, created the popular Bazaar del Mundo out of the historic Pico Motor Lodge. An attractive complex of shops and restaurants surrounding a small plaza area greatly increased the number of people coming to the area. Silberman, a powerful political force, sold his interest to become California's secretary of business and transportation and eventually finance director under Governor Jerry Brown. Powers—also a successful decorator in the San Diego area—converted the Bandini House (later the Cosmopolitan Hotel) into a picturesque restaurant. The state's overall concept for Old Town is to reconstruct the houses standing during the interpretive period (1821-1872) in phases over the next 25 years. In 1980, annual visitors to San Diego's historic center totalled more than four million.

THE P. D. FIVE: A contemporary musical group composed of policemen plays for the local community as part of their regular duties. Left to right, Edward Kunold, Bill Allen, Carlos Garcia, John Fung and Greg Drilling are seen at Montgomery Junior High School.

OLD TOWN AND BALBOA PARK: Heritage Park (top), Bazaar Del Mundo (center left), tobacco shop (above) and Casa de Estudillo (bottom left) in Old Town; California Tower (top right), feeding the pigeons (left inset), lily pond (center inset) and lawn bowling (right inset) in Balboa Park.

The history of Balboa Park during the 1970s was one of success and sadness. In 1967, Bea Evenson and the Committee of 100 began a successful drive to preserve the Spanish Colonial architecture of the 1915 Exposition buildings. When the old Food and Beverage Building was demolished, the committee spearheaded a campaign to raise funds and pass a bond issue to allow authentic reconstruction. The ornamental facade was exactly reproduced. Completed in 1971 and renamed the Casa del Prado, the building is used for many community programs. Funds were requested for restoration of other exposition buildings, but the public turned down a second bond proposal in 1972. The City Department of Parks and Recreation then planned a phased remodeling effort. New additions included the Reuben H. Fleet Space Theatre and Science Center completed in 1973 and donation to the city in 1976 of the Mary Marston family home and surrounding 4½ acres adjoining the north end of the park. A grant from the federal Economic Development Agency provided $5 million for reconstruction of the Electric Building that housed San Diego's Aerospace Museum and Hall of Fame.

By mid-February 1978, workers from Ninteman Construction Company had finished removing the last of 200 unique molds on the building from which the entire new façade (originally inspired by the Casa Consistorial in Palma, Mallorca) was to be duplicated. Just ten days later, on the night of February 22, the building went up in flames. All the treasures of the museum, including the only flyable replica of the "Spirit of St. Louis," the Ryan M-1, the Consolidated PT-3, the Luscombe Phantom and many others were destroyed. In addition to irreplaceable Lindbergh memorabilia and other priceless items, aviation researchers lost an important library and archives. Out of the charred remains, some things were saved—three wrought-iron balcony railings, a moon rock and contents of the Hall of Fame office. Under the leadership of Chamber President Richard Capen and Lee Grissom, who became the Chamber's 39th executive vice president in 1975, the organization promptly raised $110,000 to rebuild the Spirit of St. Louis replica. Other funds began pouring in to replace the rest of the collection and the aerospace exhibits formally moved into the renovated 1935 Ford Building early in 1980. The rebuilt Electric Building, known variously as the Canadian Building and Palace of Electricity, has been approved to house the museum and headquarters of the San Diego Historical Society, the Model Railroad Club, the Hall of Champions and other civic groups.

Just two weeks after the Aerospace Museum disaster, another major Balboa Park fire sent shock waves through San Diego. The incomparable Old Globe Theater—the revered reproduction of Shakespeare's original built for the 1935 California-Pacific Exposition—was totally gutted. Director Craig Noel's first thoughts turned toward the upcoming productions, especially the Shakespeare Summer Festival, one of San Diego's most popular attractions. With more than 600 performances annually on its two stages and on tour, the Old Globe had one of the heaviest annual production schedules of any theater in the United States. The emotional support of the beloved theater was so great that $6 million equally divided between private and public support was raised in a little over one year. Some controversy developed over plans to rebuild the theater because its small size caused many people to be turned away. Nevertheless, the theater is being faithfully reconstructed with only slight modifications to seat some 525 to 550 people. In the meantime, the city approved construction of the Festival Stage, an outdoor theater set in the canyon to the east of the Carter Center Stage. Architect Robert Mosher had planned the outdoor facility in 1974, but it failed to become a reality. The city granted the new theater a temporary permit only since it removed land from what some people considered appropriate park use. The Old Globe's projected completion is June 1981, and the city has

Mary G. Marston — her family home and surrounding 4½ acres were donated to the city in 1976.

With more than 600 performances annually on its two stages and on tour, the Old Globe had one of the heaviest annual production schedules of any theatre in the United States.

CULTURAL HUB: On Balboa Park's del Prado (right), eight museums are walking distance apart - Museum of Man, Natural History Museum, Museum of San Diego History, Hall of Champions, San Diego Museum of Art and Timken Gallery, Botanical Building and the Reuben H. Fleet Space Theater (top) where visitors take a simulated swing around Saturn in the year 2350. Dancing outside the Old Globe Theater (above) which was built for the 1935 Exposition and is being "faithfully reconstructed" after a 1978 fire.

MONUMENTS TO THE PAST: Serra Museum
dedication (above) as the focal point of Presidio
Park (inset); San Diego Mission (left); and Cabrillo
National Monument (above).

COLORFUL ATTRACTIONS:
Ranunculus flower fields (top right) in north San Diego County; Torrey Pines Golf Course (left); and thoroughbreds racing on grass course at Del Mar (above).

extended the permit for the Festival Stage, which seats 750, until 1983. The Old Globe Association and many theater-goers hope it will be permanent. Other Balboa Park considerations involved restoration and repair of other exposition buildings and appropriate use of all areas within the park.

In September 1978, somber headlines rivaling those of the 1905 Bennington disaster emanated from San Diego when PSA Flight 182 from Sacramento collided at 9 a.m. with a private airplane over North Park and crashed, claiming 144 lives. It was the United States' worst air disaster up to that time. The *Evening Tribune's* extensive coverage of the crash earned the newspaper a Pulitzer Prize. As a result, the whole issue of air traffic control came under heavy scrutiny in San Diego and a TCA (Terminal Control Area) Class 2 was finally established at Lindbergh Field in 1980.

The United States National Bank of San Diego, one of the oldest and largest financial institutions in the city, was declared insolvent by the comptroller of the currency on October 8, 1973. Founded in 1913 and purchased by C. Arnholt Smith in 1933, the bank had grown to the 26th largest in the nation with 62 branches in southern California and deposits in excess of $1 billion. A lawsuit commenced by the Securities Exchange Commission in May 1973 charged Smith and other officers of Westgate California Corporation with improper actions. This precipitated the collapse of USNB. Westgate, formed in 1960, was a Smith-controlled conglomerate of tuna boats and canneries, airlines, taxicabs, insurance companies, real estate holdings, hotels and other businesses. In the wake of the USNB failure, Westgate filed Chapter X proceedings in February 1974. Smith—a civic leader and a former "Mr. San Diego"—pleaded *nolo contendre* in Federal District Court to violations of the national banking laws. A fine of $30,000 and a suspended jail sentence were imposed. Subsequently, after a two-year trial in state court during which 58 counts were dismissed, Smith was found guilty of income tax violations. Extensive civil litigation included a class-action suit by USNB minority shareholders against Smith and members of his family that resulted in a $29 million jury award in Federal District Court. Appeals to higher courts from both jury decisions are still to be resolved.

Smith, principal owner of the San Diego Padres, sold the baseball team to Ray Kroc, owner of the McDonald's fast food chain, in 1974. After a shakeup in management (both in the front office and on the field), the Padres picked up momentum. With star pitchers Randy Jones (Cy Young Award winner in 1976) and Gaylord Perry (the winner in 1978), the Padres developed a loyal following. Although their position in the standings was never spectacular, players like All-Star outfielder Dave Winfield made it possible for the Padres to become competitive in the National League. Their first winning season came in 1978. Young president Ballard Smith, Kroc's son-in-law, had a promising team when the player strike was averted in May 1980.

Professional football told a brighter story. Tommy Prothro—selected by principal owner Eugene Klein to be head coach of the San Diego Chargers from 1974 through 1978—directed a major rebuilding effort that reached fruition under San Diego's "own" Don Coryell. Coryell led the San Diego State University Aztecs through twelve winning seasons (including a 31-game winning streak) from 1961 to 1972. He returned to San Diego after a five-year coaching stint with the St. Louis Cardinals. Coryell's Chargers were guided by quarterback Dan Fouts and backed up by such top-quality pass receivers as Charles Joiner and John Jefferson. They won the American Football Conference's Western Division in 1979 with twelve victories and emerged as one of pro football's strongest teams.

As both Charger and Aztec fans began to jam the stadium for home games, the parking lot became a veritable sea of tailgating picnics on Saturday nights and Sunday afternoons. This became an increasingly

Freeman Williams, guard for the San Diego Clippers.

The San Diego Chargers won the American Football Conference's Western Division in 1979.

competitive participant sport. Creative portable feasts ranged from simple hibachi hot dogs or hamburgers with potato chips and beer to such epicurean delights as cracked crab or beef bourguignonne with cucumber salad and just the right wine. Festive tables and colorful T-shirts added a new dimension to San Diego football.

Basketball fans greeted the arrival of a long-awaited National Basketball Association team for the 1978-1979 season when owner Irv Levin moved the former Buffalo Braves to the city. Under Coach Gene Shue, the San Diego Clippers (with the league's second-leading scorer Lloyd Free) had an exciting first season but missed the playoffs by two games. Their second year at the Sports Arena brought the often-talked-about hometown hero Bill Walton back to San Diego. The Clippers paid dearly to secure the former Helix High School center, who was a three-time UCLA All-American and the NBA's most valuable player of 1976. Injuries to Walton and others again spoiled playoff hopes. The departure of Shue and contract disputes gave the Clippers a shaky beginning in 1980.

The San Diego Sockers, representing one of southern California's fastest growing sports among young and old, took their place among the other professional teams at San Diego Stadium in 1978. The Sockers gained steadily in support and, in both 1979 and 1980, came within one playoff game of reaching the championship Soccer Bowl.

Tennis has always been popular in San Diego with many public and private courts available throughout the county. Tennis centers, camps, clubs and clinics, together with related fashions and equipment, are big business. The San Diego Friars of World Team Tennis had one of the nation's best attendance records in 1978 before the folding of franchises elsewhere caused its demise. The almost overnight success of racquetball

FUN IN THE SUN: Surfing the day away at Ocean Beach Pier (above); sunning at La Jolla Cove Beach (left inset); wading at Pacific Beach (right inset); and sand castle building at Coronado Beach (left).

CITY CENTERPIECES: Old Point Loma Lighthouse (top); the Convention Center (left); and the Chamber of Commerce building (above).

was felt strongly in San Diego. Predicted by some to become the largest participant sport in the nation by the mid-1980s, the sport has outpaced some of the more traditional games.

Another popular activity that returned to San Diego during the 1970s was the shooting of films for movies and television. Although La Mesa and Coronado had housed some of the earliest movie companies in the United States, Hollywood outdistanced its southern rivals during the 1920s and 1930s. Union regulations then made it economically unsound to make films in San Diego because extras from Los Angeles had to be brought in and maintained. When the television series "Harry O" starring the late David Janssen moved back to Los Angeles in 1975, the Chamber of Commerce formed the San Diego Motion Picture and Television Bureau with city funding and support. The bureau succeeded in establishing a local office of the Screen Extras Guild so that extras could be hired locally. They also cut through other red tape and enabled the local industry to thrive once again. San Diego attracted major movie, television and commercial productions because of its natural scenery and suitable climate. Several big-budget movies were filmed in the city while television's Perry Como Easter Special of 1978 and the Dean Martin Christmas Special in 1979 gave the rest of the nation a good look at Sea World, Torrey Pines and San Diego's sunshine.

The *San Diego Union* continued to grow in circulation during the 1970s, and has become the area's strongest daily newspaper. Longtime publisher James S. Copley died in October 1973, just as the press moved into its new headquarters in Mission Valley. His widow Helen took charge of the Copley newspaper chain. She made a number of policy changes to modernize the *Union* and *Evening Tribune* and broaden their scope of news coverage. In 1975 she hired as editor Gerald L. Warren, who had been deputy press secretary in the White House and a former assistant managing editor of the *Union*. The San Diego *Daily Transcript* continued to expand as a daily business paper, and in 1978 the *Los Angeles Times* launched a San Diego County edition, providing new competition for the local dailies. The successful *San Diego Magazine* celebrated its 30th anniversary with special pictorial issues in November and December 1978. A new publication, *San Diego Home/Garden*, appeared in 1980, as did the weekly *San Diego Business Journal*.

The economic forecast for the San Diego region in the coming decades is more optimistic than for the nation as a whole. As in previous years, the county's trends are expected to follow state rather than national patterns, but high housing costs may slow population gains significantly. Declines in government payrolls because of tax-cutting initiatives and other measures limiting public spending will add a degree of uncertainty to the region's employment opportunities. Nevertheless, the Chamber of Commerce, and a revitalized Economic Development Corporation, have attracted new industries and corporate headquarters to San Diego. The purchase of the historic San Diego & Arizona Eastern Railway by the San Diego Metropolitan Transit Development Board (MTDB) provided 108 miles of fixed-rail right-of-way and cleared the way for a light-rail transit system. The first leg will operate 15.9 miles from the Santa Fe Depot to San Ysidro, making eleven intermediate stops. A new West Terminal was added to Lindbergh Field in 1979 to ease passenger congestion, but some feel the airport needs to be moved to an outlying area. No alternative site has yet been agreed upon.

San Diego, no longer isolated but still blessed with a highly desirable climate and location, faces a number of future challenges. These involve principally water, energy, transportation, growth and the region's relationship with Mexico. Continued careful planning is essential. With a solid base in economic progress and a people proud of cultural and intellectual achievement, San Diego will continue to solidify its position even more firmly as California's cornerstone.

THE SILVER SCREEN: Making movies at Balboa Park, circa 1920 top; movie director Allan Dwan (bottom) in front of "Flying A" movie studio on La Mesa Boulevard, circa 1910.

The economic forecast for the San Diego region in the coming decades is more optimistic than for the nation as a whole.

A CITY BY THE SEA: Fog invades Ocean Beach Pier (top left); San Diego skyline (left); San Diego Harbor from Point Loma (above), early 1900s; and Point Loma from the air, 1979 (left).

Chronology of events

Group at Squire family home, 1896

1492 - 1541

The Empire of Spain reaches a zenith under the Hapsburg monarchs; discovery and exploration of the New World is carried on by Spain, Portugal and other European powers; Spaniards introduce the horse and the planting of wheat, vineyards, sugar cane and other products into America; the Indians give corn, tomatoes, potatoes, chocolate, tobacco and quinine to the Europeans; heavily populated Indian civilizations are found in Central and South America.

1492 - Columbus reaches New World and claims Indies for Spain; he is greeted by native Americans whose ancestors arrived 12,000 - 15,000 years before.

1512 - Vasco Nuñez de Balboa discovers Pacific Ocean.

1519 - Expedition of Ferdinand Magellan, a Portuguese sailing for Spain, circumnavigates globe.

1519 - Hernán Cortés conquers Aztecs of Tenochtitlán (Mexico City) and establishes Spanish control.

1533 - Fortún Jiménez tries to gain foothold at La Paz, Baja California, but fails.

1535 - Antonio de Mendoza becomes Viceroy of New Spain; Cortés attempts to colonize Baja California but unsuccessful.

1539 - Francisco de Ulloa explores Gulf of California and west coast of Baja California, proving California not an island, but idea remains.

1540 - Francisco Vásquez de Coronado explores southwest as far as Kansas; Melchior Díaz reaches Colorado River and crosses into Alta (Upper) California.

　　　- Hernando de Soto explores southeast from Florida to Mississippi River.

A 1650 French map showing California as an island

1542 - 1700

England, France and the Netherlands gain New World holdings; Roman Catholic missions established to Christianize native Americans; Spain opens a Pacific route used by Manila galleons sailing between Philippine Islands and Acapulco; England challenges Spain's power in New World and Europe; France gains territory in Canada and explores Mississippi Valley.

1542 - Juan Rodríguez Cabrillo sails into San Diego Bay on September 28, names port San Miguel.

1553 - University of Mexico founded.

1565 - Spain extends conquest to Philippines.
　　　St. Augustine, Florida founded by Spanish soldiers.

1579 - Francis Drake lands on coast of California and names area near San Francisco Bay Nova Albion.

1588 - San Diego de Alcalá (St. Didacus) canonized in Rome. English defeat Spanish armada.

1595 - Sebastián Rodríguez Cermeño explores California coast, wrecks galleon near Drakes Bay.

1602 - Sebastián Vizcaíno heads expedition to explore California, sails into Cabrillo's San Miguel and names port San Diego de Alcalá to honor saint whose day is celebrated November 12.

1607 - English found Jamestown Colony on Chesapeake Bay.

1608 - French establish Quebec on St. Lawrence River.

1609 - Santa Fe founded by Spain in New Mexico.

1615 - Private entrepreneurs seek wealth in Baja California through pearl fishing; pearls too few for sufficient profits.

1683 - Father Francisco Eusebio Kino and Isidro Atondo y Antillón attempt to establish settlement at San Bruno, Baja California, and cross peninsula overland to Pacific coast.

1697 - Jesuit missionaries under Juan María Salvatierra establish first permanent settlement in Baja California with Mission Nuestra Señora de Loreto.

1701 - 1770

The throne of Spain passes to Bourbons; colonial rivalries continue among European powers in Americas, Asia and Africa; the thirteen English colonies solidify position on East coast of North America; Vitus Bering explores strait separating Asia from North America; George III becomes king of Great Britain and Carlos III king of Spain; Carolus Linnaeus of Sweden develops system of scientific nomenclature; eighteenth-century enlightenment felt on both sides of the Atlantic.

1701 - Father Kino reaffirmed that California was not an island after exploring the area at the headwaters of the Gulf.

1701 - Jesuit missionaries found ten missions in southern portion of Baja California peninsula.

1735 - Indians at four Baja California missions lead uprising against Spaniards.

1746 - Father Fernando Consag explores northward along gulf coast of Baja California in search of mission sites.

1763 - Treaty of Paris ends Seven Years' War; France expelled from North America, Louisiana ceded to Spain, Florida passes to Great Britain.

1766 - Father Wenceslaus Linck explores Baja California's northern portions.

1767 - Santa María de los Angeles, northernmost Jesuit mission in Baja California, founded.
Gaspar de Portolá appointed Governor of Baja California with headquarters at Loreto.

1768 - Jesuit missionaries expelled from Baja California for political reasons.

1769 - Arrival in San Diego of maritime and land expeditions gives Spain foothold in Alta California.
Father Junípero Serra blesses Presidio Hill as site of Mission San Diego de Alcalá July 16.

1770 - Spanish soldiers and priests found Presidio of Monterey as capital of Alta California and Mission San Carlos Borromeo June 3.

Raising the Spanish flag in California, 1769

1771 - 1780

British colonies in North America declare independence July 4, 1776; separate viceroyalties set up by Spain for La Plata (Argentina) and Nueva Granada (Colombia, Venezuela and Ecuador) to join Peru and New Spain; Daniel Boone leads settlers westward into Kentucky; Captain James Cook, English navigator, discovers Hawaiian Islands and visits Pacific Northwest coast.

1772 - Spain divides missions of Baja California and Alta California between Dominican and Franciscan Orders at point just south of present boundary between United States and Mexico.

1774 - In August Mission San Diego de Alcalá moves to present site six miles inland from presidio. Juan Pérez sails to 54° 40' north latitude to claim the Pacific Northwest for Spain.

1775 - Local Indians attack and burn Mission San Diego, killing Father Luis Jayme November 5.

1776 - Juan Bautista de Anza travels overland to Mission San Gabriel from Tubac, Arizona, with colonists destined for Monterey and San Francisco. San Francisco Presidio and Missions San Francisco de Asis and San Juan Capistrano founded. First baptism at rebuilt Mission San Diego held in December.

1777 - San José de Guadalupe, first civilian settlement in Alta California, founded.

1779 - A *Reglamento* (code) for governing California issued by Governor Felipe de Neve.

San Diego Mission in ruins, late 1800s

1781 - 1790

Treaty of Paris of 1783 recognizes American independence and returns Florida to Spain; Spaniards expand mission efforts in northern Mexico and Californias; Russians establish trading post on Kodiak Island; United States Constitution adopted (1787); Royal Botanical Garden founded in Mexico City.

1781 - California's second town — El Pueblo de Nuestra Señora la Reina de Los Angeles — founded September 4. Indians at Yuma attack Spanish colonizing party, closing overland route from Arizona to California.

1783 - Father Fermín Francisco de Lasuén reports 966 baptisms, 232 marriages and 210 deaths at Mission San Diego.

1784 - Father Junípero Serra dies at Mission San Carlos Borromeo (Carmel). Governor Pedro Fages grants the first private ranchos in California to soldiers having served at San Diego Presidio.

1785 - Father Lasuén becomes Father President of the California missions.

1786 - Count of La Pérouse, French navigator, first foreign visitor in California.

1788 - First American ships — *Columbia* and *Lady Washington* — sail to Pacific Northwest coast.

1790 - San Diego Presidio has population of 212; Mission San Diego houses 933 Indians.

1791 - 1800

George Washington and John Adams become presidents of United States; French Revolution occurs in 1792, Napoleon rises to power; Spaniards withdraw from Nootka Sound on Vancouver Island because of British pressure; Russians establish post at Sitka, Alaska; Treaty of San Ildefonso in 1800 returns Louisiana to France from Spain.

1791 - Spanish expedition of Alejandro Malaspina surveys California to gather scientific information on around-the-world journey.

1793 - British Captain George Vancouver visits San Diego and finds it poorly protected.

1795 - Padres discover spring near Mission San Diego to increase water supply. School at San Diego Presidio has 22 pupils under Sergeant Don Manuel de Vargas.

1796 - *Otter* from New England arrives in Monterey to establish trade with California.

1797 - Mission San Diego becomes most populous in California with 1,405 Indians.

1798 - Wine pressed from grapes raised at Mission San Diego. Mission San Luis Rey de Francia founded June 13 and dedicated to St. Louis IX, king of France in the mid-thirteenth century. Dominican missionaries from Baja California visit San Diego.

1800 - First American ship, the *Betsy*, arrives in San Diego.

1801 - 1810

Thomas Jefferson and James Madison serve as U. S. presidents; most of Europe begins to unite against Napoleon; French place Joseph Bonaparte on throne of Spain; United States purchases Louisiana from France; Lewis and Clark reach the mouth of Columbia River overland; Daniel Boone leads settlers to Missouri; Father Miguel Hidalgo issues call for Mexican independence at pueblo of Dolores near Queretaro.

Ramona and Allesandro from Ramona *by Helen Hunt Jackson*

1803 - American brig *Lelia Byrd* fired upon from Point Guijarros (Ballast Point).

1804 - Lieutenant Manuel Rodríguez, commandant of presidio, supervises reburial of bodies of Fathers Luis Jayme (d. 1775), Juan Figuer (d. 1784) and Juan Mariner (d. 1800) between two altars of new church April 26. Missionaries continue to work on dam and aqueduct system to obtain good water supply from San Diego River.

1806 - 1810 Lieutenants Francisco María Ruiz and José de la Guerra y Noriega and Captain José Raimundo Carrillo serve as presidio commanders at San Diego.

1808 - Construction of new San Diego mission church structure begins.

1809 - Russians establish few buildings at Bodega Bay.

1810 - San Diego's presidial population approximately 350, with 1,611 Indians at Mission San Diego and 1,517 at Mission San Luis Rey.

1811 - 1820

United States and Great Britain fight War of 1812; James Madison and James Monroe serve as U. S. presidents; Napoleon defeated at Waterloo; Fernando VII resumes throne of Spain; Mexico began fight for independence along with most of South America; The Missouri Compromise allows entry of Maine as free state and Missouri as slave state.

1812 - Earthquake shakes much of California causing major destruction at Mission San Juan Capistrano. Russians found a colony at Fort Ross, north of San Francisco.

1813 - Church at Mission San Diego completed and dedicated by Father José Barona.

1813 - 1816 Padres build dam in Mission Gorge and aqueduct system to supply the mission with water.

1816 - *Asistencia* (sub-mission) founded at San Antonio de Pala (and continues to serve Indians in district).

1818 - *Asistencia* founded at Santa Ysabel with oldest two bells in California (1723 and 1767). Hipolyte de Bouchard attacks California coast in name of independence from Spain.

1819 - Adams-Onis Treaty transfers Florida and Spain's claim to Pacific Northwest (54°40') to United States.

1820 - Indians at Mission San Diego number 1,567; Indians at Mission San Luis Rey total 2,603.

1821 - 1830

Mexico achieves independence from Spain; James Monroe, John Quincy Adams and Andrew Jackson are U. S. Presidents; Santa Fe Trail opened between Missouri and New Mexico; Americans move into Texas; Monroe Doctrine formulated; Boston trading ships sail along Pacific coast.

1822 - California swears allegiance to government of Mexico. Luis Argüello becomes first elected native-born governor of California.

1822 - Presidio families begin move down hill to build houses below (Old Town) in San Diego County.

1823 - First private rancho (Los Peñasquitos) granted Francisco María Ruiz.

1825 - Governor José María Echeandía moves capital of California from Monterey to San Diego.

1826 - Jedediah Smith, fur trapper, first American to arrive in San Diego via overland route.

1827 - French sea captain Auguste Bernard du Haut-Cilly visits San Diego in *Le Héros*.

1829 - Fur trapper James Ohio Pattie and several companions imprisoned at San Diego presidio. First hide house built at La Playa (Point Loma).

1830 - San Diego's presidial population 520; 7,294 Indians in district; Mission San Diego lists 1,544 and Mission San Luis Rey 2,776 residents. Mission San Diego has 7,630 head of cattle and 16,120 sheep; Mission San Luis Rey has 25,000 head of each and 2,210 horses.

Pendleton House, frame and adobe dwelling built by Don Juan Bandini in the mid 1800s

---

1831 - 1840

Andrew Jackson and Martin Van Buren are presidents of United States; Antonio López de Santa Anna dominates Mexican politics; American settlers move into Oregon Territory; Texas declares independence from Mexico; fur trappers enter California from New Mexico.

1831 - Jonathan Trumbull (later Juan José) Warner reaches California. Capital of California returned to Monterey; rivalry develops between northern and southern California.

1832 - Father Antonio Peyri leaves Mission San Luis Rey for home in Spain.

1833 - Act to secularize California missions passed in Mexico.

1834 - 1836 Secularization of Missions San Diego and San Luis Rey carried out; providing land for granting ranches.

1835 - San Diego officially becomes pueblo (town); presidio effectively abandoned. Richard Henry Dana visits San Diego aboard a hide and tallow trader from New England.

1836 - Indians attack rancho settlements.

1838 - San Diego loses pueblo status and becomes subprefecture of Los Angeles.

1839 - Russians sell Fort Ross to John Sutter who moves it to confluence of the Sacramento and American rivers.

1840 - San Diego's population is 150; 2,250 Indians still live at former mission.

1841 - 1850

William Henry Harrison, John Tyler, James K. Polk and Zachary Taylor serve as U. S. Presidents; "Manifest Destiny" becomes theme for westward expansion; Mormons reach Utah; U. S. and Great Britain settle the Oregon boundary question at 49th parallel; U. S. and Mexico go to war over Texas boundary question; Samuel Morse invents telegraph; California has population of 92,597 in 1850.

1841 - First American immigrant wagon train reaches California over Sierra Nevada.

Bishop García Diego y Moreno, first bishop of California, visits San Diego and confirms 125 people at old presidio chapel.

1842 - Governor Manuel Micheltorena visits San Diego on way from Mexico to Monterey.

1844 - John C. Fremont's U. S. military mapping expedition reaches Sutter's Fort.

1845 - 1846 Donner party suffers serious losses on overland trek to California.

1846 - Group of American settlers declare California's independence as Bear Flag Republic June 14. Commodore John D. Sloat raises American flag at Monterey July 2. Captain Samuel F. Dupont orders U. S. flag raised in San Diego July 29. Battle of San Pasqual fought near Escondido December 6.

1847 - Capitulation of Cahuenga ends war in California January 13. Mormon battalion arrives in San Diego January 27.

1848 - Gold discovered at Sutter's Mill by James Marshall January 24. Treaty of Guadalupe Hidalgo signed February 2 ends Mexican War; California becomes part of United States.

1849 - U. S. Boundary Commission arrives in San Diego.

1850 - California admitted to Union September 9 as 31st state, upsetting equal balance of free and slave states. of San Diego incorporated (with population of 650), becomes first county created by California legislature. Joshua Bean becomes first American mayor of San Diego. William Heath Davis starts New San Diego by waterfront.

Battle of San Pasqual

1851 - 1860

Millard Filmore, Franklin Pierce and James Buchanan are U. S. presidents; Peter H. Burnett is first American governor of California; Gadsden Purchase brings southern Arizona into Union; several transcontinental railroad surveys made; Commodore Perry opens trade with Japan; expansion of slavery issue becomes irrepressible conflict; silver discovered in Nevada; California's population reaches 379,994 in 1860.

1851 - *San Diego Herald* begins publication.
Indians led by Antonio Garra attack Warner's Ranch.

1852 - Phineas Banning and D. W. Alexander start stage line between Los Angeles and San Diego.

1853 - Lieutenant George Derby plans to turn San Diego River into False (later Mission) Bay.

1854 - San Diego & Gila, Southern Pacific & Atlantic Railroad organized. County public school system organized.

1855 - Heavy rains wash out dam on San Diego River.

1857 - James Birch opens first transcontinental overland mail route (Jackass Mail Line) from San Antonio to San Diego.

1858 - Butterfield Overland Stage begins regular service from Missouri to San Francisco. Church of the Immaculate Conception dedicated in Old Town.

1860 - San Diego's population is 731; county totals 4,324 (1,249 white, 8 black, 3,067 Indian).

1861 - 1870

Abraham Lincoln serves as president until his assassination April 1865; Jefferson Davis becomes president of Confederacy; Civil War ends with Lee's surrender at Appomattox; Andrew Johnson succeeds Lincoln and fights with Congress over Reconstruction; French intervene in Mexico; U. S. purchases Alaska from Russia;

transcontinental railroad completed from Council Bluffs, Iowa to San Francisco.

1861 - All stage travel over the southern route discontinued because of Civil War.
Storms, earthquakes and flood tides damage San Diego.
1862 - Abraham Lincoln signs order returning title to mission buildings at San Diego to Catholic Church together with 22.2 acres of surrounding lands. Drought, smallpox epidemic and locust plague hit San Diego area.
1863 - *Star of India* launched as *Euterpe* at Ramsey, Isle of Man (England).
1865 - President Lincoln signs order returning mission buildings at San Luis Rey to Catholic Church together with 64 acres of surrounding lands.
1866 - General William Rosecrans surveys San Diego for railroad depot.
1867 - Alonzo Horton arrives April 15 and, by May 10, has purchased 960 acres of New Town for $265.
1868 - Construction begins on Horton's Wharf. Kimball brothers lay out National City on northwestern corner of old Rancho de la Nación. First school opened in New San Diego. Land (1,440 acres) set aside for large city park (Balboa Park).
1870 - San Diego Chamber of Commerce founded in January. Gold discovered near present-day Julian. San Diego's population is 2,300; there are 4,324 in county and 560,247 in state.

Home of Juan Maria Marron, owner of Rancho Agua Hedionda, built in 1842.

1871 - 1880

General Ulysses S. Grant and Rutherford B. Hayes serve as U. S. presidents; Reconstruction ends; Salvation Army is organized; first major baseball league is formed; Alexander Graham Bell invents telephone; F. W. Woolworth opens five and ten-cent-store.

1871 - County seat moves to Horton's Addition (New Town).
San Diegans lay cornerstone for new county courthouse.
San Diego Union begins daily publication March 20.
1872 - First Jewish synagogue organized in house of Marcus Schiller.
Fire destroys much of Old Town in April.
San Diego Fire Engine Company No. 1 organized.
1873 - San Diego Water Company formed.
1874 - City receives its final patent to pueblo lands.
1875 - Chamber of Commerce arranges for U. S. Cavalry post.
1876 - Southern Pacific Railroad connects San Francisco with Los Angeles.
1877 - San Diego River diverted into False Bay.
1878 - First telephone demonstrated in city.
1879 - California adopts new constitution.
1880 - San Diego's population reaches 2,637; there are 8,618 in county and 864,694 in state.

1881 - 1890

James A. Garfield, Chester A. Arthur and Grover Cleveland are U. S. presidents; Clara Barton establishes Red Cross; Apache chief Geronimo finally captured in Arizona; American Federation of Labor and Interstate Commerce Commission formed; Chinese Exclusion Act passed.

1881 - San Diego Gas Company organized.
1882 - San Diego's first public library opened. California Southern

Railroad service begins with San Diego's connection to Santa Fe Railroad.

1883 - Kate Sessions becomes principal of Russ School. Leach's Opera House, first in the city, opened. John Montgomery makes first controlled glider flight.

1884 - First transcontinental railroad reaches San Diego.

1885 - Group of German-Americans found Olivenhain.

1886 - Construction of Hotel del Coronado begins. Electric lights installed in downtown San Diego.

1887 - National City incorporated. San Diego and Old Town electric street cars begin operating. Chamber of Commerce urges engineering plan for 1,400-acre city park (Balboa Park). *The Golden Era* magazine promotes San Diego.

1888 - Cities of Escondido and Oceanside incorporated. San Diego High School organized. Sweetwater Dam completed. San Diego Flume brings water to city.

1889 - San Diego becomes fourth-class city under new charter; Douglas Gunn elected mayor.

1890 - San Diego's population declines from estimated 40,000 in 1887 to 16,159; there are 34,987 in county and 1,213,398 in state.

Bar in unknown saloon, circa 1890

1891 - 1900

Benjamin Harrison, Grover Cleveland and William McKinley are U.S. presidents; Marconi patents wireless; Panic of 1893 results from economic depression; automobiles begin to be manufactured in Detroit; Spanish American War is fought over Cuba and United States annexes Philippines, Puerto Rico and Guam as a result; Hawaii also becomes a part of United States.

1891 - Chilean insurgent transport *Itata* is seized at San Diego. City of Coronado secedes from San Diego. W. H. Carlson elected mayor.

1892 - John D. Spreckels buys transit system. Klondike gold rush begins.

1893 - Riverside County is formed from large slice of San Diego County.

1894 - Chamber of Commerce urges establishment of state normal school.

1895 - The *San Diego Evening Tribune* founded.

1896 - Harbor fortifications begun at Point Loma.

1898 - D. C. Reed elected mayor. One of first movies, "San Diego Street Scene," filmed in city.

1899 - Edwin M. Capps elected mayor.

1900 - John D. Spreckels opens Tent City in Coronado. San Diego's population reaches 17,700; the county numbers 35,090.

1901 - 1910

William McKinley (assassinated 1901), Theodore Roosevelt and William Howard Taft are U. S. presidents; Henry Ford organizes motor company and Wright Brothers complete successful flight; San Francisco earthquake and fire kill 452 people; Admiral Robert E. Peary reaches North Pole; California population is 2,377,549 in 1910.

1901 - Imperial Valley canals filled from Colorado River. San Diego purchases water systems within city.

1902 - Katherine Tingley invites Cuban children to her Theosophical Community on Point Loma.

1903 - 1904 San Diego County Hospital built.

1905 - 1906 Flood waters pour through the Colorado River bank for 16 months to create Salton Sea.
U. S. S. *Bennington's* boiler explodes in San Diego harbor, killing 60 and injuring 47.

1906 - John D. Spreckels and others form corporation to build San Diego and Arizona Railroad.
Dr. Lee DeForest operates first wireless in San Diego.
Chamber of Commerce appropriates funds for harbor improvements.

1907 - Imperial County formed from 4,089 square miles of San Diego County.

1908 - Cities of El Centro and Calexico are incorporated.
Chamber of Commerce board increased from 21 to 30 to include representatives from county communities.
Nolen Plan for city development presented for approval.
Great White Fleet visits San Diego December 5.

1909 - Historian William E. Smythe begins Little Landers Colony in the South Bay area.

1910 - U. S. Grant Hotel, dedicated October 15, replaces Horton House.
San Diego's population reaches nearly 40,000.

W. A. Begole Stoves, Tin and Hardware

1911 - 1920

Woodrow Wilson follows Taft as president in 1912; Mexican Revolution ousts Porfirio Diaz and pledges social reform; National Association for the Advancement of Colored People (NAACP) begins and Boy Scouts of America founded; Congress institutes federal income tax; Panama Canal completed and World War I begins in Europe; 18th amendment (Prohibition) is ratified; women achieve right to vote; League of Nations formed after surrender of Germany in 1918 but U. S. refuses to join; Roald Amundsen reaches South Pole.

1911 - City of Chula Vista incorporates.
Glenn Curtiss starts flying school on North Island.
American Film Company (Flying A) sets up studio in Lakeside, then La Mesa.
Voters assure harbor development by approving bonds.

1912 - El Cajon and La Mesa incorporated.
Essanay Western film company makes several Bronco Billy pictures in La Mesa while Ammex produces movies in National City.
The I. W. W. free speech controversy climaxes with expulsion of Emma Goldman.

1913 - Congressman William Kettner and Chamber of Commerce helps obtain appropriations for naval coaling and radio stations.

1914 - Morena Dam purchased by city for $1.5 million.

1915 - Panama-California Exposition dedicated, and Balboa Stadium opens.
Charles Hatfield, "The Rainmaker", commissioned to fill Morena Reservoir.

1916 - Heavy flooding washes out Otay Dam and Old Town Bridge.

1917 - Louis J. Wilde elected mayor.
Camp Kearny established; U. S. Marine Base and Naval Hospital approved; Rockwell Field and Naval Air Station set up on North Island.

1918 - Chamber of Commerce raises $280,000 to buy land for first major Navy base.

1919 - San Diego and Arizona Railroad completed.

1920 - Phil D. Swing of Imperial County elected to Congress.
San Diego's population reaches 74,683.

Warren G. Harding, Calvin Coolidge and Herbert Hoover serve as U. S. presidents; *Time* Magazine and *Reader's Digest* begin publication; first all-weather transcontinental highway dedicated; J. Edgar Hoover appointed to head FBI; Mickey Mouse created by Walt Disney; The Roaring Twenties end abruptly with the stock market crash October 29, 1929. California has 5,677,251 people in 1930.

Lieutenant J. W. McCloskey, Curtiss instructor and hydroplane

1921 - Edward, Prince of Wales, addresses 25,000 San Diegans in Balboa Stadium.

1922 - Nine radio stations licensed in San Diego; only KFBC (KGB) remains continuously on air.
County population reaches 100,000.
Barrett Dam completed on Cottonwood Creek.
U. S. Navy dedicates hospital in Balboa Park.

1923 - Lieutenants Oakley Kelly and John Macready make first non-stop transcontinental flight from New York to San Diego in 26 hours and 50 minutes.

1924 - Electric railway line opened to Mission Beach and La Jolla.

1925 - Ryan Airlines establishes first regular air passenger service in the U. S. between Los Angeles and San Francisco.

1926 - Radio station KFSD (KOGO) begins broadcasting from the U. S. Grant Hotel.
Fine Arts Gallery opened in Balboa Park.

1927 - Charles Lindbergh completes his flight from New York to Paris in Spirit of St. Louis, built by Ryan in San Diego.

1928 - Ira C. Copley purchases the *San Diego Union* and *Evening Tribune.*
Lindbergh Field, San Diego's municipal airport, dedicated.

1929 - Presidio Park and Serra Museum dedicated July 16; 160th anniversary of Mission San Diego's founding.
$1.8 million Fox Theater dedicated.

1930 - Dr. Albert Einstein visits San Diego.
County population reaches 209,659; the city numbered 147,995.

1931 - 1940

Franklin D. Roosevelt serves as   president of U. S.; Adolph Hitler becomes chancellor of Germany and Benito Mussolini rises to power in Italy; Congress creates Social Security system; Prohibition ended by 21st amendment; New York World's Fair opens; trans-Atlantic air flights begin; Boulder Dam completed on the Colorado River; Hitler invades Poland.

1931 - San Diego adopts new city charter for city manager form of government.
New San Diego State College campus dedicated.

1932 - San Diego County has 16,000 persons unemployed and 4,000 on relief.
Chamber of Commerce helps Consolidated Aircraft move to San Diego from Buffalo, New York, beginning today's aerospace industry.

1933 - Long Beach earthquake kills 121 persons.

1934 - The California Institute of Technology acquires 160 acres on Mount Palomar to install a telescope.

1935 - El Capitan Dam, capacity — 38 billion gallons, dedicated.
California Pacific International Exposition opened May 28 in Balboa Park.

Gambling banned in Mexico.
Consolidated Aircraft dedicates new plant at Lindbergh Field.
1936 - Federal government approves construction of the County Fair Grounds at Del Mar.
1937 - The Right Reverend Charles Francis Buddy installed as Bishop of the newly created Roman Catholic Diocese of San Diego.
1939 - Metropolitan's Colorado River aqueduct completed to Lake Mathews.
1940 - All American Canal formally dedicated in Imperial Valley.
San Diego County numbers 289,348; city's population reaches 203,341.

La Jolla beach scene, circa 1929

1941 - 1950

U. S. President Franklin Roosevelt dies in his fourth term and is succeeded by Harry Truman; Japan's bombing of Pearl Harbor causes U. S. entry into World War II; rationing of food and other essentials begins; Earl Warren becomes governor of California; Germany surrenders in 1944 and Japan in 1945 after atomic bombing of Hiroshima and Nagasaki; Philippines granted independence; United Nations Charter adopted; India becomes independent and Israel created; U. S. enters Korean War.

1941 - San Diego Naval Air Station begins training pilots for U. S. Air Force (a total of 31,400 during World War II.)
1942 - Western Defense Command removes nearly 2,000 persons of Japanese descent from San Diego to relocation centers.
Wartime housing constructed at Linda Vista.
Consolidated Aircraft merges with Vultee to become Convair.
Camp Pendleton area (Santa Margarita Rancho) purchased by Navy for marine base.
1943 - Chamber of Commerce begins planning San Diego's postwar economy.
1944 - City Manager Walter Cooper killed in airplane accident; Mayor Harley E. Knox injured.
San Diego County Water Authority formed with nine member agencies.
1945 - U. S. ratifies a treaty giving portion of Colorado River water to Mexico.
Voters approve bond issue of $2 million to develop Mission Bay.
San Diego experiences slight recession as World War II ends.
1946 - San Diego County Water Authority annexed to Metropolitan Water District and city of Coronado withdraws.
1947 - San Diego Aqueduct completed to bring Colorado River water to city.
1948 - *San Diego Magazine* begins publication.
The 200-inch Hale telescope completed on Palomar Mountain.
1949 - San Diego broadcasts first television show on Channel 8.
Mission Bay aquatic park formally dedicated.
Portugal donates statue of Juan Rodríguez Cabrillo to stand at Cabrillo National Monument on Point Loma.
University of San Diego receives its charter from state.
1950 - San Diego's population reaches 334,387.

1951 - 1960

Harry Truman and General Dwight D. Eisenhower serve as U. S. presidents; General Douglas MacArthur removed as far-east commander; U. S. Supreme Court bans segregation in education;

NASA organized; jet airline passenger service inaugurated; Fidel Castro takes over government of Cuba; Alaska and Hawaii admitted to Union; Edmund G. "Pat" Brown follows Goodwin J. Knight as California's governor; California's population reached 15,717,204.

1951 - John D. Butler becomes first native San Diegan elected mayor.
       Conversion of tuna clippers to purse seiners begins.
1952 - California Western University opens on Point Loma.
       Carlsbad incorporates as a city.
1953 - Chamber of Commerce urges formation of a unified port district.
1954 - Kearny Mesa industrial center established.
1955 - Bonds voted for construction of the Tenth Avenue Marine Terminal.
       Councilman Charles C. Dail elected mayor.
1956 - General Dynamics takes over Convair.
       Fiesta del Pacífico begins as tourist attraction (it ran four summers).
       Torrey Pines city park becomes California State Park Preserve.
       Campus in San Diego-La Jolla area proposed for the University of California.
       City of Imperial Beach incorporated.
1957 - First Atlas missile built at San Diego successfully test-fired.
1958 - City Council approves zone change to allow May Company department store to be built in Mission Valley.
       Chamber of Commerce leads successful bond issue to establish University of California, San Diego.
1959 - City of Del Mar incorporated.
1960 - A $1.75 billion bond issue for State Water Project approved statewide and supported 4 to 1 by San Diegans.
       Military payroll reaches $280 million, making San Diego second largest military establishment in U. S.
       City population reaches 573,224; county tops million mark at 1,033,011.

Kit Carson School, Linda Vista, 1943

1961 - 1970

John F. Kennedy, Lyndon Johnson and Richard Nixon serve as U. S. president; Peace Corps organized and space program launched; U. S. involvement in Vietnam escalates and antiwar protests rise across nation; civil rights movement gains steady ground; counter-culture is born, and the Beatles cause a musical sensation; the UC Berkeley campus and others erupt with student demonstrations; John Kennedy, Martin Luther King and Robert Kennedy assassinated; Neil Armstrong walks on moon; State Water Project makes headway on Feather River and Ronald Reagan elected governor of California.

1961 - City Council moves to acquire downtown land to centralize public buildings.
1962 - Salk Institute opens in La Jolla.
       Senator Hugo Fisher becomes secretary of State Resources Agency.
       Voters approve $12.6 million in bonds for Mission Bay.
1963 - Frank Curran elected mayor.
       Vista and San Marcos incorporated.
       Chamber of Commerce helps establish Economic Development Corporation.
1964 - Sea World built on Mission Bay.
       University of California opens 1,000-acre campus at La Jolla.
1965 - Charles Dail Community Concourse and Civic Auditorium opened.

1966 - Voters approve $30 million to construct a second pipeline of the second San Diego aqueduct.
Voters approve construction of $27 million sports stadium in Mission Valley.
San Diego Zoo attracts 2.6 million visitors.
Old Town becomes State Historic Park.
1967 - San Diego's Opera company gives American premiere of Hans Weiner Henze's *The Young Lord.*
1968 - Pennsylvania Railroad purchases 1,180 acre Scripps Miramar Ranch for development.
United States International University opens Elliott campus.
1969 - San Diego celebrates 200th birthday July 16.
San Diego Coronado Bay Bridge connecting San Diego with Coronado completed.
1970 - San Diego County's worst brush fires in history blacken large areas of the back country.
San Diego became fourteenth largest city in United States (second largest in California) with 696,769 population.

1971 - 1980

Richard Nixon, Gerald Ford and Jimmy Carter are U. S. presidents; Nixon successfully tours Red China; Watergate causes Nixon to resign; U. S. withdraws from Vietnam; price of oil quadruples with organization of petroleum exporting countries (OPEC); steady inflation felt across nation; Jerry Brown, son of Pat, elected governor of California; Proposition 13 passes in state, severely limiting property taxes; Ronald Reagan obtains Republican nomination for president and California's population reaches an estimated 22,911,000 at end of 1979.

1971 - San Diego State College becomes part of state university system.
The Sherman-Gilbert house becomes first building moved to Heritage Park.
Assemblyman Pete Wilson elected mayor of San Diego.
National University founded in San Diego.
1972 - University of San Diego merges its College for Women and College for Men.
1973 - Point Loma College established by Church of the Nazarene.
Second pipeline of second San Diego aqueduct (Pipeline 4) completed to Miramar Reservoir.
1975 - Centre City Development Corporation founded.
1976 - San Diego participates in U. S. Bicentennial celebration; *Star of India* sails in its honor July 4.
Chamber of Commerce establishes San Diego Motion Picture & Television Bureau.
San Diego experiences serious drought but water supplies sufficient.
1977 - City of Lemon Grove incorporated — fourteenth in county.
Economic Development Corporation revitalized through major industrial marketing plan devised by Chamber of Commerce.
1978 - Mayor Pete Wilson enters race for governor of California.
Fires in Balboa Park destroy Aerospace Museum in Electric Building and Old Globe Theater.
Chamber of Commerce raises $110,000 to rebuild Spirit of Louis replica.
1979 - City population estimated at 833,000; county at 1,767,450
Balboa Stadium demolished over protests from the City Council.
San Diego Chargers win American Football Conference Western Division Championship.

Placing of cross on Church of the Immaculata, University of San Diego, May 1958

San Diego experiences heavy rains and flooding throughout city and county.

1980 - The San Diego Trolley, first link in light rail transit, dedicated.

Mission Bay: 4,600 acres of land and water area, 27 miles of shoreline

Cabrillo celebration: Chamber of Commerce float 1894.

Partners in Progress

Frye, Garrett and Smith Print Shop, circa 1903.

Growing together ...

There were eight of them in 1870,
businessmen who knew they wanted a better San Diego.
They gathered in the back of David Felsenheld's store
at Sixth and F streets to form the San Diego Chamber of Commerce.
It became an official organization January 22.

From the beginning, these men in the private sector led the way.
They wanted to strengthen the economy through free-market enterprise.
They wanted a city in which to live and work —
a city that was pleasant and rewarding.
And they set goals to see that it was accomplished.

They wanted to increase trade,
and they knew that meant increased transportation connections.
They pushed for railroad service,
for a steamship line to San Francisco,
for roads to San Bernardino and Yuma.
Within a few months, they turned out their first promotional pamphlet
and raised $10,000 for a turnpike to Arizona.

For three years, the Felsenheld store was the meeting site.
When they outgrew it, they gathered in the
City Trustees meeting hall.
That lasted until 1883.
The first permanent site was the Consolidated
Bank Building.
There were others — the Elks Building at
Columbia and Broadway
from 1908 to 1931;
the Chamber of Commerce Building at
Columbia and Broadway
from 1931 to 1967;
the Centre City Building at Third and A
streets.

The Elks Building, home of the Chamber of Commerce from 1908 to 1931.

They moved into their twelfth home —
the Chamber Building (formerly Charter Building) at First and C streets —
in December 1978.

During its 110 years, the Chamber had 39 chief executives.
Many are still remembered —
T. C. Macaulay held the post from 1929 to 1946 (except for service in World War II);
John F. Borchers followed from 1954 to 1975;
he was succeeded by Lee Grissom.

The Chamber's strength and vitality has been its membership —
The leaders who backed the Chamber
were men and women who knew what they wanted for the city
and set out to achieve it. One hundred ten Chamber presidents have risen
from these ranks, from Aaron Pauly in 1870 to H. Cushman Dow in 1980.
All the dedicated volunteers represented firms committed to a free marketplace,
a fair profit and a strong economy.
Their financial support has helped sponsor *San Diego: California's Cornerstone.*
Many of their histories are recorded in the book.
Some of them have grown up with the city, others are relatively new.
But they are all dedicated to San Diego — to its economic,
social and cultural growth.
They are all partners in the work of a great city.

Atlas Hotels Inc.

The idea that succeeded

"A man with a new idea is a Crank, until the idea succeeds."

— Mark Twain

To San Diegans in the 1950s, Charlie Brown was not the bumbling hero of the Charles Shultz comic strip, but an enterprising, if seemingly-eccentric, seaman-turned-entrepreneur.

Charles H. Brown had run a number of successful ventures in San Diego, and in 1953 he took a gamble which more than paid off: he opened a 46-room motel in the unlikely location of Mission Valley — a spot off the beaten track.

Despite the dim prognoses offered at the time, that hotel, the Town and Country, would become the cornerstone of a moderate-sized corporation serving the Southwest with quality leisure services and employing some 2,600 persons, of whom 1,800 work in San Diego County.

Brown's vision of Mission Valley proved to be right, and in the next decade others followed his lead. Camino de la Reina became Hotel Circle. Of the hotels there, two had been built by Brown and two more acquired by his companies from competitors.

By the time Charles Brown died in 1966, he left behind an impressive, eclectic consortium: the four hotels in Mission Valley (Hanalei Hotel, Kings Inn, Mission Valley Inn, Town and Country); a fifth hotel in Los Angeles (Carriage Inn); a construction company; three development companies (Mission Valley Development, Sample-Brown Enterprises and Town and Country Development); San Diego's first UHF television station (Channel 39); the city's first cable television company; Courtesy Products Corporation (distributor of Courtesy Coffee to hotels nationwide); and a hotel management company — Atlas Hotels Inc.

When Charles' son, C. Terry Brown, succeeded the interim president in 1968, it became apparent that his loosely-knit inheritance would have to be reorganized in order to remain viable.

Although the hotels were managed by Atlas, they were actually owned through the development companies. The Kings and Carriage Inns were held through Sample-Brown Enterprises; the Mission Valley Inn and undeveloped land south of Interstate 8 were controlled by Mission Valley Development; the Hanalei, Town and Country and undeveloped land north of Interstate 8 by Town and County Development; the television interests by San Diego Telecasters.

There was a lot more country than town to Mission Valley when Charles H. Brown opened the first of Atlas' hotels, the 46-room Town and Country, shown here as it appeared in the early 1950s.

Twenty-five years after it opened, the Town and County sported the dimensions of a small city. If all facilities were filled to maximum capacity, 13,418 persons could be accommodated at receptions in the hotel's meeting and convention rooms, 852 patrons could be seated in the various restaurants and lounges, and more than 3,000 guests could occupy hotel rooms.

Under a sweeping realignment, the three development companies were dissolved and their assets and liabilities assumed by Atlas Hotels, the sole surviving entity. San Diego Telecasters became Omni Video, a wholly-owned subsidiary of Atlas.

There were more changes in the offing. Atlas divested itself of its telecommunications enterprises, and decided to concentrate its efforts on its hotel operations.

The company went public, and $3.6 million was raised through the sale of stock. With this and a $7 million loan, the company built the city's first convention center, which was opened in 1970. As a result, the

company's assets jumped from $10 million to $20 million almost overnight.

In the 1970s, Atlas again expanded. A hotel (the SunBurst in Scottsdale) was purchased in Arizona; another (the Ramada Inn) was leased in San Diego; a third (the Pacifica Hotel in Culver City, California) was run under a long-term management agreement.

Atlas also began to diversify again. It opened a membership health spa in San Diego. It acquired the San Diego based Picnic 'N Chicken fast-food chain and expanded it into the Sacramento area. It opened a theme restaurant (Crystal T's Emporium) in San Diego and acquired Blackbeard's Restaurants in Lahaina (Maui), Hawaii and Newport Beach, California.

By the end of Atlas' silver anniversary year, its holdings included: eight hotels with 2,500 rooms; convention complex and seventeen hotel restaurants and coffee shops; the Picnic 'N Chicken chain; the Atlas Health Club; a seafood restaurant in Hawaii; and three theme restaurants.

In addition to its profit centers, Atlas maintains a number of supporting subsidiary operations, including Atlas Air-Conditioning; Atlas Bakery (which supplies most of the company's breadstuffs); Atlas Courtesy Card (a credit company); Crest Advertising; and Mutual Hotel Supply (a procurement and distribution firm).

The Atlas innovative spirit continues into the 1980s as plans are made which include tripling the number of Picnic 'N Chicken outlets; construction of a ninth hotel as part of San Diego's downtown redevelopment drive; doubling the number of theme restaurants; and expansion of three existing hotels (Hanalei, Mission Valley Inn and Town and Country).

Avco Community Developers, Inc.

Rancho Bernardo making history as a model 'New Town'

Rancho Bernardo Road, looking east, circa 1964.

Rancho Bernardo today.

Twenty-three miles north of downtown San Diego, still within San Diego City limits, a contemporary "city within a city" landmarks a valley filled with historic prominence.

This trend-setting 5,800-acre development of Rancho Bernardo — privately-financed, molded and sculpted by Avco Community Developers, Inc. (ACD) — is applauded by world economists, public officials and fellow developers as a model 'New Town.' Rancho Bernardo balances beauty and function to masterfully serve a range of socio-economic groups from young families to retirees. People from all 50 states and many countries make their homes here.

Rancho Bernardo has long been a coveted spot. During the 18th century, villages of the Kumeyaay Indians lined its San Bernardo River. Spanish explorers arrived and raised some of the county's finest cattle in its knee-high pastures.

In 1847, the Battle of San Pasqual, a turning-point battle of the Mexican-American War, took place nearby. Troops clashed again two days later at Mule Hill, a knoll overlooking Rancho Bernardo. Famed scout Kit Carson brought reinforcements from San Diego to force a Mexican surrender, a victory which opened the doors for California statehood.

After Rancho Bernardo lands opened for public sale, property titles reveal that famous authors, prize home builders, retiring company presidents and men the "San Diego Sun" praised in 1882 as "the great industrialists of our time," bought land in Rancho Bernardo. The valley — with its natural beauty and temperate climate — drew the visionaries.

Recent history holds no exception. In 1961, the rolling grasslands were chosen for the site of today's renowned concept-to-conclusion development, envisioned at its completion as home for 50,000 people in 17,000 homes. The land was purchased and ground was broken in 1963.

Acquired by Avco Corporation in 1968, this new community of Rancho Bernardo, under the leadership of Avco Community Developers, Inc. President R. Barry McComic, gained in recognition as one of the world's finest examples of a privately-planned, financed and developed "New Town."

From the outset, the nation's leading experts in land planning, recreational-facility planning and housing design were tapped to assure that Rancho Bernardo would mature into something much more than just another master-planned development. Painstaking attention was given to the physical, emotional, educational, commercial, recreational and cultural needs of a broad spectrum of potential residents.

The result is impeccably-planned neighborhoods where singles, families and retirees; renters and home buyers; sports enthusiasts and devotees to the more leisurely arts; students and entrepreneurs, all share distinct yet compatible pursuits and lifestyles. ACD has produced a wide variety of housing from luxury custom homes to moderately-priced single-family homes, condominiums, duplexes and apartments.

The success of Rancho Bernardo lies not only in housing plans that encourage a happy coexistence of people at all stages of career and income. From the start, ACD retained a functional perspective about the development, providing funds for facilities and services that a developer usually does not provide — for example, payment in excess of $7 million for a sewage system. Such detail stabilized the "New Town" before its growth and popularity soared.

Rancho Bernardo was built from the core out — from the basics to embellishments. Its logical design makes each neighborhood an adjunct to the other, incorporating shopping centers, recreational facilities — even light industry — within a framework that regards visual aesthetics as highly as it does workability.

The site has earned the attention of several major corporations, bringing to its 635-acre Bernardo Industrial Park a base of "clean" industry. Hewlett-Packard, National Cash Register, the Burroughs Corporation, Oak Industries and America's first Sony plant occupy space here.

The Mercado, a quaint Spanish complex with cobblestoned courtyards that house boutiques and pubs, The Saddle Club and The Rancho Bernardo Inn with its year-round golf and tennis activities are a haven for "snowbird" visitors and residents alike.

Rancho Bernardo has become one of the prized vacation spots of California.

Grand stretches of natural terrain and greenbelts throughout make it a trophy of urban environmental enhancement. Strict architectural and land use controls insure its

beautification for generations to come. Under Avco Community Developers' careful direction, and reflecting its residents' pride and sense of community, Rancho Bernardo is a tribute to its historic valley and is one of San Diego's richest assets.

California First Bank

A history of firsts in San Diego

In 1883 when San Diego was a rough and tumble whaling town with almost 3,000 residents, Jacob Gruendike, owner of the town's leading general store, decided to branch out into banking.

Gruendike started the First National Bank of San Diego (California First Bank's predecessor) with a capital investment of $50,000. First National opened for business in a one-story brick building on the corner of Fifth and E Streets on July 2.

Gruendike's First National was not San Diego's first bank, but it outlasted competitors to become the "oldest, largest and strongest commercial bank in San Diego," as an early motto proclaimed.

From the very start, First National was to be "first" in many areas. One of Gruendike's initial ventures was to pioneer the financing of fishermen and boat builders — two of San Diego's most important trades. In 1885, the Santa Fe Railroad came to town, linking San Diego with the east for the first time. Again, First National was there first with the financing.

Around the turn of the century, when the bank's deposits were nearing $1 million, First National became the first bank to finance automobiles in San Diego County.

The year 1910 saw San Diego's population reach 40,000, with First National growing right alongside the city. In 1917, the bank's growth caused its move to a new, bustling location at San Diego's main intersection, Fifth and Broadway. The first electric lights in town illuminated Broadway and an electric streetcar connected the Plaza and Old Town.

That same year, sugar magnate John D. Spreckels purchased controlling interest in the bank. At one time, he owned most of downtown San Diego and a good part of Coronado, the San Diego Gas and Electric Company, the streetcar and ferry systems, the San Diego Union and three hotels.

In 1921, First National became the county's first bank to offer neighborhood branch offices. Its deposits had grown to over $15 million.

Panic swept the country in the '30s as

The original First National Bank building on the corner of Fifth and E Streets. 1883.

The lobby of the Fifth and E office, featuring marble, brass and mahogany. 1883.

depositors rushed to their banks to withdraw cash and gold. Within a short time, 5,000 banks had failed. Interest rates on savings accounts dropped to 1 percent and the prime rate plunged to 1½ percent.

Despite this, First National not only survived, it even managed to continue its

pioneering in financing. In 1936, it became the first bank in San Diego County to finance private airplane ownership.

By 1942, First National's deposits were nearly $56 million. In this year, it became the first bank west of the Rockies to establish a common trust fund. During the next decade, First National was the first bank in San Diego County to install electronic data processing equipment.

First National experienced its most dramatic growth in the '60s. In 1966, its headquarters moved into a modern, 25-story building — just two blocks away from the location it had occupied for almost 50 years. Today, California First's San Diego headquarters is housed in this building at Fifth and B Streets.

In 1969, First National became the principal subsidiary of Southern California First National Corporation — a one-bank holding company — and was renamed Southern California First National Bank.

The Bank of Tokyo of California, a subsidiary of The Bank of Tokyo, Ltd., acquired Southern California First National Bank in 1975. Southern California First's 75 branches were teamed with the Bank of Tokyo of California's 25 branches to form California First Bank.

The Bank of Tokyo of California was established in 1952, with offices in San Francisco and Los Angeles. Its parent institution, The Bank of Tokyo, Ltd., evolved from the Yokohama Specie Bank, which had opened a San Francisco office in 1886, three years after Gruendike founded his First National Bank of San Diego.

California First offers customers the convenience of full service banking throughout California, plus international expertise through its affiliation with The Bank of Tokyo, Ltd.

In 1977, California First Bank dedicated a new, 22-story headquarters building in San Francisco.

The state's seventh largest bank in terms of deposits, California First Bank now has more than 100 offices throughout the state and four facilities overseas. It has come a long way from Gruendike's one-story brick building at Fifth and E.

Copley Newspapers

San Diego's newspapers — a history of family dedication

The San Diego Union moved to this building at Fourth and D (now Broadway) from Old Town. The photograph, looking south, was taken from the Horton House which was located on the site of the present U.S. Grant Hotel. That is the Plaza in the right foreground. Note camera and tripod lower right. The Union was published here from July 1, 1870 to June 1, 1878.

The San Diego Union and The Evening Tribune are part of the story of the Copley Newspapers, a story that was begun by a father, passed along to a son, and is being continued by a wife and her son.

Colonel Ira C. Copley founded the organization that was to become The Copley Press, Inc., in Illinois when he purchased The Aurora Daily Beacon in 1905. Over the years he expanded his group of newspapers in two of the nation's key states, Illinois and California, to such an extent that individually and collectively they have grown to become an important voice in journalism.

In addition to the two newspapers in San Diego, Copley newspapers are located in Los Angeles County, California, and in Illinois. Also, the newspaper organization operates Copley News Service, the world's largest supplemental news agency. CNS provides in-depth news coverage and diversified features to more than 2,000 newspapers in this country and abroad.

Colonel Copley died in 1947 at the age of 83. Upon his death, his son James S. Copley took over the direction of the newspapers. He became chairman of the corporation in 1952 and sole owner of the newspaper group in 1959. When he died in 1973, he left behind a testimony to a man who had made a lasting impact on the American press and the American way of life.

Jim Copley was succeeded by his wife, Helen K. Copley, who today is chairman and chief executive officer of The Copley Press, Inc., and publisher of *The San Diego Union* and *The Evening Tribune*. Her son, David, serves as assistant to the president of the corporation, Hubert L. Kaltenbach, and as a director of The Copley Press, Inc.

The San Diego Union is a pioneer newspaper. It was founded in 1868 and took its name from the conflict fought to *unify* the nation, the Civil War.

The *Union*, a morning newspaper, and the *Tribune*, an evening newspaper, were purchased by the Copley organization in 1928. Together, they became the first two of a long history of Copley Newspapers in California.

In 1973, the *Union* and the *Tribune* moved from their downtown location into a new

In 1973, the Union *and* Tribune *moved into this $24 million facility in Mission Valley.*

$24 million facility in an area that has become a prime artery of the business and tourist life of San Diego — Mission Valley.

The Evening Tribune is, in every sense, the arch competitor of the *Union*. The two newspapers are located on different sides of the same building, but in the operation of their editorial departments they are completely separate. They have different editors and different staffs. At times they back opposing political candidates and differ in their recommendations on ballot propositions.

The *Tribune* was established in 1895. In 1939, after it had become part of the Copley organization, it absorbed the *San Diego Sun* and became the *Tribune-Sun*. In 1950 it acquired the name, features and circulation

list of the *San Diego Daily Journal* and once again became *The Evening Tribune*.

In their news policies, *The San Diego Union* and *The Evening Tribune* are committed to the highest standards of professional journalism. They seek to present an objective and restrained portrayal of the news without innuendo, sensationalism or any indication of the personal views of the writer, the publisher or the editorial policy of the newspapers.

The foundation of the Copley Newspapers' editorial policy is a dedication to the strength, endurance and welfare of the United States of America, its people and its institutions. The newspapers are basically independent in their initiative, which characterizes the American spirit.

In speaking of the newspaper organization, Helen Copley has said:

"Copley newspapers today face the future in a position of economic strength and continued dedication to the principles of good journalism and the American private enterprise system.

"We are a unique newspaper organization, not only because we are privately owned, but also because in all of our areas of publication we serve strong, dynamic markets. We bring to these markets, which include some 50 communities, the heritage of an established newspaper family and the dedication of concerned, corporate citizenship."

Del Mar Thoroughbred Club

Bing's baby is a giant — and still growing

Bing Crosby hadn't been to Del Mar racetrack in more than 30 years when he dropped in unexpectedly on that quiet July day in 1977.

A visitor to the area because his son was competing in the National Junior Golf Championship at nearby Torrey Pines course, he was given a nostalgic tour of the racetrack of which he was the guiding founder and its first president.

"I'm amazed at how beautiful it is," he said. "Just look what's been done with the growth and expansion. The development has been great. And the infield, what a change. It's as fine as any track in America."

Crosby's words complimented Del Mar Thoroughbred Club, which initiated a 20-year lease of the facilities with the State of California in 1970. Under its banner, the picturesque seaside course has become one of the country's 10 most popular tracks.

Indeed, the 1979 season was Del Mar's

With newsreel cameras there to record the historic moment, Del Mar racetrack opened July 3, 1937. Bing Crosby, guiding founder and first president, was on hand to welcome the track's first customer, Mrs. W. R. Richardson of Long Beach, through the gates, inset.

finest, attracting 750,311 patrons during its 43-day stand for a daily average of 17,449, seventh highest nationally. Mutuel handle totaled $115,953,710 for an average of $2,696,598, fifth in America.

As Crosby strolled the grounds, his mind must have recalled the days when Thoroughbred racing at Del Mar was only an idea.

In 1936, Crosby, nearing the zenith of his career, spent his leisure as something of a country squire at a newly-purchased ranch in Rancho Santa Fe. An acquaintance, William A. Quigley, a resident of La Jolla, approached Crosby with the notion that racing could prosper at Del Mar. Both were aware of the early success of Santa Anita which opened on Christmas Day, 1934.

They submitted a proposition to the 22nd District Agricultural Association, operator of the San Diego County Fair and proprietor of the state-owned fairgrounds.

Essentially, the deal evolved as a racing franchise in exchange for the loan from Crosby and associates of enough money to construct a grandstand, clubhouse, racing strip and stable accommodations. The loan would be repaid from a percentage of profits.

In early May, 1936, at a meeting at Warner Bros. studios in Burbank, the Del Mar Turf Club was formed, with Crosby heading the board as president and Pat O'Brien named vice president. An offering of stock in the fledgling enterprise at $100 per share was met cooly by prospective investors who questioned if a track situated 100 miles from the major population mecca of Los Angeles could survive.

Del Mar's management team in the track's infancy was headed by, from left, William A. Quigley, director of racing; Bing Crosby, president, and Pat O'Brien, vice president.

Nonetheless, equity was acquired enabling the new company to sign a 10-year lease for $100,000. Six weeks after signing of the lease, however, the 22nd District ran out of funds for building. Borrowing against life insurance policies, Crosby and O'Brien loaned more than $400,000 at no interest, the money to be repaid from rents due.

With paint still wet and confusion rife, Del Mar opened in Hollywood premiere style July 3, 1937. Dressed casually in yachting cap and loose-fitting sports shirt, with pipe in place, Crosby personally greeted the first customer when the gates opened at 10:40 a.m.

Four hours later, the now nattily-attired Crosby addressed the assembled 15,000 fans:

"We hope you enjoy the meeting — and have a measure of success at the pay-off windows."

In the more than 40 years since that memorable day, there have been countless highlights created by many of the Turf's greatest stars. Among historic moments are Seabiscuit's 1938 triumph over Ligaroti in their $25,000 winner-take-all match race, an event which put Del Mar "on the map;" John Longden's 4,871st winner which bettered Sir Gordon Richard's record for career victories in 1956; and Bill Shoemaker's 6,033rd win which eclipsed Longden in 1970.

Crosby sacrificed his interest in Del Mar in 1946 due to show business commitments, resulting in a succession of managements before Del Mar Thoroughbred Club. The latter, a non-dividend paying corporation, has a board of directors comprised of notable breeders and owners who serve without remuneration, dedicated to promotion of the sport.

Crosby and his fun-loving cohorts set a style — relaxed and friendly — which became a tradition. And, every day, before the first and after the last races, his mellow voice is heard, singing the song which he co-wrote, "Where the Turf Meets the Surf."

FedMart*

Growing by innovation... meeting the challenges of the '80s

An abandoned warehouse served as the first location for a small membership store which offered federal employees a mart in which to shop for quality merchandise at low prices. This was how "FedMart" derived its name. From its humble beginning in 1954 at Main Street and Division in downtown San Diego, it grew into one of the nation's largest mass merchandisers.

FedMart's second store opened in 1955 in Phoenix, and a third opened shortly thereafter in San Antonio. But FedMart began its commitment early to the San Diego economy. In 1958 a second store in San Diego opened in Kearny Mesa at Convoy and Othello Streets. This facility still serves area shoppers today, while a portion of the building was used as the corporation's cen-

FedMart's flagship store on Sports Arena Boulevard is the third largest store on one floor in the United States.

185

tral headquarters and warehouse for many years.

The '60s saw more San Diego FedMarts open and the dropping of its membership requirement. The company grew in stature, became a public company, and in 1969 its stock began trading on the American Stock Exchange. Today FedMart stock is also traded on the Pacific Stock Exchange and the company has more than 3,700 shareholders across the U.S.

To meet the expanding needs of Fed-Mart's growing chain of stores, the company constructed a 300,000 square foot distribution center north of San Diego on Miramar Road in 1971 to service its stores in California and Arizona. This is still a major company facility and the base for part of FedMart's large fleet of trucks.

In 1975 FedMart had 44 stores spanning California, Arizona, New Mexico and Texas in the rapidly growing "Sunbelt," with annual sales of $381 million. That year, a West German retailer named Hugo Mann acquired controlling interest in Fed-Mart. Shortly thereafter, an extensive remodeling and construction program began as existing stores were upgraded with new fixtures and new display and merchandising techniques, modern materials handling equipment and sophisticated computer operations.

In early 1978 a major expansion took place with the company's acquisition of 26 large stores from other retailers. Within a

FedMart Corporate Headquarters on Rosecrans Street in Point Loma.

year most of these were completely remodeled and reopened as full line FedMart stores. As a result, FedMart doubled in size to a total of more than 5,000,000 square feet of store building space in 68 stores. Five of the acquired stores were located in San Diego. The store on Rosecrans Street became the corporate headquarters in 1978, and now employs more than 600 people.

Also located in San Diego is the company's flagship store on Sports Arena Boulevard. This facility became the third largest store on one floor in the U.S. after it was expanded to 208,000 square feet in 1979. In nearby Mission Valley is FedMart's photofinishing plant, operating under the name "TruColor Foto, Inc." This facility employs 130 people and produces in excess of 40 million color prints annually.

The company's strategy is spearheaded by

an aggressive merchandise mix that offers one-stop shopping with 30-plus departments under one roof, including a complete supermarket. Both food and general merchandise are checked out through electronic cash registers at the front of the stores. This approach to merchandising is eminently suited to the need to save consumers time and gasoline; it also positions the firm well to meet the opportunities of the new decade. FedMart also vigorously pursues a policy of minimizing operating costs in order to keep prices low on quality products. To meet this objective, it has pioneered new techniques of product presentation, distribution, computerized ordering and inventory control.

Another step recently initiated by Fed-Mart to meet the pressure of inflation on consumers was the introduction in 1979 of a full line of no-frills food and household generic products called "Bright Yellow Wrap," FedMart was the first retail chain to bring this type of merchandise to San Diego.

Today, FedMart is one of San Diego's largest employers, with more than 4,000 employees in San Diego and 11,000 employees throughout the company. Its annual sales exceed one billion dollars, making it a leader in the industry, and one of the largest firms making its home in the city. And FedMart, like San Diego, continues to grow with confidence and energy directed toward meeting the challenges of the '80s.

Foodmaker, Inc.

A leader in food service innovation

The new-found affluence of the '50s created an environment in which consumers fervently embraced innovative new products and services: The automobile provided unprecedented access to new experiences and markets; and with the postwar populace mobilized, speed and time assumed a new importance.

Food service across the country responded to these trends with the drive-in restaurant. San Diego not only kept pace but offered its answer to those demanding fast-food service, the "drive-thru."

The concept was introduced by Robert O. Peterson, proprietor of the successful Oscar's, in 1951 with the opening of the first Jack In The Box. Located at 63rd and El Cajon, Jack In The Box offered a limited menu with the traditional American hamburger for just 18 cents. Customers could

The Boathouse, located on scenic Harbor Island, San Diego.

order from the convenience of their cars through speaker devices and be on their way within minutes, order in hand. Or, they could order from the service window and dine on the outdoor patio in the mild Southern California climate.

In 1968, Ralston Purina Company of St.

Louis purchased and consolidated Jack In The Box, a Commissary division, and several other businesses to form Foodmaker, Inc., headquartered in San Diego. The move made regional expansion of Jack In The Box a reality and by the end of the '70s decade more than 800 units were operating,

Jack In The Box, located on Mission Gorge Road, San Diego.

concentrated in the western United States.

The innovative customer service that successfully launched the Jack In The Box system was just one of many original ideas which marked its historic growth. New products have made possible a variety of combinations for breakfast, lunch and dinner from scrambled eggs, pancakes and French toast to a deluxe line of sandwiches and Mexican-style food. Jack In The Box was the first in the industry to offer onion rings, a steak sandwich and breakfast sandwich.

The Ralston Purina food service interests were further diversified in the early '70s. Continental Restaurant Systems (CRS) was formed as a subsidiary corporation to operate 7 theme restaurants — the Jolly Ox, Tortilla Flats, Hungry Hunters in San Diego, and Boar's Head, The Dock and Tortilla Flats in the Midwest — plus the Boat House and Stag & Hound restaurants. CRS merged with Foodmaker, Inc. in 1975 and became an operating division. In just a few short years, Foodmaker, Inc. was operating 65 restaurants in the Midwest and West under 14 popular themes, serving a variety of menus emphasizing beef and seafood, and combinations in a fine dining atmosphere. Some of these popular restaurants serving San Diego are: The Boat House, Hungry Hunter, Monterey Whaling Company, Monterey Jack's and London Opera House.

Foodmaker's involvement with the culture and people of California, specifically San Diego, has been a deep commitment over the years. Its donations to philanthropic and educational foundations such as the San Diego Symphony, Zoo and San Diego State University, its sponsorship of events such as the Jack In The Box Invitational track and field meet have brought countless benefits to the public.

Foodmaker, Inc. is a part of the very large customer service industry. Its business is providing food, atmosphere and service to the public through its numerous restaurant facilities. From sit-down dining to fast-food drive-thru dining, Foodmaker, Inc. continues in the innovative spirit in which it began nearly 30 years ago.

General Atomic Company

"A multitude of applications in the service of society"

The late John Jay Hopkins, chairman of General Dynamics, (on platform) and Dr. Frederic de Hoffmann, (extreme right) host 1956 groundbreaking ceremonies for General Atomic facilities on Torrey Pines Mesa.

Those were dedicatory words of Dr. Niels Bohr, Nobel Laureate and a giant in the emerging new world of nuclear energy, for General Atomic's handsome new research center on Torrey Pines Mesa. The date, June 25, 1959, followed by some three years the founding of General Atomic (then a division of General Dynamics Corporation) by John Jay Hopkins, chairman of GD, and Dr. Frederic de Hoffmann, General Atomic's first president.

Before the move to its 400-acre headquarters on a lee slope of the Torrey Pines cliffs, General Atomic's home, appropriately, was in an unused schoolhouse on Barnard Street in Pt. Loma, where classrooms had become offices and places of research.

By June 1959, General Atomic was already well along the path it had set for itself in the still-young nuclear industry. Its staff was nearly 700. The first TRIGA research reactors had been built, and one had even been operated at the 1958 "Atoms for Peace" conference in Switzerland.

Scientists and engineers were working on the High Temperature Gas-cooled Reactor

concept for a nuclear power plant with safety, economy and environmental advantages not possible with other systems then already further along. A group of 52 electric utility companies became sponsors and in the summer of 1959 Congress authorized the prototype 40,000-kilowatt HTGR at Peach Bottom, Pennsylvania.

General Atomic's pioneering work in controlled fusion also was under way, supported then by 11 Texas utility companies. Another project, with sponsorship from the U.S. government, was Project Orion, involving the use of nuclear energy pulses for

Aerial view of General Atomic's 425-acre headquarters and research facilities, where more than 2000 persons work at development of advanced energy systems.

space propulsion.

The employee and consultant roster was a "Who's Who" in nuclear science: Bohr, Edward Teller, Harold Urey, Ted Taylor, Hans Bethe, Lothar Nordheim, Peter Fortescue, Ed Creutz.

Through the decade of the 1960s GA continued to grow and to broaden its horizons. In 1965 it contracted to build a commercial-size HTGR plant for Public Service Company of Colorado and looked at the application of gas-cooled reactor technology to nuclear breeders.

Two of the most important events in GA's history occurred in 1967. Peach Bottom achieved operational status, proving the viability of the HTGR concept. And late in the year Gulf Oil Corporation acquired General Atomic. In 1970, Gulf General Atomic became a part of Gulf Energy and Environmental Systems Company, which was headed by C. A. Rolander, Jr., a GA veteran with nuclear power experience dating from the wartime Manhattan Project. One year later the company entered the nuclear power plant market on a fully commercial basis and in a few years had commitments for 10 HTGR systems.

In 1973, Gulf sold a half interest in GE & ES to a member company of the Royal Dutch/Shell Group and the name became General Atomic Company. W. W. (Bill) Finley, a Gulf executive with considerable overseas experience, became president of GAC.

During these years, General Atomic's versatile staff brought forth numerous innovative ideas. A membrane that applied osmosis to the purification of brackish water became ROGA (Reverse Osmosis General Atomic). This technology was later sold to Universal Oil Products. Another major product resulted when GA metallurgists discovered the dense graphite coating for HTGR fuel was bio-compatible and developed Pyrolite and a family of artificial heart valves and other prosthetic devices. This business was sold in 1979 to Intermedics, Inc., also of San Diego. The use of very strong magnetic fields to shape metal evolved from GA's fusion experiments and became Magneform, a business now licensed to another company.

The general downturn in public and business attitudes toward nuclear energy forced a realignment of General Atomic's business goals in the mid 1970s and it was decided to withdraw the HTGR from the commercial area. Power plant contracts were terminated and GAC returned to a strong research and development position with R&D efforts covering the spectrum of nuclear fission and fusion and solar energy as well, with support from industry, government and overseas interests. A fixed-mirror solar concentrator developed by GAC is part of the nation's first demonstration of electric power production using a solar heat source. Commercially, the company applied its expertise in electronics to become one of the largest manufacturers of nuclear instrumentation and producing equipment for automated self-serve gasoline stations and bulk petroleum product distributors.

In early 1979, Dr. Harold Agnew, former director of the Los Alamos Scientific Laboratory, became president of General Atomic. Later in the year, the company signed agreements with the U.S. Department of Energy and the Japan Atomic Energy Research Institute, making the Doublet III fusion project an international quest for this most important energy source of the future.

With the world's conventional energy sources dwindling ever more rapidly and of uncertain supply, General Atomic's 2000 employees and diverse activities are fulfillment of Professor Bohr's dedicatory prophesy.

General Dynamics Corporation

A heritage of aviation leadership

Some 30,000 of San Diego's 170,000 residents turned out on October 20, 1935 to welcome Consolidated Aircraft to the "city of aviation firsts."

Under founder Major Reuben Hollis Fleet, Consolidated had been formed 12 years earlier through a merger of Gallaudet Aircraft and Dayton-Wright. After moving the company from Rhode Island to Buffalo, N.Y. in 1924, Fleet decided that San Diego was the answer to his need for year-round flying weather and ice-free seaplane testing waters.

Consolidated — which in 1943 would become Consolidated-Vultee Aircraft Corporation and, in 1954, the Convair Division of General Dynamics — began in a 300 by 900-foot factory bordering Lindbergh Field and built on a wet San Diego Bay tideland. Within six years, the company doubled its floor area 16½ times. Today, that original building is a small part of the company's spacious Lindbergh Field plant, and is a half-mile distance from bay waters.

Since beginning as a builder of primary training planes in the '20s, Convair has produced a wide range of military and commercial aircraft.

During World War II, Convair operations expanded to 13 divisions in ten states — with a peak employment exceeding 101,000 (45,000 in San Diego). Thirty years later, founder Reuben Fleet would recall:

"Across our largest building in San Diego we painted our motto 'NOTHING SHORT OF RIGHT IS RIGHT' and improved the quality of our products to the point where they earned an unexcelled record for strength, ease of maintenance, reliability and safety."

Between Pearl Harbor and VE Day, the company delivered more than 33,000 military aircraft, including thousands of B-24 Liberators (6,726 built in San Diego), L-5 Sentinel liaison aircraft, PBY Catalina and PB2Y Coronado flying boats, BT-13 Valiant trainers and PB4Y Privateer patrol bombers.

In March 1953 General Dynamics Corp. acquired a controlling interest in Convair from the Atlas Corp. which, in 1947, had purchased the majority shares from Avco Manufacturing (formerly Aviation Manufacturing Co.). Convair was officially merged into General Dynamics in 1954.

Post-war activities at Convair included production of the Air Force F-102A Delta Dagger and F-106A Delta Dart supersonic interceptors, as well as experimental aircraft such as the XFY-1 Pogo vertical takeoff fighter and the XF2Y-1 Sea Dart, first delta-wing seaplane. The commercial Convair-Liners, of which more than 1,000 were built at Lindbergh Field, became the standard medium range transport for some 40 domestic and foreign airlines in the late '40s and '50s.

At the same time, Convair's plant in Pomona began production on Tartar and Terrier, two shipboard tactical guided missiles which had their genesis in San Diego. In this dawn of the space age, Convair marked its 25th birthday in 1948 with the first launch of the MX-774, forerunner to the giant Atlas, world's first intercontinental ballistic missile. While the original MX-774 program stalled for lack of funding, the missile technology inherited from it was resurrected in 1951 when the U.S. Govern-

Tomahawk cruise missile during testing.

ment evinced interest in rocket studies. The program took on a "crash" status in 1954 and on Dec. 17, 1957, Convair's first Atlas thundered into the skies at Cape Canaveral.

In later years, Atlas played a double role — as an ICBM and as a launch vehicle for the National Aeronautics and Space Administration and Air Force programs. In its first two decades of operation, Atlas successfully lofted some 400 payloads. Another Convair product, the high-energy, upper-stage Centaur booster, was first used in 1963 and has since combined with Atlas for a long record of successes. In 1973, the Atlas-Centaur combination sent Pioneer 11 on its dramatic probes of Jupiter and, more recently, Saturn.

Today, San Diego operations of General Dynamics' Convair Division embrace facilities at three major plants and four specialized test sites. These facilities cover more than 10,000 acres with more than six million square feet, representing a capital investment of more than $120 million.

Convair's Kearny Mesa plant includes executive and administrative offices, as well as engineering, laboratory and test facilities. Manufacturing at Kearney Mesa includes work on three versions of the cruise missile, one of the nation's high priority defense programs. Adaptable to launch from land, sea, air and underwater, the cruise missile has the potential for becoming one of the longest-term programs to date at the division.

At the company's Lindbergh Field plant, fuselage sections for the wide-bodied tri-jet DC-10 are built and shipped to the Long Beach plant of McDonnell Douglas for final assembly. Convair also produces fuselages for the Air Force tanker/cargo KC-10.

San Diego is the home for two other divisions of General Dynamics: DatagraphiX, Inc., and the Electronics Division.

DatagraphiX, worldwide leader in the computer output microfilm (COM) industry, has its headquarters and other facilities in the San Diego area. The General Dynamics subsidiary manufactures a broad range of products here for generating and retrieving computer-generated data on microfilm.

The Electronics Division of General Dynamics, co-located with Convair at Kearny Mesa and at Lindbergh Field, develops and manufactures electronic systems for military and government users. Among current programs are avionics test equipment for the F-16 multirole fighter (built by GD's Fort Worth Division) and range measuring systems for the Army, Navy and Air Force.

The M. H. Golden Company

Partners in building America's finest city

The Old Globe Theatre in Balboa Park was built in 1935 in 28 working days.

There are few names more synonymous with San Diego than "Golden." While the name conjures up many of the images that describe "America's Finest City," Golden also has another familiar meaning in San Diego: Construction.

For three generations, the Golden family has placed its indelible mark on hundreds of San Diego County cornerstones, ranging from public and private buildings to military installations and highways. Today, the M.H. Golden Company is a leading Southern California general contracting, construction management and community development firm.

The story began in 1927 when Morley H. Golden founded the company with a handful of Navy contracts and a payroll usually consisting of only a carpenter, laborer and Golden himself. Partly due to the Navy's high expectations and requirements, the M. H. Golden Construction Company's reputation for integrity and quality craftsmanship became widespread in San Diego. Although the annual work volume in early 1930 was about $300,000, it quickly increased to $1 million by the end of the same year. By mid-1945 the annual volume reached nearly $6 million and today it exceeds $50 million.

It was Golden's meticulous attention to detail that soon led to other types of contracts. St. Patrick's Church and Sacred Heart Church, both built in 1929, are examples of the company's highly detailed and quality work, as is the Elks Club at Fourth and Cedar, now the law school of United States International University. The Mayan architecture of the Federal Building was completed in 30 working days by Golden in 1935 as San Diego rushed to prepare for the California Pacific International Exposition. In that year, Golden also built the replica of England's Old Globe Theatre with 165 men in only 28 working days.

By 1945, the Golden Company had built more than 200 structures and was firmly established as the largest Navy and marine contractor in San Diego. Yet it never limited itself to any one type of construction. For example, the firm built the San Diego Police Department headquarters and jail as well as the Skyroom atop the El Cortez Hotel. It built the post office, the Coast Guard base and Sweetwater Dam in San Diego, along with two naval facilities in San Francisco. It was the Navy work that led the company into heavy marine and bridge construction, including piers as well as an ex-

The San Diego Masonic Temple.

The San Diego Union/Tribune Building in Mission Valley.

tensive water filtration plant.

Civilian and military construction continued to be the company's mainstay after World War II and through the Korean war. In 1956, Morley H. Golden retired and turned the company leadership over to his son, Robert. Prospects for added business were expanded as the company launched simultaneous forays into new construction fields, new markets, innovative internal management systems and computer technology.

A system of project management was initiated that provided full Construction Management (CM) services long before CM became a recognized facet of contemporary development. (Construction Management involves coordinating the activities of the builder, developer and architect on a project.)

Also, the company expanded its base of operations beyond California to the East Coast, Midwest, Southwest and Hawaii. It applied computerized technologies to nearly all its internal and external systems and services. By the end of the 1950s and through today, the company had assumed the posture of a major general contractor as well as developer-owner.

In 1976, Robert Golden's son, Morley R., became company president and the firm earned acclaim for a $5 million planned residential development, Lake Helix. A separate Construction Management Division was established which managed the construction of the Mira Mesa, Junipero Serra Junior/Senior High Schools and Oxnard Community College. To its long repertoire of building projects were added several hospitals, banks and high-rise office buildings.

Today, the M. H. Golden Company continues its growth as an innovator in the building trades industry and as a partner in San Diego's dynamic future. Its principles of integrity and quality craftsmanship combined with a progressive spirit have become a tradition, reflected throughout America's Finest City.

Home Federal Savings & Loan Association of San Diego

Company built on the foundation of liberties

Home Federal's founder, Charles K. Fletcher, never intended to go into business. He was more interested in politics and diplomatic service. His father, Colonel Ed Fletcher, was a state senator who felt he, too, was destined for politics.

Although many people told him he would be smarter to first try business and then go into the political arena, he was stubborn in his personal commitment — until the Depression hit and the Homeowners Loan Act was initiated to help people survive the times.

One section of the act created the Federal Savings and Loan Insurance Corporation. With an idea in mind, Fletcher took a two-week vacation in San Diego to explore possibilities — and ended up taking out an application to charter his own business, Home Federal Savings and Loan.

"I named it Home because I had always liked that word," he explained. "I loved my home. The articles by which all federal savings and loans are born use the words 'home ownership' and 'thrift.' I still believe the home is the foundation of our liberties."

Fletcher opened his office in a corner of his father's place of business, borrowing a desk and chair. He started with $2,000 of his own and $7,500 from 50 San Diegans pledged to support his venture. He then phoned everyone he knew, hired a secretary and began building the business. That was in 1934.

Now Home Federal has more than 75 branches scattered throughout California, with more than 2,300 employees.

The first Home Federal office was opened in a corner of founder C. K. Fletcher's father's place of business. Charlie Fletcher borrowed a desk and telephone and went to work.

1938-55

Home Federal later moved to its own office on Seventh Avenue, where it was based for 17 years.

Fletcher, now retired, admits he didn't have any idea his project would grow to such great proportions. He expected it to be a profitable venture and insured that by bringing in the best personnel he could find. He wanted his employees to feel they were part of the family.

Home Federal, now headed by Fletcher's son, Kim, still prides itself on its family philosophy. Employees, including top management, are encouraged to remain on a first-name basis. The Home Federal policy is still based on promoting from within and providing educational programs to help employees achieve their goals.

Charlie's son, Kim, joined Home Federal in 1950, beginning his career as a teller, then working into loans. In those days, tellers performed a variety of functions and were familiar with many aspects of the financial business. Home Federal was still a small office run by a handful of people. In 1955, a new office was built on the corner of Seventh and Broadway, but the business had outgrown it by the time it moved. A year later, the first branch at North Park opened, with about one added each year after that. In the early '60s Home Tower was built.

In those early years, services were limited, so Home Federal's success depended greatly on the home and family philosophy with which it was born.

"We had no frills," says Kim, who was appointed executive vice president in 1959 and assumed the duties of president in 1964. "We gave away matches, a few counter statements, but not much else. We've added so many services over the years and I see more on the way. We'll be branching further and further into Home Federal country."

In the immediate future, he predicts further branching in a few areas outside San Diego County, with much of Home Federal's branching happening outside the county within two years. There still remain

Kim Fletcher

holes to fill in Los Angeles and Orange counties for Home Federal, as well as extension into surrounding communities. Most of the branching is expected to be in areas where Home Federal already has a foothold.

Home Federal is now the third largest federally-chartered savings and loan in the nation; sixth largest savings and loan overall.

"Credit has to go where credit is due," Kim adds. "It has to go to the people who carried it on and did — and do — a marvelous job... and to Home Federal's customers."

Hotel del Coronado

A resort that would be "the talk of the Western world."

From the top of the San Diego-Coronado Bridge, visitors can look across the Coronado Peninsula to the Pacific Ocean. Dominating the skyline is an intriguing Victorian castle-like structure; this is the world renowned Hotel del Coronado.

Generally considered to be the last of the extravagantly conceived seaside resort hotels, it stands as a monument to the past with its turrets, cupolas, hand carved pillars, and magnificent Victorian gingerbread. In recognition of its architectural beauty and historical significance, the famed hostelry has been designated as an historical landmark by the City of Coronado, the County of San Diego, the State of California, and in 1977 was selected by the Department of the Interior as a National Historical Landmark. The Del has also been listed in the National Register of Historic American Places and has been included in nearly every significant list of America's finest resort hotels.

Before the hotel was built, the Coronado Peninsula was uninhabited except for jackrabbits and coyotes. The entire tract of land — more than 4,100 acres — was valued at $1,000 (25¢ an acre!) prior to 1870. Suddenly people began to realize the potential of the area and property values skyrocketed. By 1885, when Elisha Babcock of Indiana and H. L. Story of Chicago purchased the peninsula, the acreage was valued at $110,000. Even at that price, Babcock realized that he had gotten a fantastic deal. As he looked over the land, he daydreamed. It was then he decided to build on the Coronado Peninsula a resort hotel that would be the "talk of the Western world."

Railroad architects James, Watson, and Merrit Reid were commissioned to design the great resort. Construction was hastily begun in March of 1887. A great many obstacles had to be overcome to permit the completion of Babcock's dream. Laborers were recruited in the San Francisco area and transportation systems (both a railroad and ferry boat system) were set up to facilitate the movement of workers and supplies to the work site. Working mostly from rough drawings and verbal instructions the immense 3½ million square foot building was sufficiently completed to permit opening the hotel only eleven months later, February 19, 1888. Another two years, however, were required to complete all the finish work on the structure. The cost of building and furnishing the hotel was approximately $1 million.

The first guest to sign the register was Nelson Morris, the cattle king. Since then the hotel's guest register has grown into an autograph collector's dream. Early visitors included the Tiffanys, Armours, duPonts,

Elisha S. Babcock, right, whose dream became "the talk of the Western world." The hotel under construction below.

Main entrance, Hotel del Coronado — when Sarah Bernhardt arrived, she had only one word for it — "Charmente!"

Astors, and Vanderbilts who claimed entire sections of the Del as "home" for months at a time. Other famous visitors included Thomas Edison, who designed the hotel's original electrical system, Ella Wheeler Wilcox, William Jennings Bryan, and U.S. Presidents: Harrison, McKinley, Taft, Wilson, F. D. Roosevelt, Eisenhower, J. F. Kennedy, Johnson, Nixon, and Carter.

When southern California became the world capital of the movie industry, the Hotel del Coronado became one of the stars' favorite hideaways. Many films were made in the San Diego area and often the Del was used as a location. Gloria Swanson was a frequent visitor, and other performers who starred in films made at the Del such as Johnny Downs and Anita Page decided to stay and have since made Coronado their home. Other films made at the Del include: *Wicked, Wicked; Stuntman,* and *Some Like it Hot;* as well as portions of television series: *Ghost Story, Love – American Style, Hunter,* and *Captains and Kings.* In 1975, Viking Press released Richard Matheson's novel *Bid Time Return,* a delightful romantic story set almost entirely at the Del.

Though the Del stands as a magnificent reminder of past eras of elegance, this grand lady by the sea has also kept up with the times. Three fine buildings; the 208-room Ocean Towers, Grande Hall Convention Center, and the 96 room Poolside addition have been added to expand the Del's capacity. These buildings have been tastefully designed to complement the elegant main building.

The hotel is presently owned and operated by the Hotel del Coronado Corporation, headed by M. Larry Lawrence, which acquired the property in 1963. Previous owners include John Alessio, Barney Goodman of Kansas City, John D. Spreckels who owned the hotel for 50 years, and of course, Elisha Babcock whose dream remains to this day "the talk of the Western world."

E. F. Hutton Life Insurance Company

A story of innovation and growth

E. F. Hutton Life Insurance Company, the only life insurance company headquartered in San Diego, had its genesis in an Oakland investment club in the 1930s. That organization grew into a mutual fund, Insurance Securities Trust Fund, and was limited to insurance stocks. Insurance Securities Incorporated, advisor and manager of the trust fund, achieved substantial success and, early in the 1960s, looked at its unique expertise and wondered if it should organize and operate its own insurance company. The affirmative answer led directly to Life Insurance Company of California, the original name of the company, then based in San Francisco.

On its first working day of 1963, Alan Richards, now president and chief executive officer, came on board. Within 18 days, the company had its Certificate of Authority in California and Richards was soon showing his genius at innovation. He created the "California Special" — a life insurance plan with a totally new concept. It was easy to understand, readily marketable, and held broad appeal.

The following September, a drive was initiated that exploded into $17 million in sales in one month's time! The first full year of sales operations was concluded with more than $85 million worth of insurance in force. The figure went to more than a quarter billion dollars by 1965, a half billion in 1971, and reached the billion dollar mark during 1974. At the start of 1980, Hutton Life had assets of $210 million, 53,631 policyowners, and $2 billion of insurance in force.

Not only did the company grow rapidly in the domestic market, but it acquired World-Wide Assurance Company, Ltd. of Windsor, England, which now conducts reinsurance operations in some 50 nations. Hutton Life is licensed in 49 states and the District of Columbia.

Several innovative steps contributed to growth and success. Early in 1971, a policy called split life was introduced, featuring inexpensive term coverage. The following year, a modified life plan offering low cost life insurance for continuing policyowners was introduced. The company was quickly becoming one of the success stories of American business.

Success and resulting growth created a critical expansion point when its San Francisco lease was due to expire in 1977. Considerable study of various locations throughout California led the firm to San Diego where a 17-acre site was chosen in the Torrey Pines area of La Jolla. This site has since been expanded to 31 acres. "The

Above, Alan Richards, chairman and president. Left, the low profile building, with its high ceilings and skylit central concourse, reflects a concern for the natural environment.

cooperation of the Chamber of Commerce, the Economic Development Corporation and San Diego city officials made our choice relatively simple," says President Alan Richards.

A distinctive, 52,000 square foot headquarters building was constructed overlooking the Torrey Pines golf course, and the company made its move in November of 1977. The low profile building, with its high ceilings and skylit central concourse, reflects a concern for the natural environment and at the same time meets the needs of the company's policy owners, employees and neighbors.

During 1977, negotiations were entered into with The E. F. Hutton Group Inc., the parent of one of the largest securities firms in the country, regarding acquisition by that corporation. In February, 1978, the transaction was completed, making the company part and parcel of one of the world's strongest and most highly respected financial organizations.

Hutton Life's marketing efforts have been directed toward trend-setting products

which are presented to the public by highly professional sales people. This accounts for a Hutton Life average individual life policy size of about four times the industry average. In January, 1979, a highly innovative, consumer-oriented life insurance product was introduced offering complete cost disclosure. The plan's rate of interest crediting makes it an attractive savings medium in addition to its excellent life insurance protection. Management feels this policy, called Completelife, will set the pattern for the basic insurance product of the future. "It combines inexpensive mortality coverage with an outstanding return in comparison with our competitors, plus full disclosure," notes Alan Richards. "This is a product that can compete with many other savings plans because of its good tax-sheltered savings feature in addition to its very low cost protection."

A willingness to chart a course of offering non-traditional life insurance products in response to consumers' needs has been the theme of Hutton Life's story of innovation and growth.

Imperial Corporation of America

Building the largest multi-state savings and loan

The vacating of a liquor store on the corner of Cass and Garnet Streets in 1953 may have been the reason Imperial Corporation of America (ICA) began, according to a speech once given by its founder, T. Franklin Schneider. Schneider, who traveled to San Diego in 1948 to retire from his successful real estate business in Washington, D.C., noted that the vacant store made an ideal location for a savings and loan office. On December 11, 1953, he and several associates opened Suburban Savings and Loan Association on that corner.

In October, 1956, Schneider acquired Imperial Savings and Loan in El Centro, and on November 9, 1956, a savings and loan holding company was officially chartered. Given the name San Diego Imperial Corporation to commemorate the two counties in which its offices were located, the company's origins are of special interest in view of the controversy surrounding savings and loan holding companies in the 1950s.

Traditionally categorized as a cottage industry, savings and loans could not have made the national impact on the housing field which they now command had men like Schneider failed to see the merits of holding companies. "We can move money around faster — particularly participatory loans," T. F. Schneider told reporters in 1959. "We also have the advantage of central management of the bond portfolio."

The financial talent that Schneider displayed in fostering the company's growth from an initial investment of $6 million in 1956 to assets of nearly $1 billion at his death was just one manifestation of his overall genius. An intense, scholarly man, he maintained an enthusiastic interest in his favorite hobby, astronomy. He kept a 12½" reflector-type telescope in his back yard for many years, finally donating it and its Palomar-like dome to the physical science department of San Diego State University when the growing pressure of his business made it necessary for him to relinquish pursuit of his hobby.

During its short 25 years, Imperial Corporation of America has owned 27 separate savings and loan associations. These have now been merged into four subsidiaries: American Savings of Kansas, Gibraltar Savings Association in Texas, Silver State Savings in Colorado, and ICA's largest subsidiary, San Diego-headquartered Imperial Savings and Loan, which serves all of California. Today the combined assets of these companies exceed $6.5 billion, and ICA is the nation's largest multi-state savings and loan holding company.

Corporate headquarters for Imperial Corporation of America and Imperial Savings & Loan Association in Kearny Mesa.

Thomas Franklin (T.F.) Schneider, founder of Imperial Corporation of America, San Diego's largest savings and loan holding company.

In 1959, ICA was listed on the New York Stock Exchange, the first savings and loan association to have that distinction. The firm's present chairman of the board, G. Kenneth Handley, arranged the first public offering of ICA's stock. In 1961, while Schneider still held the post of president, the company declared its first stock dividend of five percent.

After expanding rapidly outside of California under the leadership of former president Jack H. McDonald, the company changed its name to Imperial Corporation of America in 1966 to more accurately reflect its multi-state holdings. Imperial Corporation and Imperial Savings share a logo, a blue letter "i," adopted in 1971. This insignia is prominent on the four-story building in Kearny Mesa, which houses the executive offices of both companies.

In 1975, ICA declared its first cash dividend while under the management of V. L. Viskas and continued to grow in asset size and increase its earnings. During Viskas' tenure the consolidation of all of the California S&Ls into Imperial Savings and Loan was completed. Today, with a network of offices stretching from the California-Oregon border on the north and to the Mexican border, Imperial Savings is one of California's leading financial institutions.

Imperial Corporation of America enters the 1980s with a remarkable record of growth, and a strong commitment to the future. In an era when rising home prices and real estate values make home ownership difficult for many, ICA and its subsidiary associations are determined to continue providing the mortgage loans which have helped thousands of customers in four states achieve the dream of home ownership.

KGTV10

More than 25 years of broadcasting leadership

The scene on the San Diego television screen *looked* routine — a reporter telling the story "live" from the scene. But this time was unique. This time the reporter was standing in Livermore, California — several hundred miles north of San Diego — describing the aftermath of an earthquake which had shaken the Livermore Nuclear Physics Laboratory. And it was a *first* for San Diego television, accomplished with a little help from television stations in San Francisco and Los Angeles. The "live" report was beamed from Livermore to the San Francisco area, then microwaved to Los Angeles and San Diego for broadcast on KGTV10's 11 p.m. edition of The News. It had not been done in San Diego before, but "firsts" have become a style of operation for KGTV10.

Since September, 1953 Channel Ten has been serving the San Diego area. From sparse quarters in a former aircraft plant cafeteria building to the still-expanding facilities in southeast San Diego, the station has reflected the dynamics of one of the nation's fastest-growing regions.

Channel Ten's initial telecast was rather inauspicious. After a formal "sign-on" statement viewers watched the NBC televising of the old "Friday Night Fights." And Channel Ten began its broadcast history.

In the years since, KGTV10 has developed a reputation for leadership in the community as well as the industry. Vice-President and General Manager Clayton H. Brace has had a long and firm commitment to responsive and responsible broadcasting. KGTV10 was the first local station in the nation to broadcast a one-hour, local news program on a nightly basis. The station pioneered television editorials on local issues and led the area in the first live telecasts of the old San Diego Padres baseball team.

In the 1960s KGTV10 was a pacesetter in live, remote broadcasts of area events — everything from parades to pageants. The coverage was so extensive that a competitor actually carried the Channel Ten telecast of a presidential visit.

With the advent of miniaturized equipment, KGTV10 led the area in "live" Insta-Cam reports at the scene on The News and in the use of a helicopter, SKY-10, news crew.

At the same time, other programming areas at KGTV10 have demonstrated the emphasis on quality. The children's program "Words-A-Poppin' " has received national and local awards. KGTV10's Special Projects Unit has received national and local awards for such documentaries as "Traffic In Sight," about the 1978 air disas-

Right, SKY-10, San Diego's first, full-time, news-gathering helicopter.

KGTV10 pioneered the first, live, on-location news coverage in San Diego.

ter; "Eagle Of The Sea," report on a new U.S. Navy ship; and "Mission Valley: Dammed or Damned," concerning local flooding problems.

KGTV10 established a tradition of public affairs coverage with its "Political Rally" or, a lengthy, live television broadcast offering all candidates an opportunity to be seen and heard.

Over the years reporting crews from Channel Ten have crossed the nation and traveled the world to inform San Diego viewers of current events and news. Eastern Europe, the Middle East, the Far East and

The People's Republic of China are among the locations where station news people have stopped to update San Diegans. At the same time, KGTV10 has remained focused on the people here. The efforts are reflected in the many awards lining a long hallway and filling a display case in the studio building.

A keystone in McGraw-Hill Broadcasting Company, Inc., KGTV10 is affiliated with the ABC Television Network and shares in the network's leadership in innovative approaches to television broadcasting.

Kelco

Unique marine technology
fosters company growth

Prior to 1927, giant brown kelp — a seaweed (*Macrocystis pyrifera*) — was considered nothing more than a marine nuisance, a real detriment to both boating and bathing along Southern California's coastline. In that year, however, Fred Curtis Thornley came to San Diego to manufacture a hydrocolloid called algin, which was extracted from the giant brown kelp. The American Can Company contracted with Thornley & Co. to use algin in a can sealing compound, although Thornley could foresee hundreds of other applications for alginates.

Those additional applications did not develop and, as a result, the financially troubled Thornley and Co. was sold in 1929 to a group of Los Angeles area investors, headed by Arnold Fitger and commenced business as Kelco Company. The Great Depression which followed was devastating to many American businesses but it was, ironically, one reason for the survival of Kelco. Abundant manpower was available to work long hours in the Kelco plant and on the kelp harvesting barges. During those early years Kelco produced dried ground kelp for livestock feed and kelp tablets as nutritional supplements for human consumption, in addition to algin.

By the mid-'30s the company's future depended on the discovery of more applications for algin. A special research team was organized and the search produced DARILOID® and COCOLOID®, specially buffered alginates which the dairy industry bought to stabilize ice cream and to suspend chocolate in chocolate milk.

Kelco originally collected the seaweed by hand, sending crews to the kelp beds on big barges to cut and haul the long kelp strands out of the water. By the late '30s, though, the company had made several changes in mechanization and production. By adding specially designed cutting racks to its harvesting barges, Kelco was able to greatly increase the amount of kelp it could harvest. Gas-fired dryers were introduced in 1938, to eliminate the need for sun drying operations in El Cajon.

New alginate products were developed in the late 1930s and early '40s, including bakery icing stabilizers, textile print paste thickeners, latex creaming products, paper coatings, and dental impression compounds.

World War II created a shortage of imported natural gums and Kelco expanded and innovated to help meet America's needs during this time.

The Kelco office building (right), was moved by barge to Belt Street location, 1941. Kelco plant, below, located at Division Street in National City, 1929.

In 1943, the Navy's need for expanded destroyer berths in National City forced the company to move production and office buildings by barge from the original location on Division Street in National City to the present plant site on Belt Street, under the Coronado Bay Bridge.

In 1946 Kelco expanded its production facilities and added a new manufacturing building for the production of a new product, discovered by Kelco research chemists. This product, propylene glycol alginate, is still used today for beer foam stabilization and salad dressing suspensions.

As a young company in the early '30s, Kelco employed only four people in quality control and research; but it was an early indication of the firm's commitment to research. The research and development department continued to grow, and in 1957 Kelco opened a new 10,000 sq. foot research facility in Kearney Mesa.

During the years 1957-1960 an unusual trend toward warmer ocean temperatures devastated the kelp resource off Southern California. Poor kelp harvests during these years encouraged Kelco researchers to in-

Modern kelp harvester, KELMAR, at its launch in Portland, Oregon, January, 1958.

vestigate the possibility that a certain unique microorganism discovered by the U.S.D.A., produced a gum which displayed remarkable properties. After several years of testing and research, Kelco announced commercial production of an industrial grade of this biogum, which it named xanthan gum. In 1969, after further testing, the Food and Drug Administration authorized the use of xanthan gum in salad

dressings and other food products.

Today Kelco is an operating division of Merck & Co., Inc., a world leader in human, animal and environmental health care products. The struggling commercial venture of 1929 which had one product and one customer has grown to become a leading manufacturer of specialty hydrocolloids like alginates and xanthan gum, with production facilities in other locations in the U.S. and sales offices around the world.

National Steel and Shipbuilding Company

Shipyard flourished under the rigors of tough competition

National Steel and Shipbuilding Company (NASSCO) began to build marine vessels after World War II, long after East Coast shipyards were well established. Within the following 15 years, the company expanded and matured to become one of the major U.S. yards.

"It's refreshing back in Washington to see a company dig in and compete like National Steel has done," said a U.S. maritime official in 1959 when, in stiff competition with 12 yards, NASSCO won a contract for four engine-aft freighters. With this contract, the company entered the major leagues of shipbuilding.

The story begins in 1905 when what was to become the West Coast's largest shipyard was still an iron works and machine shop located in downtown San Diego. When the iron works fell upon hard times during the Depression, financier C. Arnholt Smith acquired a controlling interest.

Smith moved the company to its present home on Harbor Drive at 28th Street in 1945 where expansion into shipbuilding was realized. The company built and overhauled scores of fishing boats during the next 14 years. By the early '50s, however, tuna imports began to cut into the thriving U.S. tuna business.

Meanwhile, other shipbuilding markets were opening. In 1951, the company signed its first of many military contracts. In excess of $10 million, it included minesweepers, tugs and barges. Employment swelled to several hundred workers and adjacent parcels of waterfront land were acquired for expansion of building ways and berths.

In the mid-'50s, general manager Milton F. Fillius guided the burgeoning shipbuilder through several complex contracts: a prototype Army beach lighter, a hydrographic survey ship called "Surveyor," and the first

Formerly an iron works, NASSCO evolved into ship building in 1945 with the construction of 52-foot-long steel-hulled tuna boats like this one. Company growth paralleled the size of ships under contract. By mid-1959 NASSCO had graduated from building fishing boats to producing big commercial freighters.

offshore oil rig in the West. NASSCO now had the requisite experience to compete for "big" ships.

When the federal government unveiled a $3-billion shipbuilding program in the late '50s, NASSCO was ready. The company signed contracts for six large federally subsidized freighters. The contracts came at a time to take up the slack in employment of San Diego aircraft industry personnel. NASSCO alone added 2,000 employees, nearly quadrupling its payroll.

The backlog of big ships strained the company's capabilities; capital was needed for new facilities. A joint venture was formed to finance the expansion. Two years later, Kaiser Industries Corporation and

Morrison-Knudsen Company, Inc., each bought a 50 percent interest in NASSCO. And in December 1979, Morrison-Knudsen Company, Inc., acquired full ownership of NASSCO.

The company signed its first major Navy contract in 1961. It was for a prototype combat stores ship. The war in Southeast Asia and the phasing out of Navy shipyards led to an upsurge in Navy work. In the ensuing eight years, the company delivered six more combat stores ships and signed a contract for 17 tank landing ships, the largest Navy contract in peacetime history. "The 28th Street shipyard is now one of the most flourishing in the nation," proclaimed the *San Diego Union.*

Before engineers completed work on the Navy contracts, then-president John Banks began to capitalize on their design expertise. The outcome was two 90,000-ton oil-bulk-ore carriers. The spin-off from these was a new class of NASSCO-designed oil tanker. The timing was right; the market was ready. NASSCO sold 13 tankers in this class. A slump in the world oil market in 1975 was followed by a boom in tankers for the Alaska oil trade. NASSCO designed and built four 188,500-ton carriers for this market. When this book went to press, NASSCO had 29 tankers built or under contract.

NASSCO enters the 1980s with the capability of building eight ships simultaneously. Its employment exceeds 6,500 to complete a backlog of Navy and commercial

Leaving San Diego harbor in October 1978 on her maiden voyage to Alaska is the giant oil tanker, B.T. San Diego, one of four 188,500-ton tankers designed and built by NASSCO. The 953-foot-long vessels are the largest launched on the West Coast.

ships approximating one billion dollars.

Today there are only 600 ships in the U.S. merchant marine compared with 4,000 in

1945, largely because of competition from heavily subsidized foreign shipyards. NASSCO president C. Larry French, a spokesman for legislation that would bolster orders in U.S. shipyards, emphasizes that "not only do U.S.-built ships mean jobs for thousands of Americans, but U.S. flagships serve as a Navy auxiliary in times of national crisis."

The Navy shipbuilding picture is not much better. To maintain our Naval fleet of 600, 20 new ships a year are needed. At the end of the '70s, Navy ships were being funded at about 13 a year.

Despite the gloomy U.S. shipbuilding forecast, NASSCO's future looks good. Quality ships, on-time delivery and new designs to satisfy emerging demands continue to be NASSCO's formula for success.

National University

Forward-looking institution is a new kind of educational resource

In November, 1972, recognizing the unfilled need for college-level programs specifically designed for the mature working adult, a small group of forward-looking individuals, led by David Chigos, Ph.D, current president, founded National University.

The group had discovered that the actual availability of relevant educational opportunities leading to a degree for working adults was significantly lower than commonly believed. The traditional multi-course-load programs in quarter and semester length packages with registration available at the beginning of those periods, lacked not only flexibility, but were not offered at convenient times and places. Most involved day-time classes not amenable to the schedule of busy executives. What was needed were relevant degree programs, offered in the evenings, and packaged so that students could have a reasonable expectation of attending all class meetings.

At National University, where degree programs are designed for persons interested in advancing along clearly defined career paths, registration is continuously open. Students register only once for their entire program, which is taken one course at a time. Many professionals feel that only intensive study which is directly relevant and profitable to them is attractive. A degree at National, therefore, requires significant intellectual commitment on the part of the student for the educational payoff to be both immediate and apparent. Each course is

National University

completed in approximately one month through attendance two evenings per week and an occasional Saturday. It is possible for a student entering the M.B.A. program to earn a degree in about 15 months.

From its earliest stirrings of existence, with 27 students attending business administration classes in a General Dynamics conference room in Kearney Mesa, the university has been acutely aware of the effects of changing conditions on its constituency. For example, the university responded to the oil embargo of 1973-74 by accelerating the establishment of Learning Centers close to students' homes and work places, thus contributing to the conservation of energy.

This brought about rapid growth in facilities and in student population. The university now serves more than 5,000 students attending classes which cover a variety of disciplines at more than 25 locations in San Diego and Orange Counties. It is not only one of the largest independent nonprofit institutions of higher learning in the state of California accredited by the Senior Commission of the Western Association of Schools and Colleges, but it is the fastest growing. Contributing to growth and its proper control have been policies designed to properly support the student. Most of the faculty have earned doctorates and 10 years

School of Law

of professional experience, and almost all of the non-teaching staff have earned graduate degrees or are in that process.

At present, the availability of undergraduate and graduate degree programs includes such areas as general business studies, personnel management, education, counseling, marketing, law, criminal justice, real estate, public administration, information systems, accounting, finance and human behavior.

At the School of Law, in addition to programs leading to the J.D. degree, a combination M.B.A. and J.D. is available.

In what is believed to be a first in the

U.S., National University offers to the hispanic community the M.B.A. program taught entirely in Spanish.

National University is engaged in a continuing quest for opportunities to serve the advancement of scholarship and to transmit knowledge, understanding and perspective to the community in the most efficient and effective ways possible.

The strivings by the university to offer programs of academic excellence at convenient times and places have struck a responsive chord in the community. As the decade of the 1970s waned, many other longstanding institutions of higher learning across the U.S. found themselves with lowered enrollments and in financial distress; some were forced to close their doors, merge with others or become an additional burden to the taxpayer by going public. National University's enrollment, however, continued to climb rapidly.

The decade of the 1980s will present further challenges to the ingenuity of the educational community to stay abreast of areas of educational need generated by economic, cultural and technological changes. National University will, as it has in the past, be in the forefront of innovation and public service, blazing educational trails for others to follow.

Pacific Southwest Airlines

Low fares and a smile: a continuing success story for PSA

What humbly began with a leased DC-3 and a handful of employees with wide-eyed aspirations has become one of the most phenomenal success stories in the airline industry.

The year was 1949. Kenneth Friedkin and his flight training school faced a diminishing number of students after World War II and decided to start an airline. Long on determination, short on cash, Pacific Southwest Airlines (PSA) was formed and began scheduled service on May 6, 1949. The founding principle of the little airline was that air transportation should not just be for the wealthy, but for everyone.

On that May morning, PSA's first flight departed San Diego's Lindbergh Field for Burbank and Oakland with 21 passengers and a dream for the future.

Although the first few years were not financially rewarding, PSA gained a reputation throughout much of California for charging very low fares while offering professional service with an uncanny sense of humor. In those early years, PSA carried so many military personnel between the large

By late 1951, PSA had expanded service and increased its fleet size to four DC-3 aircraft. Here the entire PSA fleet is pictured before beginning the daily operation with service to four California cities.

Naval bases in San Diego and Oakland that many jokingly referred to the little carrier as PSA — "The Poor Sailor's Airline." While the number of jokes in the early days usually out-numbered the year-end earnings, PSA continued to expand during the 1950s, becoming a major force in California air travel.

By the late 1950s, PSA was operating a modern fleet of Electra prop-jets and was ready to tackle the "big boys" in the highly competitive Los Angeles-San Francisco market. And by 1964, it was carrying more than 50 percent of all passengers between the two cities.

Under J. Floyd Andrews' leadership, who took over the top executive post after Kenneth Friedkin's death in 1962, service was added to the California cities of San Jose, Oakland, Ontario and Sacramento.

By the end of the decade, PSA had become the world's largest intrastate airline as well as the "hottest" airline in the industry, complete with flight attendants wearing mini-skirts and hot pants. A fleet of brightly-painted PSA Boeing 727 aircraft traversed California.

While the outward appearance was flashy, the PSA operation was based on efficiency. The airline had become a nonconformist in an industry and age of conformity. PSA shunned the traditional airline amenities such as first class sections, food service and galleys. Instead, it opted for all-coach seating with no food service while offering fares about 50 percent below those being charged on comparable routes outside California. PSA was soon carrying more than 60 percent of all air travel in California.

PSA's approach to air transportation was

PSA's famed fleet of smiling Boeing 727s now serves four Western States with more than 200 daily flights. PSA has become the nation's twelfth largest airline in terms of passenger volume with nearly nine million annual passengers.

Since 1949 when PSA first flexed its wings in California, the airline has been noted for smiling employees. Here, one of the early flight crews poses before boarding a DC-3.

so successful in California that in 1976 the airline, now headed by William R. Shimp, looked outside the state to extend its unique service throughout the Western States. However, because of government regulations, PSA was unable to expand into interstate markets until the passage of the Airline Deregulation Act of 1978.

During the first year of airline deregulation, PSA expanded service to Las Vegas, Reno, Phoenix and Salt Lake City. Fares on the new markets were lowered by an average of 30 percent below competitors' rates and the traveling public responded. On most of PSA's interstate routes, the passenger volume doubled or nearly doubled within 90 days of PSA's inauguration of service.

By the end of 1979, PSA had become the nation's twelfth largest airline, carrying nearly nine million passengers between 15 cities, a record unparalled in the airline industry.

PSA's expansion throughout the Western United States continues into the 1980s, with the airline aspiring to become the leading carrier in the Western States by the end of the decade.

PSA will become the first U.S. airline to receive delivery of the DC-9 Super 80 aircraft, the quietest and most fuel efficient aircraft developed. With the DC-9 Super 80 and present fleet of Boeing 727s, PSA plans expansion to Seattle, Portland, Denver, Houston and Dallas, plus Puerto Vallarta and Mazatlan, Mexico.

While PSA's growth and expansion continue, the goal of the airline and its employees remains the same as in the days of the leased DC-3 — a deep commitment to offer the public comfortable and friendly service at the lowest possible price.

Rohr Industries, Inc.

A place to work... to live... to grow

On the morning of August 5, 1940, five men gathered around a conference table in a San Diego law office to translate into reality a dream that had obsessed a man named Fred Rohr for many years.

Besides Rohr, the other men were J. E. Rheim and E. M. Lacey, who had recently resigned from Ryan Aeronautical Company, where Fred Rohr had for five years been factory manager; F. H. Nottbusch and his son F. H. Nottbusch, Jr., attorneys. This was not their first meeting. They had spent hours around the dining table in Rohr's home, planning and discussing their future. In the law office conference they formally

The first home of Rohr Aircraft Corporation was Eighth and J Streets, San Diego, 1940-1941.

Power packages for the Consolidated B-24 were assembled at the Chula Vista plant during World War II. At the peak of production, Rohr produced 64 of these units (16 ship sets) per day. In three years, 1942-1945, Rohr produced 38,000 power packages for the B-24 and the PBY series of flying boats.

The Chula Vista Main Manufacturing Plant and Corporate Headquarters covers 2.4 million square feet – 161 acres.

founding, Joe Rheim in 1961 and Fred H. Rohr in 1965. Burt F. Raynes succeeded Rheim as the corporation's new president and general manager. In the late '60s and early '70s the company embarked on extensive product diversification programs involving such products as automated warehousing and mail handling equipment, microwave relay antennas, marine construction, advanced gas turbine engines, precast concrete building materials, and most notably, virtually the full gamut of transportation systems which included buses, rapid transit cars, inter-city vehicles such as turbine-powered passenger trains for Amtrak and people movers. Whereas these ventures were progressive in concept and appeared to fit the national needs of the period, they were not financially successful. As a result, the company suffered substantial losses in its 1975 and 1976 fiscal years.

In 1976, under the guidance of Fred W. Garry, who had joined Rohr as president in 1974 and subsequently succeeded Raynes as chairman of the board and chief executive officer, an essentially new management team charted the course to remarkable recovery. It accomplished this by disposing of unprofitable or marginal sidelines and concentrating on what Rohr knew best — building hardware for military and commercial aircraft.

Another product area it retained was the manufacture of solid rocket motor case components for the NASA Space Shuttle program, and the Titan III space launch vehicle.

Today Rohr operates a large assembly operation in Riverside, California which contains one of the industry's largest and most modern adhesive bonding facilities, plus Arlington and Edgemont, two smaller satellite assembly plants located in the Riverside area. Rohr also has an assembly plant in Auburn, Washington and a subsidiary in France, as well as its principal fabrication and assembly facility in Chula Vista, California.

Total employment is more than 9,000 and fiscal 1978 revenues amounted to $299 million.

Rohr Industries, Inc., functions primarily as a component supplier to prime manufacturers in the aerospace industry. The corporation's principal activities include the manufacture of aircraft engine pods, or nacelles, thrust reversers and other structural and engine components for commercial, military and business jet aircraft. The company also remains involved in the manufacture of components for large rocket motors.

approved Articles of Incorporation, and Nottbusch left with them for Sacramento that afternoon. When the Articles were approved the next day by the Secretary of State, Rohr Aircraft Corporation was added to the roster of California industry.

The next step was to find a factory or a site upon which to build one. Rohr preferred the Chula Vista area on the shore of lower San Diego Bay, approximately 12 miles south of downtown San Diego. In the interim, he leased a three-story building in San Diego's wholesale district — a brick structure containing 15,000 square feet, formerly occupied by a firm of cabinet makers, and the company commenced work on its first contract. This was an order for de-

sign and installation of Sperry bomb sites on six military airplanes, the LB-30s, which was the British version of the B-24.

Suitable property became available in the Chula Vista area and the company moved into its buildings on June 15, 1941. During the war years that followed, the company achieved notable recognition in the aircraft industry for its specialized development of the "power package" concept for military and commercial aircraft.

In 1945 Rohr Aircraft Corporation, through an exchange of stock, became a subsidiary of International Detrola Corporation. The companies separated in 1949 when Fred Rohr and a group of stockholders purchased the assets of the Chula Vista firm and returned it to independent ownership and control.

In the early '60s death took the two men who had headed the company since its

Roman Catholic Diocese of San Diego

A spiritual and physical presence that began more than two centuries ago

With a growing fear that Russia would move down the coast from Alaska into California, Charles III, the King of Spain, determined to occupy Alta California. For religious purposes he invited Father Junipero Serra to join the Portola Expedition of 1769. On July 16, 1769, Serra founded and established in San Diego the first in a chain of 21 missions.

The inaugural mass was offered on the hillside near the Presidio. In 1774, it was deemed more advantageous to locate Mission San Diego on its present site near the San Diego River and the Indian village of Cosoy.

Despite unfriendly Indians, who proved difficult for the early missionaries to convert, San Diego had, by 1839, the largest population of any of the California missions. The Church progressed slowly for the next 28 years, however, and no substantial progress was made until the coming of Alonzo Erastus Horton in 1867. Horton bought 960 acres of land at public auction and planned the modern San Diego. As part of this plan, he donated land upon request to any religious denomination.

By this time the Catholic Church showed remarkable growth. Father Antonio Ubach of Spain, a vigorous individual who had great compassion for the Indians, had been appointed the fifth pastor of San Diego. He is spoken of in Helen Hunt Jackson's novel, Ramona, as "Father Gaspara." Father Ubach spent 41 of his 47 priestly years in San Diego. At the time of his death in 1907 three parishes had been established in San Diego: Immaculate Conception, Old Town; St. Joseph, New Town; and Our Lady of Angels. Mission San Diego did not receive the status of a parish until Feburary 2, 1941.

When San Diego's first bishop, Charles Francis Buddy, arrived in 1936, there were 100,000 Catholics in the newly formed diocese. He labored for 30 years and founded numerous parishes, missions and schools. He fostered one diocesan newspaper, founded the University of San Diego and the diocesan seminary. His famous "Crusade for Souls" brought many into the Church.

On March 6, 1966, Bishop Francis James Furey succeeded to the title of Bishop of San Diego and served in that position for three years. During that short time, he was among the first bishops in the United States to organize and encourage a senate of diocesan priests to advise him in his duties. He encouraged the establishment of parish councils, founded an Ecumenical Center at the University of San Diego, and often invited rabbis and ministers to participate in Catholic functions.

Bishop Leo Thomas Maher was named the third Bishop of San Diego on August 27, 1969. Since that time, he started 14 new parishes and ordained more than 45 priests and 35 permanent deacons. The number of Catholics in the Diocese surpassed 590,000.

In 1978 the continued growth of the diocese brought about a separation of the four counties into two separate dioceses, each containing two counties. The new Diocese of San Bernardino comprised the counties of Riverside and San Bernardino; the Diocese of San Diego was comprised of the counties of San Diego and Imperial.

With growth and reorganization came construction of new facilities, including Cathedral Plaza in downtown San Diego — a residence built especially to house the elderly.

Progress was made also in the area of assistance to the people of Hispanic heritage. The Padre Hidalgo Center was established to help meet the Mexican-Americans' spiritual and social needs and the Southern Cross diocesan newspaper started printing church news in Spanish.

The "excellence in education" was a position long taken by the Roman Catholic Diocese of San Diego. In 1972, the College of Men, the College of Women and the School of Law of the University of San Diego were combined into a university that evolved into a leading institution of higher learning. Bishop Maher serves as chairman of the board of trustees.

From the first mission of California to the newest parish church, the Roman Catholic Diocese of San Diego forges ahead into its third century of spiritual leadership and service.

Mission San Diego de Alcala was established in 1769, left. One of the first parishes in San Diego was St. Joseph Church, bottom, now a cathedral, circa 1954.

San Diego Federal Savings & Loan Association

A simple principle of thrift and home ownership

In 1885 San Diego Federal's first office was housed in the Morse, Whaley & Dalton Real Estate Company at 809 Fifth Avenue, left. San Diego Federal moved into its new 24-story headquarter building in 1974, below.

In 1885, San Diego was experiencing a land boom. The discovery of gold in California and the new arrival of the Santa Fe Railroad were rapidly transforming a tiny hamlet of a few hundred citizens into a thriving seaport. Families were arriving at such a fast clip that homes and schools could not be built fast enough.

It was against that economic backdrop at 8 p.m. on July 11, 1885, that a group of 10 men sat down in a small room in downtown San Diego. Gas lamps flickered in E. W. Morse's high-ceilinged office at 809 Fifth Avenue as the meeting was called to order. Two hours later, the birth of Southern California's first building and loan association had been recorded and its by-laws formed. The name chosen: San Diego Building and Loan Association.

The simple principle expressed by those men in their first meeting became a guideline for the Association over its next 95 years of business: San Diego Federal would be in business to encourage thrift and promote home ownership.

Moses A. Luce, Congressional Medal of

Honor winner and one of San Diego's premier attorneys, was elected general counsel. More than 80 years later his grandson, Gordon C. Luce, would assume the presidency of the Association and lead it through its greatest period of growth and prosperity.

By 1917, as American boys prepared for the voyage to Europe to fight in the Great War, San Diego Federal began the first of three major moves in the downtown area, finally culminating in new quarters in the Southern Title building at 3rd and Broadway. Directly across the street that year, General Grant's son was building the U.S. Grant Hotel.

Following the establishment of the Federal Home Loan Bank System by Congress in 1932 and the authorization of federal savings and loan charters a year later, the stage was set for the sound growth pattern which continues to this day. On December 30, 1936, San Diego Building and Loan converted to a federal association and became known for the first time as San Diego Federal Savings and Loan Association.

The close of World War II brought our

country face to face with the most acute housing shortage in the nation's history. Since many returning servicemen had discovered San Diego, the city and county experienced a building and land development boom which continued through the decades of the '50s and '60s. In 1952, to better serve those housing demands and the needs of an increased customer base, San Diego Federal moved to a large, new headquarters building at 1265 Sixth Avenue.

In 1969, with the sudden passing of Association President Jack Thompson, the board of directors turned to a new management team headed by Gordon C. Luce and James C. Schmidt. Luce was named president and Schmidt executive vice president. Soon, a vigorous new expansion program was embarked upon. In the next five years, Association assets grew from $312 million to more than $800 million and 23 new branches were added.

To make San Diego Federal a more dynamic, competitive force in the community, a new branching strategy was formulated, directed at areas where savings penetration was low. A distinctive arhictectural style was developed and San Diego Federal's name became synonymous with patriotism and genuine concern for the environment. The theme was symbolized by a new logo featuring seagulls on the field of blue and red.

During this period, San Diego Federal originated programs to assist lower-income areas of San Diego, expanding later to other parts of California. The Association led the way with inner-city offices, bringing savings and loan services to communities which would otherwise have gone without them.

In 1974, San Diego Federal moved into a new, 24-story headquarters building in the heart of downtown San Diego. The offices are just a stone's throw from where it all began back in 1885 — San Diego Federal had grown from a "hometown" savings and loan to one of the nation's largest and most successful.

In 1975, the Association passed the $1 billion mark in assets and by 1979 had doubled to more than $2 billion.

Late in that year, Gordon Luce was elected chairman of the board and chief executive officer and James Schmidt elected president.

At the beginning of 1980, with growth that has mirrored the acceleration of California's economy, San Diego Federal's statewide branch network was at 70, with a projection of 100 offices within a few years.

With strong financial ratios, sound deposit growth, good cash flow management, and one of California's finest branch networks, San Diego Federal is well prepared to serve the current and future needs of its more than 300,000 customers — and to continue its adherence to the principle of thrift and home ownership set forth by its founders almost a century ago.

San Diego Gas & Electric

A century of service to Southern California

When five San Diegans formed San Diego Gas Company in 1881, the City of San Diego's population had just passed 3,000. There were only 89 gas customers. Not everyone wanted or trusted gas for heating and lighting. Whereas kerosene was cheap and something they knew about, natural gas was odorless and dangerous. It was a time well before horses began pulling streetcars through downtown, and folks were skeptical about new-fangled conveniences like telephones and gas.

In 1885, the stockholders considered adding an electric plant to the system, but the idea was dropped due to lack of enthusiasm. But in 1887, responding to increased demands for both gas and electricity, San Diego Gas took over a struggling electric company and changed its name to San Diego Gas & Electric Light Company. Old timers still call SDG&E "the gas and light."

Soon, electricity began to illuminate homes, streets and businesses all over America and the possibilities for gas in homes and businesses took on new dimensions. The homemaker found that gas could be utilized in cooking, waterheating and clothesdrying. In years to come, homes and businesses came to be heated and air conditioned with gas and/or electricity.

As early as 1918, SDG&E began looking to the north and to other utilities in order to be certain of always providing reliable service. In its first major electric interconnection, the company tied in with Southern California Edison, just up the coast from San Diego at San Juan Capistrano. In 1932, SDG&E tied in to Southern California Gas Company's natural gas pipeline, phasing out its own gas plant in San Diego.

In the '40s, the company expanded and began to serve the developing communities in San Diego's metropolitan area. Today, SDG&E serves all of San Diego County and parts of Orange and Imperial Counties.

San Diego County and SDG&E grew steadily but slowly after the second world war. However, in the early '60s the company began planning for major growth on its system. In 1963, the company signed an agreement making it a 20 percent owner of the San Onofre Nuclear Generating Station at San Clemente, at the time the largest nuclear power plant in the U.S. That same year, SDG&E joined the California Power Pool, an important linkup of utilities in California that allowed members to transfer and sell power among themselves, saving money for customers and improving each system's reliability.

In 1964, work began on the Liquified Natural Gas (LNG) Plant, which stored natural gas in a liquified state during off-peak periods, thereby saving the company and its customers millions of dollars in natural gas costs.

Also in 1964, the company put into operation its largest power plant, South Bay 3. With the addition of power plants like South Bay 3 and stable prices for inexpensive natural gas and oil, SDG&E was able to make significant *reductions* in the cost of energy to its customers.

Since 1964, SDG&E had added three new oil-fired power plants and has reaped the benefits of less expensive, clean nuclear power from San Onofre which has been in operation since 1967.

Through the '60s and '70s, San Diego has

been one of the most popular places in the country to live. Indeed, since 1962 the number of SDG&E customers has more than doubled, to 750,000, and is growing at the rate of nearly 35,000 customers a year, making it the nation's fourth fastest-growing utility.

SDG&E today is a dynamic, forward-moving company, well-respected among utilities across the country for its innovative programs in conservation and its unique approach to attaining energy from a variety of sources. SDG&E is constantly looking for ways to provide for the ever-increasing population's electricity needs, using a variety of sources of power.

The company is trying to develop geothermal facilities in the Imperial Valley, east of San Diego, and its work in the research, and development of solar energy has put it at the forefront of solar research in the country.

SDG&E has played a significant role in making San Diego County one of the most desirable places to work, play and raise a family in the entire U.S. Today more than ever before, energy is critical to maintaining San Diego's high standard of living and level of productivity.

Although all utilities face many problems in the years ahead, SDG&E is confident that with public support, it will solve the problems and serve the community for another 100 years in the same innovative, enterprising spirit that has characterized its service in the past.

San Diego Trust & Savings Bank

Institution is San Diego's largest and oldest locally-owned bank

San Diego was a small city of 16,000 when Joseph Sefton, a successful businessman from Dayton, Ohio, opened the San Diego Savings Bank in 1889 at Fifth and E. The initial authorized capital in the new bank was $200,000.

Sefton established a tradition of first-class banking principles and of community involvement that continues to this day. "Believing in the future of San Diego," President Thomas Sefton, the founder's grandson, recently stated, "my grandfather wanted his bank to do its share toward furthering the community's progress. A long term commitment of service was introduced; the confidence of its patrons was soon obtained; and a sound and profitable institution arose."

The bank was well established in 1893 when the national banking crisis swept across the nation, closing many banks in its path. In San Diego, Sefton confronted the crisis squarely and informed customers that his bank would not close. The panic diminished on his premises when depositors were paid on demand.

When this upheaval was over, the bank prospered, catering as it did to small depositors and providing the means to finance homes and commercial buildings. In 1894 it was necessary to move into larger quarters at Fifth and F.

San Diego entered the 20th century determined to achieve metropolitan status; pitching in its share of enthusiasm and determination was San Diego Savings, which assisted in community efforts designed to attract permanent residents and new business enterprises. Myron Gilmore, who was cashier at the founding, became president on the death of Sefton in 1908. At the same time Joseph Sefton, Jr. assumed the vice-presidency. In 1913, to accommodate its expanding business, the bank moved into

San Diego Trust & Savings Bank Building, Broadway at Sixth Avenue, San Diego, California. Wm. Templeton Johnson, Architect, right. Thomas W. Sefton, president and chief executive officer – the third Sefton to occupy the presidency of San Diego Trust & Savings Bank, below.

spacious quarters in the Watts Building.

The bank's resources were marshalled to assist in the development of the Panama-California Exposition of 1915, a milestone in the development of the city which required six years for planning and construction.

In the 30 years between 1890 and 1920 the bank's assets steadily increased to $7 million, while population of the city rose to 75,000.

San Diego Savings anticipated new opportunities for development at the start of the '20s. New areas of service for customers were introduced when the bank's charter was amended to include trust and commercial accounts. "Trust" was added to its name in 1925.

In the '20s, the "great western migration" was underway in the United States, with the automobile transporting a flood of people into Southern California. In those flourishing years the population of San Diego doubled; and San Diego Trust provided financial support to the expanding military population and to the nascent aviation industry that would build the "Spirit of St. Louis." In 1928, the bank's lofty headquarters building, a notable architectural landmark, was completed at Sixth and Broadway.

Although the next decade was scarred by an economic depression, San Diego Trust's substantial resources provided a solid base for support to the community in that difficult period. In 1935 Joseph Sefton, Jr. took command of the bank.

The economy surged with the advent of World War II. War Bonds were dispensed over the bank's counters, as were Liberty Bonds in World War I.

By mid-century assets had climbed to $30 million and the bank again experienced a time of expansion. The first branch office was opened in 1956, and many were to follow, spreading the institution's geographical influence throughout the city and county.

Electronic data processing equipment was introduced along with other innovative banking services: installment loans, compounding of interest daily, personalized checking, drive-in banking. Perhaps the most dramatic example of the bank's commitment to lead is its Automated Teller Machine ("7/24") network.

In 1960 Thomas Sefton took the helm as president and a new era of measured expansion and advanced customer services was initiated.

San Diego Trust & Savings Bank has maintained throughout its history a consistent growth rate while meeting firmly the challenges of war, depression, soaring inflation and stagflation, regulatory action and inaction.

San Diego Trust enters its 10th decade determined to continue its tradition of quality service as the largest and oldest locally owned bank in San Diego, a stature achieved without merger or acquisition. In addition to proven leadership and management and a well-trained staff, resources now include 34 banking offices in San Diego County and nearly $600 million in total assets. With the continued backing of its loyal patrons, who number in the thousands, these human and physical resources will be used aggressively — now and in the future — for the benefit of the community.

Science Applications, Inc.

Science meeting the challenge of a changing world

Science Applications, Inc. (SAI) was founded in La Jolla, California, on January 31, 1969 as an organization whose primary business was to be top quality scientific and technical research on nationally important issues. Dr. J. R. Beyster, the founder, felt that employee participation in deciding the company's future was the best way to attract top technical and management talent and to stimulate SAI's growth. San Diego's universities, institutions, and businesses were and still are endowed with a rich abundance of the specialized professionals needed for such growth. The founding concept of SAI was a very new way of thinking for professional services companies at the time, but it flourished in the receptive climate of San Diego where a tradition of supporting high technology and scientific enterprises proved to be ideal for the SAI approach.

The people who joined the fledgling company were independent-minded professionals with specific ideas of what they wanted to do. The freedom from outside influence along with the flexibility of the SAI organization allowed them to pursue areas of their own personal interest and to locate near their customers. In this way, SAI grew from a single office in San Diego housing 20 employees in 1970, to 40 principle offices from coast-to-coast and in Europe housing 3500 employees in 1980, producing annual sales of $150 million.

The specific areas of technical work in

The old Scripps Clinic on Prospect Street in La Jolla now houses SAI offices and research facilities. This complex was started in 1924.

San Diego has provided the perfect setting for SAI's growth.

SAI reflected Dr. Beyster's initial idea of addressing nationally important issues. Thus, business areas grew at SAI to reflect the ability of science to meet the challenge of changing world needs in *national security, energy, environment,* and *health.* SAI's initial contracts were in the national security areas in which sophisticated calculations of nu-

206

clear weapons effects were performed for the Defense Nuclear Agency. This area has grown steadily to encompass all aspects of national security and today accounts for half of SAI's business.

Health got its big push in 1972 when the "war on cancer and heart disease" was announced with a greatly accelerated biomedical research program. SAI staff helped to design and manage this complex long-range process and later expanded to work on the health care delivery problems.

Environmental issues gradually became more important during the decade of the 1970s as more and more regulations were created by the federal government. SAI engineers worked on design problems to help industry meet new regulations; SAI

laboratories measured the toxic effects of substances.

Energy issues became an economic, technical, and political reality to the world with the 1973 oil embargo. But SAI's energy work had already begun in 1970 with some of the nation's first comprehensive research on nuclear security and safety issues. SAI's energy program rapidly expanded towards its current involvement in energy conservation and the development of alternative energy sources for the future: solar, nuclear fusion, coal liquification, oil shale, biomass conversion, and others.

Today, SAI is one of the top five scientific and technical professional services firms in the world. Approximately one-fourth of its staff is located in the San Diego area with

corporate headquarters at the La Jolla Cove location where SAI was founded. SAI's share of the U.S. market for its kind of professional services is growing at twice the rate of the total professional services market — a market that itself is growing at twice the rate of the gross national product (GNP). Thus, the future looks optimistic for SAI and for San Diego, with major growth potential on the business horizon for both.

The exciting success of the SAI story underscores the boldness of thought and dedication of the SAI founders and staff in pursuing their new idea at just the right time in history. San Diego's role in this story is simply being the ideal place where this idea could happen.

Scripps Clinic and Research Foundation

Medical research/medical care partnership was key to growth

The original Scripps Clinic just prior to its opening in 1924. The structure had formerly housed a sanitarium.

On December 11th, 1924, the townspeople of La Jolla gathered on one of the coastal village's quiet streets to observe the official opening of a special, but unimposing medical facility. To be called "Scripps Metabolic Clinic" in honor of its founder and one of La Jolla's leading citizens, Ellen Browning Scripps, the 15-bed institution was chartered as a center for the study and treatment of disease.

In 1976, almost 52 years to the day later, more than 3000 people from throughout the U.S. and abroad were on hand when Scripps Clinic and Research Foundation dedicated a sprawling medical-scientific complex that today includes one of the world's largest medical research institutes and a medical center whose reputation for excellence attracts patients from Boston to Bangkok.

The transformation of Miss Scripps' small clinic into a front-ranking institution employing the talents of more than 2000 physicians, surgeons, medical researchers and support personnel did not take place overnight. In fact, after an initial growth spurt that occurred between its founding and the early 1930s, the Clinic grew only slowly for almost a quarter of a century.

It was not until the 1950s, when improved air and ground transportation had shattered San Diego's relative isolation from the country's mainstream, that Scripps Clinic began to fully realize the potential envisioned by its founders.

Beginning in 1955 and continuing through the next decade and a half, change became a near-constant in the institution's life.

Scripps Metabolic Clinic (center) circa 1930. In later years, the clinic would expand into the community hospital (left) and nurses home (right), as well as into many smaller structures behind these buildings.

The commitment to the study of disease made almost 30 years earlier blossomed into a major medical research effort. Leading scientists were recruited from across the country and a large new laboratory facility built to accommodate them. By the late 1960s, Scripps' contributions in a host of areas ranging from allergies to cancer to rheumatoid arthritis had earned it world-wide prominence.

The institution also had launched an advanced training program for young physicians and scientists. Begun in 1958 with a mere half dozen people, Postdoctoral Fellowships at Scripps soon became a much sought after credential, annually attracting hundreds of young men and women from around the globe.

At the same time, Scripps' clinical program was burgeoning, offering specialized medical services first in six, then 12, then 18, and, later, more than two dozen medical and surgical fields. The original clinic building long since had been replaced by a complex of large and small structures consuming more than five acres in La Jolla's central district.

The relatively far-flung reputation garnered during the institution's early years continued to grow. Building on its "bench strength" — the sophisticated analytic capabilities afforded by its research —

Scripps Clinic and Research Foundation's medical-scientific center in northern La Jolla. The complex, completed in 1977, now houses most of the institution's research, patient care and educational activities.

Scripps gradually became nationally and even internationally known for excellence in medical care.

Throughout the '60s, the Clinic found increasing numbers of people were coming to its doorstep from across the U.S., from Canada, Mexico and Europe. By the end of the decade, more than two-thirds of its patients hailed from outside San Diego County's borders.

Indeed, Scripps' achievements had earned widespread reknown. It had been selected by the National Institutes of

Health to serve as one of 12 National Asthma and Allergic Disease Centers, as a Special Cancer Center, and as one of three U.S. institutions spearheading work on multiple sclerosis and other neurologic diseases.

But Scripps' evolution was far from complete. In fact, the 1970s marked the start of a new era for the then half-century old institution. While it continued to serve growing numbers of patients from distant locales, increasingly, people from San Diego were coming to Scripps for all their health care needs. Grown steadily more comprehensive over the years, the Clinic's historically specialized services diversified still further to accommodate rising demands of local patients.

A far cry from its comparatively tiny predecessor, Scripps Clinic and Research Foundation in the 1980s remains an institution on the move. Now housed principally in the northern La Jolla complex completed in 1977, Scripps recently has launched new programs in research, in disease prevention and community-oriented health care, and in both patient and professional education. Combined, these new initiatives are opening a still newer, and possibly even more dramatic, chapter in the institution's history of service to people in San Diego and around the world.

Solar Turbines International

Growing with San Diego for more than 50 years

Solar Turbines International is recognized as the world's leading manufacturer of industrial gas turbine engines and related equipment, a position attained through foresight, technical competence and a determination to overcome early adversities.

Although more than 50 years old, the firm today is full of youthful vigor and is continuing to grow as its products help meet the world's never-ending quest for energy.

Founded in 1927 as the Prudden-San Diego Airplane Company, the firm built three of the first all-metal airplanes manufactured in the United States. When the Great Depression ended this venture, the young business, then called Solar Aircraft Company, began working with new metal alloys. Under its president, Edmund Price, Solar developed the first successful stainless steel aircraft engine exhaust manifolds, which far outlasted those made of other materials and added to flight safety.

Although the company struggled through the early and mid-1930s, by the end of that

Solar's first product: The MS-1 all-metal, eight-passenger sesquiplane at San Diego's Lindbergh Field, circa 1930. This was one of only three airplanes ever built by Solar.

Solar's newest product: The highly efficient 10,600-horsepower Mars industrial gas turbine driving a gas compressor on a natural gas pipeline in Idaho.

decade Solar had 200 employees and was producing nearly three-quarters of the aircraft exhaust manifolds in the United States.

With the advent of World War II, Solar doubled and tripled its work force. By war's end, the company had produced more than 200,000 manifolds and won three Army-Navy "E" Awards for its efforts.

A peacetime economy brought with it sweeping changes and a diversification into such unrelated product lines as stainless steel milk truck tanks, caskets and midget race car bodies. And, although layoffs continued, Solar's dedication to high quality

research, through studies on metallurgy, gas flow and sound effects, began to reap rewards.

Solar developed the first successful U.S. jet engine afterburner and entered the gas turbine industry by introducing the 40-horsepower Mars engine, designed to power portable fire pumps on Naval vessels and to provide auxiliary power on large military cargo aircraft.

Through the Korean conflict and into the late '50s the company's reputation continued to grow. Products included turbines, controls, missile and jet engine parts, industrial expansion joints and honeycomb metal structures.

In 1956, Herbert Kunzel was elected Solar's second president and in 1957 the Navy signed a contract with Solar calling for the development of a 1000-horsepower

gas turbine to be used for small boat propulsion. To be named the Saturn, the engine ultimately led Solar into preeminence as the world's leading manufacturer of industrial gas turbines and related equipment.

The year 1960 ushered in a new era. Solar became a subsidiary of International Harvester Company; the rugged Saturn turbine entered production and saw its first commercial applications being used to drive electrical generators; and Solar developed its own natural gas compressors.

In the late '60s, the Centaur turbine engine was introduced. Now rated at 3,830-horsepower, the Centaur accelerated the firm's move into overseas markets. Its success helped shape the decision that changed Solar's destiny, namely to sever its traditional ties to the aerospace industry; and in 1973 Solar began concentrating on its gas turbine markets.

Also in 1973, Solar's current president, O. Morris Sievert, assumed the reins from Herbert Kunzel, who retired after more than 27 years with the company.

In the mid-1970s, the pace quickened: ground was broken for a new $20-million manufacturing plant on Kearney Mesa; a $25-million order was won for Centaur turbine compressors for the Soviet Union. In 1975, sales topped one-quarter of a billion dollars, and Solar announced another new engine: a 10,600-horsepower industrial workhorse that would assume an old name from the firm's history — Mars.

Now an Operating Group of International Harvester, Solar Turbines International is a worldwide supplier of rugged gas compressor, generator and mechanical drive units. Nearly 80 percent of its markets are outside the United States, primarily in the petroleum industry. And the company broke ground for another new plant in 1979 to accommodate the growing demand for its aircraft auxiliary power units, now produced in ratings up to 275 horsepower.

So what began as a struggling aircraft manufacturer more than 50 years ago today is a dynamic force helping to produce the world's energy supplies and developing advanced equipment and technology for the future.

Spectral Dynamics

Analyzing vibration resulted in company's smooth, steady growth

The process of spectrum analysis — a practical, near automatic process which measures and analyzes vibration — was an idea born 20 years ago in the mind of a young engineer at the General Dynamics

aircraft plant in Ft. Worth, Texas. Laurie Burrow's device, the "dynamic analyzer," was the solution to the problem of measuring and analyzing vibration in the faster, heavier planes then coming on line at G-D.

Although "spectrum analysis" is not a term you're likely to hear in normal conversation, it is the basis for the innovative, high-technology organization of Spectral Dynamics in San Diego. And, it is a process

"DYMAC" instruments help prevent breakdowns of expensive machinery by giving early warning of impending troubles.

Spectrum analyzers aid scientists in designing underwater detection gear by studying a porpoise's "speech" pattern.

how complex the product being studied. Instead of going through laborious and costly trial-and-error methods, an engineer can go right to the specific part of a machine causing the problem and redesign it. All of which translates to longer product life, fewer breakdowns ... and far greater customer satisfaction.

Aggressive marketing — actually, technical missionary work of carrying the gospel of spectrum analysis throughout industry — and a steadily expanding product line soon carried Spectral Dynamics far beyond its original aerospace limits. Today, the home washing machine and the outboard motor owe as much of their silent, dependable operation to Spectral's instruments as did yesterday's rocket.

Where smooth, noise-free products were only a luxury a few short years ago, today they are demanded by the public in every area and on every price level. And these demands are backed by a considerable body of health and environmental laws and regulations. Compliance virtually demands the use of spectrum analysis.

Under the leadership of Hugh Ness, co-founder and now company president, Spectral has grown both in size and breadth. One self-contained division — DYMAC — was established to extend vibration analysis and measurement to the "predictive maintenance" of industrial machinery. DYMAC equipment, working around the clock and always "on-line", spots where a machine has a potential problem; for example, a gear that's chipped or a bearing that's beginning to wear. By warning the machine's operator of such troubles when they first start, DYMAC enables them to avoid future breakdowns. Maintenance can be scheduled realistically on the basis of need rather than on regular time periods, when tear-down and inspection may not even be necessary. This time and money saving procedure is now standard in power plants, pipelines, refineries, paper mills and petrochemical plants, using DYMAC equipment.

Another division established under Hugh Ness's leadership — Special Contracts — carries the process of spectrum analysis on shipboard, under the sea and into the air. Here, the same basic techniques used to design quiet farm machinery and to check the condition of petrochemical compressors are employed for detection, identification and classification of space, oceanographic and undersea naval information.

In 1978, the company merged with Scientific-Atlanta, a Georgia-based firm and a leading supplier of satellite ground terminals and equipment for cable TV systems, energy management and home security. All San Diego operations remain under the guidance of Hugh Ness, whose worldwide organization of 800-plus people is still dedicated to making the world "run silent, run smooth."

that affects just about every product used in industry and in everyday life. For, what you don't hear and what you can't feel in these products is largely due to Spectral's pioneering efforts.

When you enjoy a smooth, quiet ride in your car ... when your refrigerator operates silently and dependably year after year ... when the engines on your jetliner speed you safely across country, chances are that spectrum analysis played an important part in their design, production or maintenance.

A short time after development of the analyzer, Burrow and the patent were moved to San Diego by G-D. His en-

thusiasm for the product and its broad applications even beyond the aircraft industry were shared by his new San Diego colleague, Hugh W. Ness. Together, they purchased the patent and the small inventory of analyzers that had been built by G-D, and Spectral Dynamics Corporation was on its way ... a one-product company in a 2,500 square foot store-front type facility.

From that product and that store front came the entire science of spectrum analysis, one of the cornerstones of present-day engineering. Briefly, it enables engineers to "decompose" noise and vibration, to break it down into individual areas called frequencies or "tones". Once these have been precisely determined, it becomes relatively easy to trace each noise and each vibration back to its exact source, no matter

The Sumitomo Bank of California

Looking to the future without discarding the traditions of the past

Before the colonization of North America in the mid-16th century and while Japan was still caught up in the throes of feudal conflict, a samurai warrior by the name of Masatomo Sumitomo decided to renounce his nobleman status and enter the Buddhist priesthood.

Following a period of meditation and self-reflection, Masatomo left the church and opened a small shop in Kyoto, then the Japanese capital, specializing in medicine and books. It was his conviction that this new endeavor would help him better serve his fellow man and contribute to the public good.

Masatomo gained a reputation of honesty, reliability, and deep community attachment; a credo which was to become the guiding principle underlying all Sumitomo enterprises in the centuries that followed.

Masatomo Sumitomo's descendants ventured into various fields — mining, industry, commerce, and finance. The financial activity commenced around 1670, during the early years of the Edo Period in Japan, when the Sumitomo clan began to privately finance copper mining operations on the island of Shikoku.

In 1895 Japan experienced an economic boom that was attendant upon her emergence into industrialism. This boom provided the opportunity for the establishment of The Sumitomo Bank, Ltd., which was founded on the same principle of community trust and dependability engendered centuries earlier by Masatomo.

As the bank expanded its scope of business activity (The Sumitomo Bank, Ltd., today is one of the largest in the Free World), its attention was naturally drawn to international markets. In the early 1900s, the large migrations of Japanese to California resulted in a tremendous corporate need for financial aid in business and agricultural pursuits. Sumitomo seized the opportunity to provide that assistance.

In the mid-1920s, the first Sumitomo Bank in California was established, only to have to cease operations completely with the outbreak of hostilities in the Pacific in 1941. With the war ended, Sumitomo applied for and was granted a State Charter in November 1952, and thus was reborn The Sumitomo Bank of California.

On February 2, 1953, it opened two relatively small banking offices — one in San Francisco and one in Los Angeles — with a handful of employees and total assets of not quite $6 million. At the outset, Sumitomo's activities concentrated upon international commerce financing and assisting California's growing Japanese population with its financial needs. Japanese Americans, re-establishing themselves after World War II, found Sumitomo responsive to their requirement for capital to start their own businesses and to purchase family homes.

Today, of course, with 46 offices throughout the Golden State, Sumitomo is represented in communities which reflect the broad spectrum of California's people. With assets and deposits both well in excess of $1 billion, it is the 10th largest bank in the

San Diego Office of The Sumitomo Bank of California.

state and in the "top 80" of some 15,000 banks in the United States. The majority of the more than 2,000 shareholders are California residents.

Sumitomo's headquarters are in San Francisco, but it also maintains Northern and Southern California divisional headquarters — the latter based in Los Angeles.

The San Diego Office of Sumitomo, opened in September 1972 at 410 A Street, is one of the bank's largest and is considered by many as "one of the real jewels" in Sumitomo's statewide crown.

In that relatively short span, the San Diego office has played a significant role in providing the financing for large commercial developments in the city as well as San Diego's sizable medical community. Moreoever, the cosmopolitan staff of more than 40 men and women provide valuable support to city officials and business leaders in attracting new Japanese investment in order to bolster and diversify San Diego's economic base.

Sumitomo uses as its trademark the "Igeta," which in Japanese represents an ancient well frame. It is traced to a distant ancestor of the House of Sumitomo, who, it is said, came from the district of *Izumi* (or "well.") Thus, the stylized *Igeta* is symbolic of the "continuation of the freshness and substance that is akin to the never-ending flow of a spring."

Teledyne Ryan Aeronautical

From the "Spirit of St. Louis" to unmanned aircraft and space

The pace-setting — and contrasting — advances in aerospace technology during the past half-century are well illustrated by the accomplishments of San Diego's pioneer aircraft company, Teledyne Ryan Aeronautical.

In 1927, Ryan Airlines, Inc., founded five years earlier by T. Claude Ryan, designed and built the world's most famous airplane, the "Spirit of St. Louis." And, by the 50th anniversary of Charles A. Lindbergh's historic New York-Paris flight, Ryan Aeronautical Company was well established as the world leader in the design and production of highly sophisticated remotely piloted vehicles.

Today Teledyne Ryan Aeronautical is recognized not only for its famed pilotless jet aircraft, but also as the free world's largest supplier of Doppler radar navigation equipment, and as an airframe subcontractor to major aerospace companies. In addition, Teledyne Ryan has expanded its electronic simulation capabilities to include the surface transportation field.

It was in 1925 that the Ryan name first attracted attention with the establishment of the Los Angeles-San Diego Air Line, the country's first year-round daily scheduled passenger airline.

The following year Claude Ryan saw the need for a more modern plane suitable for commercial airmail service and conceived the M-1, first production monoplane in the United States. It was this plane which first attracted Lindbergh to Ryan's design capability.

In addition to aircraft design and production, Ryan operated a pilot and aviation mechanics school which in 1939 began to train military pilots for the government.

With Charles A. Lindbergh at the controls, the Ryan 'Spirit of St. Louis' monoplane was flown solo nonstop from New York to Paris in 1927 in the world's most famous flight.

Without a human pilot aboard, a Ryan Firebee remotely piloted vehicle (RPV) is flown by a controller from an electronic panel hundreds of miles away during a reconnaissance mission over Southeast Asia nearly five decades after Lindbergh's historical flight.

During World War II, Ryan trained 14,000 Army Air Corps pilots, most of whom received instruction in Ryan S-T sport trainers converted to military use as the first low-wing primary trainers ever ordered by the armed services.

Ryan S-T military planes were also used extensively by friendly foreign countries, including those in Latin America, the Netherlands East Indies, Australia and China.

Another WW II project was the jet-pushed, propeller-pulled Ryan FR-1 Fireball. Designed to provide the U.S. Navy with a highly maneuverable fighter which could outperform famed Japanese

Zeros, the composite-engined Fireball was the Navy's first jet plane and the first plane with tricycle landing gear to operate from aircraft carriers.

Ryan was also a major producer of aircraft and engine components during and after WWII for such companies as General Electric, Boeing and Douglas.

After WW II the company turned back to the private airplane market and began manufacturing the Ryan Navion four-place business and personal plane, producing more than 1,200 of this tremendously popular aircraft. The military also used the Navion L-17 version as a liaison plane in the Korean theatre.

Pioneering new concepts in aircraft design, Ryan became a leader in the development of research aircraft, particularly V/STOL types — those capable of vertical and short take off and landing. This work began with the YO-51 Dragonfly of 1940 and was followed by the X-13 Vertijet (1957), the world's first jet VTOL aircraft. Others were the VZ-3RY Vertiplane (1959) and the XV-5A/B Vertifan (1964).

One of the most advanced developments in aviation today is the RPV remotely piloted vehicle, an outgrowth of the Firebee pilotless jet airplanes which Ryan designed in the early 1950s to simulate the threat of 'enemy' aircraft. More than 6,000 Firebees have been built as aerial targets to meet military requirements for weapons training and for the evaluation of the weapons systems fired against these high-speed targets. More sophisticated models provide electronic warfare systems or are able to conduct high altitude reconnaissance, carrying electronic and photo sensors on intelligence gathering flights without risking a human pilot on such missions.

The company branched out into the area of electronics for aerospace applications, developing a target seeking guidance system for the Ryan Firebird, one of the earliest air-to-air missiles. From this cornerstone of technology grew a wide spectrum of electronic systems for aeronautical, surface and space applications. The company has produced every spacecraft landing radar and altimeter on the Surveyor, Apollo and Viking programs. Thousands of the company's Doppler radars are flying in dozens of different fixed and rotary wing aircraft throughout the world.

Over the years Ryan grew steadily and soundly into one of the nation's leading corporations in the field of aviation. By 1969, when it was purchased by Teledyne, Inc., Ryan Aeronautical Company, including its Continental Motors Corp. subsidiary, was doing an annual business of more than $400 million.

Teledyne Ryan Aeronautical, the company that T. Claude Ryan founded, the company that built the "Spirit of St. Louis," continues as a pacesetter in aerospace and electronic technology.

Trusthouse Forte, Inc. and TraveLodge International, Inc.

Providing a good night's sleep — and more — throughout the Western Hemisphere

When Scott King opened his first motel in 1934, he saw a need for providing clean, affordable roadside accommodations to a nation that was just beginning its love affair with the automobile. The sprawling Southern California area was a natural place for people to begin experiencing their new mobility and King found a ready market for his "auto courts." As the roadways of America began expanding across new frontiers, a new TraveLodge was never far behind, particularly in the wide-open West. The boom gained momentum in the 1950s and 1960s as America entered the era of a new interstate highway program designed to link all of America by automobile, with nary a stoplight to hinder the onward rush. Soon, the TraveLodge name and its friendly symbol — Sleepy Bear — became familiar favorites for family and business travelers alike on the roads and superhighways of the United States and Canada. King was pleased and proud and continued his high standards into every new area. But he had little idea what the future would hold for his company when it would become part of a group that would develop landmark properties throughout the Western Hemisphere, providing quality accommodations for all travelers.

The next major era in the TraveLodge growth story started in 1968, when a consortium of companies affiliated with Trusthouse Forte Limited, of London, purchased King's interest in the company. Roger Manfred, who had been deputy managing director of TraveLodge Australia Limited, chief executive officer of its international division and who jointly organized the consortium, was brought in as president and chief executive officer of the El Cajon-based TraveLodge International. He soon launched the company on a program of growth that took many forms and began setting new standards in the lodging industry.

The company developed the now familiar Tri-Arc motor hotels — high-rise, full-service hotels which give TraveLodge guests unobstructed views from each room, provide for more efficient operation of the property and create a striking architectural addition to the communities they serve.

High standards of design are also evident in the franchise program, which now constitutes more than half of the total network and which has been growing at a rate of better than 15 percent a year.

To better manage this program of growth and enhance administrative service to its

The TraveLodge Tower at Harbor Island, San Diego, California, has 208 rooms and is located across Harbor Drive from San Diego International Airport, on a man-made island in San Diego Bay.

growing family, TraveLodge developed the most sophisticated program in the industry for monitoring labor costs and operating efficiencies. Each day, information provided to the El Cajon headquarters can give managers a precise measurement of labor activity against a standard for each property. No other lodging group has such a finite measuring system and, as a result, independent operators and franchisees from other chains have been switching to TraveLodge in ever-increasing numbers. The company also used its management expertise in taking over previously troubled properties around major airports in the United States and turning them into winners. The results: during a five-year period, TraveLodge increased its net profits by 227.9 percent on a 38.6 percent increase in sales.

The first "TraveLodge" built by Scott King, with his name also proudly showing on the building.

TraveLodge has also been an international pioneer. Its reservations center in Kansas City was the first to offer multilingual assistance to visitors from foreign countries and was named as the official host number by the U.S. Travel Service. Through its Visit North America program, TraveLodge has helped educate travelers from Europe and other countries about the sound value found in U.S. travel. As a result of its voucher program sold through the worldwide sales and reservations system of Trusthouse Forte Limited, of London, to world tour operators, the number of foreign travelers using TraveLodge properties has more than doubled each year.

Today, the number of TraveLodges in the Western Hemisphere is climbing toward 600. Its parent, Trusthouse Forte, Inc., is undertaking one of the most significant expansions in the history of the lodging industry during the next few years: adding 17 properties with almost 10,000 rooms in major cities throughout the Western Hemisphere. They include luxury properties at the Plaza of the Americas in Dallas, Canal Place in New Orleans, Kennedy Square in Cambridge, Mass., Bunker Hill in Los Angeles, San Francisco Airport, Houston, Denver, Philadelphia and other major business centers.

Food service is becoming another growth area for Trusthouse Forte. Its operation in New York serves the daily dining needs of United Nations and major institutional and corporate clients. The Colony Foods division operates more than 110 Colony Kitchen and Hobo Joe's family restaurants in the West.

Soon, a San Diego-based chain known for its friendly service and the best beds in town will have joined with its parent to become one of the most important hotel, catering and leisure operations in the Western Hemisphere, with annual sales of more than $1 billion and one of the best profit records in the history of the industry.

University of San Diego

A value-based education meets the challenge of the future

The Most Reverend Bishop Charles Francis Buddy, first Bishop of the immense diocese of San Diego (36,000 square miles), planned construction of the University of San Diego complex soon after his appointment in late 1936. Almost from the beginning, he worked with Mother Rosalie Clifton Hill of the Sacred Heart's Lone Mountain College in San Francisco. Later, in 1946, Mother Hill and a group of nuns came to San Diego and took up residence in Old Town where they could supervise the planning, design and construction of the university's College for Women.

Together the nuns and the Bishop searched for an appropriate site. They settled on the sage- and chaparral-covered mesa overlooking Mission Valley, Tecolote Canyon and the bay — an ideal site for university purposes. By 1949 Bishop Buddy had carefully and systematically acquired 167 acres. In that year, the private coeducational Roman Catholic university received its charter from the state of California.

The first unit of the liberal arts division — the San Diego College for Women — opened in 1952; it was designed, financed and equipped by the Society of the Sacred Heart, a Catholic religious order.

The College for Men, sponsored and financed by the Diocese of San Diego, began classes in 1954. The School of Law, inaugurated in 1954 in temporary quarters, opened on campus in Thomas More Hall in December, 1957.

The colleges functioned separately until the late 1960s when joint academic operations began. Plans for a merger were completed in 1972, and the College of Arts and Sciences, and Schools of Education and Business Administration were established to meet increased enrollment. In 1974 the Philip Y. Hahn School of Nursing was initiated. In the fall of 1979 the combined student enrollment reached 4,123 and the full and part-time faculty numbered 263.

The architectural style for the university buildings was determined in its early years by Mother Hill. She had been favorably impressed by the University of Alcalá de Henares near Madrid, Spain, where San Diego de Alcalá (St. Didacus) had performed his work. She, therefore, chose Spanish Renaissance architecture for the first unit of the University of San Diego and set the pattern for the buildings to follow.

Bishop Buddy, in agreement with Mother Hill's concept, vowed that the ornamentation would embody his research into Christian symbolism.

The University received many of its elegant tapestries, paintings, silver and furnishings through a bequest from the James Flood estate in San Francisco to the Sacred Heart. The College for Women, designed by architect Frank L. Hope, Jr., represented

University of San Diego School of Business Administration.

Arcade connecting Founders and Camino Halls, University of San Diego.

an investment by the Society of the Sacred Heart of more than $4 million and today houses the James Copley Library, the University Chapel, a 1,000 seat auditorium, classrooms, offices and dormitories.

Throughout the years, additional university units have been constructed, financed by private donations, gifts from parishioners and by funds raised in the community. The Greater San Diego Committee led by Murray Goodrich (a Jewish friend of Bishop Buddy), directed a campaign in the late 1950s which yielded funds of $1,230,00 and pledges of $6,870,000. A million-dollar grant, supplemented by funds from Muriel Marsh Hahn, enabled construction of the nursing building in 1978.

In 1971, Dr. Author E. Hughes took the helm as president. His leadership and the guiding hand of Sister Sally Furay, vice president and provost, and the support of dedicated scholars within the university, have assured the continuance of the school's unique community role.

The School of Law has developed an enviable record throughout the West because of the research and professionalism of its faculty, the services of its legal clinics to the community and the success of its graduates.

The University of San Diego — Catholic in the post-Vatican sense — is liberal in its outlook and encourages students of all denominations to participate in its programs. Its major goal is to help individuals develop a positive set of values and a sense of personal integrity to enable them to have fulfilling lives and make useful contributions to society. The university believes that the highest academic and intellectual standards are compatible with concern for spiritual purpose and moral values. It is dedicated to an unswerving search for truth.

Van Camp Sea Food Company

Tuna fleet lured Chicken of the Sea back to San Diego

Ancient Greeks are believed to have been among the first to seek out and capture tuna some 1500 years before Christ. "Thunnos," the Greek word for tuna, was considered to be a delicacy reserved only for the rich and influential. So endearing was "thunnos" that this ancient civilization immortalized tuna in pottery, verse and as a decorative theme for household tiles.

The first civilization in the Americas to catch tuna was the Incas of Central America. 1500 years before Columbus discovered America, the Incas were busy harvesting the vast tuna supply of the Pacific. Tuna was such a sought after delicacy that the Inca emperor had a system of iron-lunged runners who delivered tuna to the Inca capitol 130 miles inland on the same day it was caught.

In view of the fact that ancient civilizations went to such great lengths to enjoy tuna, it's easy to understand why tuna has become the most popular sea food today in the United States.

It wasn't until the early 1900s that we were given the treat of enjoying canned tuna. June 6, 1914 was the first day that the Van Camp family started to pack tuna, which wasn't always called Chicken of the Sea®. Several different brands of tuna were packed in San Pedro, California by the Van Camps. Ultimately Chicken of the Sea became the brand name tuna packed by Van Camp Sea Food Company.

On October 14, 1914, the tug "Crescent" delivered one and a half tons of tuna caught in a net that measured approximately 425 fathoms in length by 42 fathoms in depth. It was not until the early 1960s, however, that the advent of purse seine technology revolutionized tuna fishing, stimulating rapid conversion of existing bait boats, launching a boom in building larger and larger tuna vessels, and inaugurating a new era of competition among tuna boat operators. A single purse seiner today can deliver in one trip 1200 tons of tuna.

Although the first tuna cannery was operated in San Pedro, California, in 1922 it was moved to Terminal Island, California and two plants were purchased in San Diego that same year in order to increase capacity. 850 people hand packed 250 to 300 tons per day. In 1959, due to economic conditions, it was decided to consolidate the Chicken of the Sea operation into one facility, and because the plants (several by now) at Terminal Island were being underutilized, the operation was moved to Terminal Island.

Van Camp Sea Food Company's cannery at the Port of San Diego covers 18 acres.

In June 1963, Ralston Purina Company, a giant in the animal feed business, purchased Van Camp Sea Food Company. At that time, Chicken of the Sea was the largest canner of a nationally advertised brand tuna in the United States. It still is.

In 1969, Ralston Purina Company and Van Camp management decided to move their operation to San Diego in order to be in the midst of the tuna resourcing industry. San Diego is the center of the U.S. tuna fleet with the majority of the seiners operating out of San Diego. There are approximately 180 tuna fishing vessels in the total world fleet, 130 of which are in the United States with 110 of them operating out of the Port of San Diego.

Plans were soon underway to find suitable locations. The world headquarters for the Van Camp operation was established in Sorrento Valley in North County San Diego in 1974. Administrative functions for this world-wide division of Ralston Purina

Company are handled by 120 employees. A Can Manufacturing Plant was located in the Watts-Gentry Industrial Park, employing approximately 110 people, which has a daily capability to produce two million cans and lids.

Chicken of the Sea's Research and Development Center is also located in Sorrento Valley. The R&D Center employs 59, half being professionals having advanced degrees in the sciences. Within the 22,000 square foot building are housed various laboratories. The personnel and facilities are dedicated to supporting the high quality of Chicken of the Sea Tuna.

Van Camp Sea Food Company had its grand opening in May 1975 in the Port of San Diego. The Van Camp Cannery has 12 acres under roof within a total complex of 18 acres. Annually 100,000 tons of tuna are packed by approximately 2,000 people.

Chicken of the Sea brand tuna is packed in San Diego, Ponce, Puerto Rico and Pago Pago, American Samoa with various other operations in Palau, Ecuador and Ghana. Tuna comes in different sizes and packs and has many various uses. There are albacore (white meat), skipjack, bluefin and yellowfin. Each has its own distinctive delightful flavor. Tuna is a convenient contributor of high quality protein to the diet.

The Chicken of the Sea family has made a significant contribution to the community of San Diego, playing a major role in the making of America's finest city.

Sunset on the bay, 1907, looking toward Point Loma from the ferry landing.

In passing ...

San Diego is a young-old city.
Although it is more than 210 years old, it is just now coming into its own.
Its growth has not been meteoric, like the growth of Los Angeles in this century.
Nor has it been linked dramatically, like Detroit, to one booming industry.

San Diego's growth has been a steady period of advancement and development.
True, there were the occasionally-missed opportunities
that enabled other cities to become major commercial hubs on the Pacific Coast.
But what was thought to be a lack of progress has many times been opportunity in disguise.
San Diego's future and greatness are still to come.

The city has tremendous natural advantages.
It is situated on the busiest international border crossing in the world,
next to one of the largest and most important cities in Mexico.
The natural harbor — its trading potential still largely untapped —
faces the great trading partners of the Pacific Basin and the Orient.
It has the most attractive climate anywhere in the Sun Belt.
It is rapidly becoming a scientific, technological and medical center.
And it is steadily becoming more of a headquarters city for many industries and services.

San Diego has truly become an international city.
Its trading ties with Mexico are growing.
And so is the interdependence of the San Diego and Baja California economies.

A large influx of Spanish-speaking people has created a bilingual culture.
Officially, it will soon be recognized as the nation's eighth largest city.

Altogether, these facts paint a bright picture for the city's future.
But it is not without its problems.
Potentially serious energy and water shortages — increasing transportation difficulties —
these must be faced.
But such problems are challenges —
and the same determination and willpower that created the city
will gather together to mold an even more stimulating future city.

It is an exciting prospect, filled with opportunity and challenge.
And it is the result of the devotion and dedication of countless individuals
who have dreamed a dream of a great city nestled beside its magnificent Pacific harbor.

Lee Grissom
Executive Vice President
San Diego Chamber of Commerce

Index

Index

Index

Acknowledgements

The task of writing a history of San Diego was made infinitely less difficult because of the outstanding sources available. Most helpful were Richard Pourade's excellent seven volumes published by Copley Books covering San Diego's history from aboriginal times to 1970. The first comprehensive history of San Diego was written by William Smythe in 1908 and was followed by those of Clarence McGrew in 1922 and Carl H. Heilbron in 1936. Recent writers such as Arnold Klaus, Jerry MacMullen, Elizabeth MacPhail, James Mills, Neil Morgan, George Phillips, and William Wagner have also contributed significantly to the overall story. The manuscript collections of the San Diego Historical Society were the source of much of the primary material consulted and the *Journal of San Diego History,* the society's quarterly publication, provided a wealth of information. The daily issues of the *San Diego Union* and *Evening Tribune* were extremely

important in pulling together the region's chronology and placing events in proper perspective. The records and publications of the San Diego Chamber of Commerce were especially helpful in understanding the city's economic development. Finally, *San Diego Magazine* contained many timely articles covering the city's recent past. Permission to reprint the excerpt from *Cities in American History* edited by Kenneth Jackson and Stanley K. Schultz was granted by Alfred A. Knopf, Inc.

For their careful reading of the manuscript and helpful suggestions, I wish to thank Roger Conlee, Director of Communications, and Lee Grissom, Executive Vice President, of the San Diego Chamber of Commerce; Harry Kelsey, Chief Curator of History, Los Angeles County Museum; Ann Kantor, Associate Director, San Diego Historical Society; James Moss, Executive Director, California Historical Society, and San Diegans Lee F. Gerlach, Flo Henrikson and

Gail Mainarick Kunold. For her help in gathering materials, proof-reading and checking references, I am especially grateful to Cindy van Stralen. I gratefully acknowledge the assistance of my colleagues at the University of San Diego, particularly Richard Phillips, James Moriarty and Therese Whitcomb. And to all who helped in their areas of expertise, a special note of thanks.

In gathering photographic materials, Tom Scharf and I wish to acknowledge gratefully the help of Larry and Jane Booth, curators of the San Diego Historical Society Title Insurance and Trust Collection; Bill Mason of the Los Angeles County Museum; William Wagner of Teledyne Ryan; and Mary Ward, County of San Diego. We also wish to thank Ray Brandes, Steven Schoenherr, and Susan Sullivan of the University of San Diego for supplying photographs of historic sites and taking some that were needed.

Iris H. W. Engstrand

Credits

The editors and publishers are indebted to a number of people and organizations, who, over the many months of preparation and production, believed as we did that San Diego citizens and visitors should have an entertaining and pictorially interesting history.

Our special thanks, of course, to author Iris H. W. Engstrand, whose cooperation and dedication made the book a reality and to Thomas L. Scharf, Historic Photo Editor.

In addition, we wish to thank:
The staff and volunteer leadership of San Diego Chamber of Commerce for their support and assistance, including H. Cushman Dow, president; Carleton Lichty, immediate past president and Lee Grissom, executive vice president. Special thanks to

Roger Conlee, Chamber director of communications, whose continued interest and guidance was invaluable. Of course Debbie Brown, Sally Moreno, Patti Cravens, Micki Flores, and Joanna Bourgeois deserve special mention.

Thank you also to Marcella Andreoli, Anne Gay, Barbara Burow, Ruth Carlsen, Gale Sonora, Cindy Alexander, Dot Migdal, Barbara Nance and of course Doug Byrns.

For assistance and authentication of manuscript, a special thanks to James Moss, who, at the beginning of this project, was director of the San Diego Historical Society
William Wagner, curator of the Ryan Aeronautical Library, provided historical photographs and counsel, for which we are indebted.

Others who contributed to the book's success are James Blank, Caroline Johnson, Marie Flagg, Paula Sullivan, Charles Chessher, Barbara Jameson Suzie Hicks, Wally King, Kathy Wendt and the entire CHP team.

Thanks to Mary Harrison for providing a different and exciting perspective of San Diego, and Jean and Jerry Fight who added a touch of much-appreciated midwestern hospitality.

Thanks to Author E. Hughes, president of the University of San Diego for the cooperation of the University and Sara Finn, director of public relations. To the management and highly professional staff of the Hotel del Coronado, Carleton Lichty, president and Don Larson, director of public relations, thank you.

Photo Credits

Sources of photographs, maps and art appearing in this book are noted here in alphabetical order and by page number (position on the page is noted). Those photographs appearing in the chapter *Partners in Progress* pages 177 through 215, were provided by the represented firms.

Aerial Fotobank; 161 bottom.
Archivo del Ministerio de Asuntos Exteriores, Madrid: 21 top.
Archivo General de Indias, Seville, Spain: 10
Blank, James: 129 bottom left, 231 top, 140/141, 141 top left, 144 top left & right, 145 top, 148 top, middle left, bottom, 149 all, 152 inset, bottom left & right, 153 top, bottom left, 156 all, 157 all, 160 all.
Bonham Brothers Mortuary: 100 bottom.
Burgener, Clair W.: 146.
Chase, Richard Gabriel: 22 Bottom
Ciruzzi, Canice: 114 top, 115.
Clock, Teri: 140 left. 137 bottom
Coates, George: 136 top left.
Copley Books: 13 bottom, 57 top, 121.
Crosby, Joanne: 12
Del Mar Thoroughbred Club: 153 bottom right.
Englehardt: San Diego Mission: 22 top.
Engstrand, Iris W.: 21 top, 33 top.
Galvez Family Collection, Buenos Aires: 18.
Geisel, Theodor: 130, bottom.
Goodrich, Virginia, drawings from "Ramona's Marriage Place" by Edwin H. Clough: 28 top, 29, 166.
History News: 177.
Huntington Library & Art Gallery: 24,28 bottom, 110.
KCST-TV Channel 39: 135 bottom.
KGTV Channel 10: 135 middle.
Kendall/Hunt Publishing Co.: 32 middle right. 120.
Knox, William H., Naval Sketches of the

War in California: 36 middle, inset.
Los Angeles County Museum of Natural History: 6/7, 26 top, 68 bottom, 70 top, 73 top, 94 top, 161 top, 165.
McClendon, Ron: 133 bottom left & right.
Maedge, Mrs. Burnell: 62 middle right.
Mexico, New Mexico and California by Brantz Mayer, Vol. I, 1853: 32 top.
Moriarty, James: 15.
Museo Naval, Madrid: 17 top.
National Archives: 113.
Out Lady of the Rosary Church: 114,115 top
Pourade, Richard
    The Explorers, A Copley Book: 13 bottom.
    The Glory Years, A Copley Book: 57 top
Pryde, Philip, San Diego: An Introduction to the Region: 32 middle right. 120.
Random House: 130 bottom.
Ryan Aeronautical: 86 right, 112.
San Diego Chamber of Commerce: 122 bottom, 147,155.
San Diego Chargers: 134, 136 bottom.
San Diego, City of: 126.
San Diego Clippers Basketball Club: 154.
San Diego Convention & Visitors Bureau: 104, 127, 130 inset, 131, 138 middle, 151, 176.
San Diego Museum of Art: 107 bottom.
San Diego Historical Society - Library & Manuscripts Collection: 18 inset, 27 inset, 30/31, 32 left, 34 inset, 35 top, 36 left, 43 middle, 63 top, 64 bottom.
    79 bottom right, 90 top right, 106, 109 right, 128 top, 163.
San Diego Historical Society - Title Insurance & Trust Collection: 2/3, 4/5, 8/9, 11 top, 14 top, bottom 17 bottom, 19, 21 bottom, 23, 25, 26 bottom, 27 right, 32/33, 33 bottom right, 34 middle, bottom, 35 bottom, 36 top right, 37, 38,

40 top and bottom, 41, 42, 43 top left, top right, bottom, 44 top, bottom, 45 bottom, 46, 47, 48, 49 all, 50 bottom left, 50 top, middle, 51, 52 top, bottom, 53, 54 top, middle, 55 top left, top right, bottom, 56, 57 bottom, 58, 59 top, bottom, 60, 61 bottom, 62 top left, top right, middle left, bottom, 63, 64 top left, top right, 65 bottom, 66, 67, 68 top, 69, 70 middle, bottom, 71, 72, 73 bottom, 74, 75, 76 top, 77 top right, bottom, 78, 79 top, bottom left, 80, 82 left, 83 top, bottom, 84 top, bottom, 85, 86 top, 87 top, bottom, inset, 89, 90 middle left, middle right, bottom, 91, 92 top left, top right, middle, 93 top, bottom, 95, 96 top, bottom, 97, 98, 99, 100/101, 101 inset, 102, 103 top, bottom, 104, 105, 108 top, bottom, 109 top, bottom, 110, 111 top, bottom, 114 bottom, 116 top, 117 top, bottom, 118, 119 top, 122 top, 124, 129 bottom right, 133 top, 137 inset, 138 bottom, 141 bottom, 143, 144 inset, 152 top, 158, 162, 167, 169, 170, 173,174,216,224.
San Diego Maritime Museum: 145 inset.
San Diego Museum of Man: 11 bottom, 12 bottom, 20.
San Diego Padres: 136 top right. 133 bottom.
San Diego Union: 54 bottom, 90 top left, 150.
San Diego, University of: 119 bottom, 129 top, inset.
San Diego Zoo: 138 top.
Scripps Institution of Oceanography: 130 top.
Seaport Village: 142.
Stagg, R.H.: 137 top left.
United States Government Printing Office - Colorado Exploring Expedition of 1857-1858: 13 top left, top right, middle left, middle right.
Young, Milt & Richardson, Bob: 135 top.

Concept and design by Continental Heritage Press, Inc., Tulsa.
Printed and bound by Walsworth Publishing, Marceline, Missouri.
Type set in Goudy Old Style.
Text sheets are Warrenflo by S. D. Warren Company.
Endleaves are Multicolor Antique.
Cover is Kingston Linen by Holliston Mills.